LAW PARTNERSHIP

ITS RIGHTS AND RESPONSIBILITIES

GEORGE H. CAIN

ABA
SENIOR LAWYERS DIVISION
AMERICAN BAR ASSOCIATION

Cover design by Emily Fina Friel.

The materials contained herein represent the opinions of the authors and editors and should not be construed to be the action of either the American Bar Association or the Senior Lawyers Division unless adopted pursuant to the bylaws of the Association.

Nothing contained in this book is to be considered as the rendering of legal advice for specific cases, and readers are responsible for obtaining such advice from their own legal counsel. This book and any forms and agreements herein are intended for educational and informational purposes only.

Library of Congress Catalog Card Number 95-80825
ISBN 1-57073-245-0

Discounts are available for books ordered in bulk. Special consideration is given to state bars, CLE programs, and other bar-related organizations. Inquire at Publications Planning & Marketing, American Bar Association, 750 North Lake Shore Drive, Chicago, Illinois 60611.

00 99 98 97 96 5 4 3 2 1

CONTENTS

ACKNOWLEDGMENTS

Credit goes to Joseph Weintraub of ABA Publications Planning and Marketing for giving me the idea for a book on partnerships. After serving as both a member of a law partnership of substantial size and as a general counsel who had many occasions to retain law firms, it seemed to me that a volume describing the rights and duties of partners in law firms was needed. Any publication on the subject available on the bookshelves was in treatise form and not necessarily enjoyable reading. A more reader-friendly volume, I thought, would be useful to those lawyers who currently are law firm partners, as well as those aspiring to these lofty heights.

Many organizations and persons lent a helping hand in my effort. The officers and Council of the Senior Lawyers Division of the American Bar Association (ABA)—most recently led by Lester M. Ponder of Indiana, John C. Deacon of Arkansas, and Victor Futter of New York, all of whom have served as Chair—were unfailingly supportive. The staff of the Publications Planning and Marketing Division of the ABA in Chicago (Joe Weintraub, Donald J. Gecewicz, and Sandra Eitel in particular) and Elizabeth M. Rielly, Susan C. Koz, and Patricia A. Allen of the Senior Lawyers Division staff were always ready to assist.

The preparation of this book took an enormous amount of research and could not have been done without the tremendous contribution of facilities provided by LEXIS™/NEXIS™. I am extremely grateful to them.

My law firm, Day, Berry & Howard, and its partners were there with additional support and encouragement.

Many law firms throughout the country answered questions about their practices and sent samples of their governing documents. Because I pledged to each complete confidentiality and anonymity, the firms cannot be identified. But this is an opportunity to thank them publicly for their help.

And then there is my wife, Connie, my ever faithful champion and valued advisor, providing advice and encouragement to light the way as always.

Thank you, one and all.

George H. Cain

PREFACE

Partnership in a law firm is a high honor. It makes no difference whether it is in a large, big-city firm or in a small office in a rural community. A partner has achieved the American dream—a piece of the action. But, in my view, the privilege of partnership does not come lightly. Partnership also signifies duty. Most partners have been, and are, too busy dealing with client problems to ponder their own situations. Hopefully, this volume will help partners (and aspiring partners) better understand their own rights and responsibilities.

George H. Cain

CHAPTER I

The Concept of Partnership

Introduction

The aim of this book is to discuss, as succinctly as possible, the rights and responsibilities of a partner in a law firm.

It must be recognized that not every lawyer is a partner in a large law firm, nor do all lawyers even aspire to such partnership. A huge number of lawyers in the United States practice alone or with one or two other lawyers in a small firm. The *New York State Bar News* for January/February 1995 states that "nearly 50 percent of all New York bar members practice in small (2–5 lawyers) or solo firms." That being true, the other 50 percent must be practicing in larger firms, in corporate law departments, in academia, or with the government. Ward Bower, president of Altman, Weil & Pensa, a major legal management consulting firm, is quoted as saying that "lawyers need to be aware of the fact that what they are experiencing, in terms of slow or negative growth and tighter economics, is not a temporary thing; this is the way the world is going to be from this point forward."[1]

Good management in a law firm means the proper, effective, and economic delivery of services expected by clients. Law firms cannot survive if the "bottom line" is improved by unethical or illegal conduct. "Attempts to make money when the lawyer fails properly to engage in economic planning for the office are prob-

1. "Law firms need to adjust to 90s reality, says expert." Donna Ciraulo, quoting Ward Bower of Altman Weil Pensa, NEW YORK STATE BAR NEWS, January/February 1995, at 1.

lematic and result not only in ethical violations but in the continued diminution of the view of lawyers by members of the public."[2] In fact, such conduct has probably brought down many more firms than it has raised up. It behooves every partner in a law firm to be aware of his or her rights so that both reputation and financial resources may be properly enhanced.

Determining One's Rights

It is fundamental that all rights depend upon the proper exercise of one's duties and responsibilities. Consequently, before we may consider the *rights* of a partner, we must first think about his or her obligations and whether they have been adequately discharged.

In most jurisdictions, partnerships—including law partnerships—have an implied covenant of fair dealing.[3] Where the covenant exists, its coverage extends to every relationship of the partnership.

First, there is the relationship among and between the partners themselves. The covenant requires that each partner deal equitably and honestly with all fellow partners, foregoing personal aggrandizement at the expense of the partnership unit. The covenant prohibits behavior that would allow one partner to acquire a fellow partner's client base by, for example, disparagement of the fellow partner.

The covenant also regulates partners' dealings with many other groups and individuals, such as prospective partners (that is, associates), employees, and those who deal with the firm in a professional way as vendors or service providers. Partners must deal fairly with lawyers seeking to be associated with the firm, with associates hired by the firm and looking to become partners, with employees on the staff, and with those applying for employment.

Finally, the covenant requires that partners deal fairly with clients of the firm. Just as in any business dealing, there is a requirement that the customer—here, the client—receive fair treatment. Attempts to increase income by padding time sheets or raising hourly charges artificially are obvious examples of violations of the covenant of fair dealing. As stated by Justice Erickson (later

---

2. William I. Weston, *The Fee, the Fee, My Kingdom Is the Fee,* THE PROF. LAW., Nov. 1994.

3. For example, New York has an implied covenant of fair dealing in contracts, including partnership agreements, while Texas does not. *See* Reid v. Vickel & Brewer, 1990 U.S. Dist. LEXIS 11589 (S.D.N.Y. 1990).

Chief Justice) of the Colorado Supreme Court, "[i]t has been long recognized in Colorado that attorneys must act with utmost good faith toward and solely for the benefit of those who entrust their interests to them."[4] In the words of the Supreme Judicial Court of Maine, "[o]ne who undertakes to render services in the practice of a profession owes a duty to exercise that degree of skill, care and diligence exercised by members of that same profession."[5]

This hornbook concept carries through the case law dealing with law firms and law partners.

Does Malpractice Insurance Protect the Partner?

Often, a partner believes there is little cause for concern should a fellow partner violate the covenant as it relates to dealing with others: after all, the malpractice insurance policy will afford protection against third party claims. Not so. Several courts have held that if *any* partner engages in conduct he or she knows could expose the firm to a claim and yet states, on an insurance application, that he or she knows of no facts giving rise to a claim, then any policy issued upon that application is vitiated. The insurance company does not have to pay.[6]

In the *Dunn* case, a law firm partner (Mr. Cooper) was embezzling funds belonging to the firm's clients. After Cooper had commenced the embezzlement, he stated on the firm's application for malpractice insurance that he was not aware of any past or present situation that could result in the filing of a malpractice claim against the firm. Upon discovery of the theft, Cooper filed for bankruptcy. Several lawyers in the firm, including Dunn, were defendants in lawsuits brought by clients whose funds had been misappropriated; plaintiffs in the *Dunn* case claimed Dunn failed to protect funds belonging to them. Malpractice claims were filed with the insurance carrier, which denied coverage for all lawyers at the firm. The insurance company brought a declaratory judgment action asserting that the professional liability policy was null and void due to Cooper's material misrepresentation on the application. All parties agreed that the policy would not cover Cooper,

---

4. Wright v. District Court in and for Gunnison, 731 P.2d 661 (Colo. 1987).

5. Fisherman's Wharf Assocs. II v. Verrill & Dana, 645 A.2d 1133 (Me. 1994).

6. *See* Home Ins. Co. v. Dunn, 963 F.2d 1023 (7th Cir. 1992).

but the other lawyers in the firm denied any knowledge of Cooper's wrongdoing and claimed coverage. Home Insurance Company filed a motion for summary judgment. The plaintiffs in the *Dunn* case, who were also defendants in the insurance company action, moved to dismiss the declaratory judgment action. The district court granted the defendants' motion, holding that the other lawyers were innocent insureds who were still entitled to the protection of the policy. Home Insurance Company appealed.

The Seventh Circuit reversed. The policy contained a "waiver of exclusions" clause, which the defendants claimed prohibited the carrier from avoiding the policy. Home Insurance asserted that because of the fraud, no policy ever came into force and, consequently, no "waiver of exclusions" clause could apply. The carrier stated that an Illinois statute recognized that intentional misrepresentation by an insurance policy applicant could void the policy. The carrier asserted that because Cooper's misrepresentation was made with knowledge, the policy never came into effect. The court agreed with Home Insurance Company, but noted as follows:

> Further, we believe that the defendants misconstrue the statute. Illinois courts have consistently held that, under the statute, an insurance contract may be invalidated for one of two reasons. First, if a misrepresentation is made with the intent to defraud, the contract is void. Alternatively, if the misrepresentation materially effects [sic] the risks taken, the company underwriting the policy may rescind it. In this regard, the Illinois courts have held [that a] "material misrepresentation will void the contract even though made through mistake or good faith. . . . In other words, it is unnecessary for the insurer to prove that a misrepresentation was made with the intent to deceive if it was material to the risk assumed."[7]

This result is reason enough for every partner to be sure that policies and procedures to reduce the potential for claims are in place, and that they are enforced. Otherwise, you, as a partner, may awake to find that someone in your firm intentionally padded a bill or carelessly checked a title report. You knew nothing about these things, but the guilty lawyer "signed off" on the malpractice policy application. When the firm is sued, you have no protection against the cost of defending the action or paying any resulting judgment.

---

7. *Id.* at 1026.

The implications of the *Dunn* case are considered in an article by Richard P. Swanson in *The Practical Lawyer* for July 1993.[8] As Swanson notes, "[c]onsider the plight of attorneys . . . in a large firm when one partner is acting wrongfully. Every professional at the firm but one may respond truthfully to the firm's annual malpractice insurance application by saying that [he or she] is not aware of any facts that might give rise to a claim. When the policy issues, every such person believes [he or she] has coverage—but when the one person's scheme unravels every other person in the firm may find [he or she] is without coverage."[9]

Even the careful lawyer can sometimes forget and that mental lapse can void a malpractice policy. For example, if your firm is sued, defends the case and, in the process, retains local counsel but fails to notify its malpractice carrier of that retention, or fails to serve notice promptly, coverage may be lost.[10]

Theoretically, if one partner is responsible for a successful, uninsured claim against the partnership, then the other partners have a right of contribution against the guilty lawyer.[11] It is self-evident that enforcing that right may be of doubtful value, embarrassing, and expensive.

It must also be remembered that malpractice insurance will not cover a situation regarding a dispute between partners that does not involve improper provision of legal services. *TransAmerica Insurance Co. v. Sayble*[12] is illustrative. In *TransAmerica,* an associate left a professional corporation, disenchanted with its management. The associate's fellow member in the corporation then wrote letters to clients about him, which he considered libelous. He sued his fellow member, Sayble, who tendered the defense to TransAmerica and two coinsurers. TransAmerica agreed to defend, while the coinsurers declined. All three insurance companies then moved for summary judgment against Sayble. The lower court granted the motions and Sayble appealed.

---

8. Richard P. Swanson, *Guilty by Partnership: How Malpractice Coverage Vanishes,* THE PRACTICAL LAW., July 1993, at 15.

9. *See also* American Home Assurance Co. v. Morris J. Eisen, P.C., N.Y. L.J., September 4, 1992, at 22 (N.Y. Sup. Ct.).

10. Clemente v. Home Ins. Co., 791 F. Supp. 118 (E.D. Pa.), *aff'd* 981 F.2d 1246 (3d Cir. 1992).

11. Reiner v. Kelley, 8 Ohio App. 3d 390, 457 N.E.2d 946 (Ct. App. 1983); JACOB A. STEIN, THE LAW OF LAW FIRMS § 6.15 (1994).

12. 193 Cal. App. 3d 1562, 239 Cal. Rptr. 201 (Ct. App. 1987).

Although its decision was based largely upon the language of the insurance policies, the Court of Appeal reversed. It said that

> [t]he two insurance policies are malpractice policies. Thus, there must be malpractice if professional liability coverage is to apply. We reject the simplistic literalism urged on us by appellants; using the word "others" instead of "clients" is not significant. To hold otherwise would do violence to the obvious intent of the parties.
>
> We do not say that an insurance policy cannot cover both professional malpractice and legal actions arising from business disputes within a law firm, but the policies at bench do not provide such broad protection.[13]

The decision in *TransAmerica* suggests that you take a careful look at your insurance policies and assure yourself that they cover the risks you have in mind in this respect.

Relationships among and between partners vary considerably, depending upon the activity. Obligations stem from the employment process, from the compensation schedules for partners, from the conduct of the firm toward partners who decide to leave the firm for one reason or another, and from the attitude of the firm toward its senior members.

Fiduciary Duty of Partners

The unique situation of a partnership, including a law partnership, establishes each partner as a fiduciary toward the others. As one court has put it, "because of this fiduciary duty, in their dealings with one another, partners cannot fall back on morals of the marketplace."[14]

In *Avianca, Inc. v. Corriea,* a Colombian airline sued its former law firm, alleging various counts of fraud by a partner, Mark Corriea. One partner, Martin Tierney, sought dismissal from the case on the ground that he had no personal involvement with any of the allegedly fraudulent acts committed by Corriea and that he had only limited knowledge of the transactions. Tierney also urged that he not be held liable for what was tantamount to criminal conduct by Corriea.

---

13. *TransAmerica,* 193 Cal. App. 3d at 1568, 239 Cal. Rptr. at 204.
14. Simpson v. Ernst & Young, 850 F. Supp. 648, 656 (S.D. Ohio 1994).

The court, in denying Tierney's motion, took occasion to discuss the status of a partner in this situation. It said that

> Tierney attempts to hide behind the same shield that Corriea does—he claims that, because Corriea's actions were those of an entrepreneur and not a lawyer, he (Tierney) should not [sic] liable. For many of the reasons explained above, the court rejects this theory. Neither Corriea, nor his law firm, nor his partner can avoid liability by segmenting their actions into those taken as Avianca's attorney and those taken independent of that role. Defendants are being sued in their capacity as plaintiff's lawyer; Corriea & Tierney (and not simply Mark Corriea) were Avianca's attorneys. Under D. C. partnership law, Tierney may still be liable.
>
> While the court sympathizes with Tierney's argument that respondeat superior liability should not be imposed under RICO, the court notes that partnership liability is somewhat different from an employer's liability for an employee's intentional actions; whereas it may be unjust to hold a corporation trebly liable for a single employee's criminal acts, the situation changes dramatically in the partnership context, where all involved are high-level managers of the firm. Partners are routinely held jointly and severally liable for the actions of their partners.[15]

Once a partnership is dissolved, then the obligation of fiduciary duty from one partner to another ceases.[16] However, one must be careful to distinguish the dissolution of the partnership from its winding up. Fiduciary duties between partners remain an obligation until the unfinished business of the firm is completed. Citing *Beckman v. Farmer*,[17] the Maryland Court of Appeals put it this way:

> But the mutual fiduciary duties cease when the winding up is completed. Thus, "when the partners agree to settle their accounts contemporaneously with dissolution with the understanding that one or more would continue the business . . . unfinished business loses its character as partnership prop-

15. 1992 U.S. Dist. LEXIS 4709, at *45 (D.D.C. 1992).
16. Marr v. Langhoff, 322 Md. 657, 589 A.2d 470 (1991).
17. 579 A.2d 618, 634 (D.C. 1990).

erty, and the outgoing partner severs the fiduciary association that binds him to the post-dissolution entity."

Whether one is a partner becomes of vital importance in the context of a malpractice action. In a New Jersey case, *Falzarano v. Leo*,[18] a lawyer (Daunno) was sued by the plaintiff on the ground that certain security documents had not been timely filed and recorded. The actual omissions had been a failure on the part of one or more associates in the law firm. Daunno moved for summary judgment, contending that he was not a partner and, therefore, not vicariously liable for the misfeasance of the associates in the firm, but only their coemployee. Before judgment, the case was settled. Daunno then sought counsel fees against the plaintiff, pursuant to a statute allowing such recovery if the suit in the underlying case was frivolous. The court awarded such fees to Daunno. The plaintiff appealed.

The appellate court reversed. It said that the plaintiff's case was not frivolous. First, the court noted that "every member of a partnership is jointly and severally liable for torts committed by other members of the partnership acting within the scope of the firm business, even though they do not participate in, or ratify, or have knowledge of such negligence or legal malpractice."[19] It then declared that

> [a]lthough Mr. Daunno claimed during the litigation that he was not a partner in the Citrino law firm, the Citrino law firm argued to the contrary in opposing his summary judgment motion. The Citrino law firm claimed that Mr. Daunno was, in fact, a partner in the firm. Moreover, the trial court advised the parties at the hearing on counsel fees that it had denied Mr. Daunno's prior motion for summary judgment because Mr. Daunno was "a principal in the firm at that time" and was "a proper party."
>
> Furthermore, although Mr. Daunno may not have actually been a partner in the Citrino law firm, he held himself out to the public as a partner, and, thus, he could have been held liable for any partnership liability as though he were an actual member of the partnership under settled principles of estoppel.[20]

18. 269 N.J. Super. 315, 635 A.2d 547 (Super. Ct. App. Div. 1993).
19. *Falzarano*, 269 N.J. Super. at 320, 1993 N.J. Super LEXIS 890 at *8.
20. *Id.*, 269 N.J. Super. at 320, 1993 N.J. Super LEXIS 890 at *9.

There are two lessons to be gleaned from the *Falzarano* case. First, one responsibility of a partner is to assure that other lawyers in the firm—counsel, associates, and senior lawyers—do not hold themselves out as partners when, in fact, they are not. They may have apparent authority to bind the firm in ways the firm never anticipated. Second, there is the obligation to supervise associates to assure that the firm will not wind up with an obligation to discharge a judgment or satisfy a claim arising from the misfeasance of an associate.

This duty to supervise was the subject of a comment by the New York Court of Appeals. In *Clients' Security Fund of New York v. Grandeau,*[21] the plaintiff Fund was seeking from a law partner recovery of funds it had paid out on behalf of his dishonest partner. The defendant claimed that the Fund was statutorily authorized to recover only for "dishonest conduct" and, because it was his partner (and not he) who was dishonest, the Fund's claim should be dismissed. The court found that, in the underlying case, it had been determined that the defendant was censured for professional misconduct, as he "failed to oversee or review the recordkeeping of his law firm, thereby contributing to the conversion by his law partner."[22]

In the pages that follow, many of the relationships that partners have with one another, and with associates and staff, will be reviewed in greater detail. Thus, we will consider what partners must do to fulfill their end of the bargain so they may enjoy rights as partners.

Are You a Partner?

Whether one is a partner is important to know. A lawyer may be a partner in name, but not in fact, and the consequences are significant. Law firms today create distinctions between "equity partners," "nonequity partners," and "contract partners." These distinctions tend to focus upon the financial consequences of the differences among categories. But, as we shall see, there are other, often unmentioned and overlooked effects. Partnership of any nature may provide privileges, but to have other benefits in particular circum-

---

21. 72 N.Y.2d 62, 526 N.E.2d 270, 530 N.Y.S.2d 775, 1988 N.Y. LEXIS 1697 (1988).

22. *Id.*, 42 N.Y.2d at 66, 526 N.E.2d at 272, 1988 N.Y. LEXIS 1697 at *9.

stances, one must be shown not to be a partner. For example, to assert rights under some federal statutes, it is "dangerous" to be called a "partner"; only an employee may assert the statutory rights.

In today's world, lawyers band together in a variety of arrangements. Before one decides to join forces with a brother or sister lawyer, it is wise to consider the consequences. It seems that lawyers Salvatore DiMasi and Stephen Karll might have made some changes had they foreseen the consequences of their office arrangement in Massachusetts. They shared office space with lawyer Ralph Donabed. Their office stationery was entitled "Law Offices of DiMasi, Donabed & Karll, a Professional Association." Invoices were issued in the same name and listed a roll of lawyers in the left-hand margin. Atlas Tack Corporation brought suit against DiMasi and Karll on the ground that they were vicariously liable for the alleged malpractice of Donabed. Atlas claimed it paid invoices by checks drawn to DiMasi, Donabed & Karll. The trial court granted the defendants' motions for summary judgment, and Atlas appealed.

The appeals court reversed. It said that the circumstances of the case raised a question about whether a "partnership by estoppel" existed. The court explained that the defendants knew Donabed was using stationery with their names on it, and that it bore the legend "a Professional Association." In the court's view, "the use of the term 'professional association' may well suggest a partnership to the public which is unlikely to distinguish among partnerships, professional corporations and professional associations. At the very least, the use of the term in the circumstances of this case presents a question of fact as to whether a partnership by estoppel exists."[23]

After the judgments in the trial court, Donabed had settled with the plaintiff, who gave him a release; the release excepted from its terms any claim against the codefendants. The appellate court held that, in Massachusetts, a release will not discharge a vicariously liable party if there is a covenant containing an express reservation of rights against that party. The court said there was no reason not to follow that rule. Accordingly, the defendants' argument that because the tortfeasor was released, they should be released, was untenable.[24]

---

23. Atlas Tack Corp. v. DiMasi, 37 Mass. App. Ct. 66 at 70, 637 N.E.2d 230 at 233 (App. Ct. 1994).

24. *Id.*, 37 Mass. App. Ct. at 71–72, 637 N.E.2d at 233–234.

The consequences of partnership are sometimes hard to predict or, more accurately, it is difficult to predict when a particular arrangement will be deemed a partnership. In *United States v. Alderson*,[25] two Alderson brothers had farmed together for twenty years and had built the business to include six full-time employees and seventy-five employees overall. The Internal Revenue Service had demanded production of partnership records, which Jack Alderson refused to produce, invoking his privilege against self-incrimination. The trial court ordered Jack Alderson to produce the records. On appeal, the Ninth Circuit took occasion to discuss a U.S. Supreme Court case, *Bellis v. United States*,[26] which was decided on facts similar to those in *Alderson*. In *Bellis*, a three-person law firm had a separate identity despite the absence of a formal partnership agreement. The firm had existed for fifteen years and had six permanent employees, an established name, and a separate bank account. It had held itself out to third parties as an independent entity, and it had filed separate partnership returns for federal tax purposes. The Supreme Court held that, because the privilege against self-incrimination is personal, it may not be invoked to avoid producing an artificial organization's records that are held in a representative capacity. The Court decided that the law firm was such an organization. In *Alderson*, the Ninth Circuit followed *Bellis*, declaring that the brothers had a partnership despite the absence of a formal partnership agreement.

The existence of a fee-sharing arrangement is not enough to constitute a partnership. In one case, two law partners, Talley and Bagby, dissolved their partnership. They agreed that Talley would handle a certain case and that Bagby would share in the fee if the case was settled. They were sued by Helen Gibson, who alleged malpractice against them. Bagby defended on the ground that any malpractice occurred after the partnership was dissolved; Gibson claimed that the fee arrangement continued the partnership. The trial court's grant of summary judgment in favor of Bagby was affirmed. The Georgia Court of Appeals held that a common interest in profits alone was not, under Georgia law, enough to constitute a partnership.[27]

25. 646 F.2d 421 (9th Cir. 1981).
26. 417 U.S. 85 (1974).
27. Gibson v. Talley, 156 Ga. App. 593, 275 S.E.2d 154 (Ct. App. 1980).

The Test for Partnership

How do you know whether you are a true partner?

The courts have developed fairly extensive tests for determining when a person denominated a "partner" is, in fact, a partner. Richard Ehrlich sued his former partners in Sann & Howe, a New York law firm, claiming that his relationship with the firm had been terminated in violation of the Employee Retirement Income and Security Act of 1985, 29 U.S.C. §§ 1001–1461 (ERISA), and particularly the section making it unlawful for a person to discharge a participant or beneficiary for the purpose of interfering with attainment of any right to which the participant may become entitled. Ehrlich conceded that to maintain an action under ERISA, he would have to be deemed an "employee."

In the case,[28] Judge Sweet followed an earlier Southern District of New York case, which had considered whether a person was an "employee" for purposes of the Age Discrimination in Employment Act, 29 U.S.C. § 630(f) (ADEA) and Title VII of the Civil Rights Act of 1964, 29 U.S.C. § 2000(e) (Title VII). The earlier case involved a certified public accounting firm with over 1,350 partners, but Judge Sweet noted that there the court held that it "looks to the 'individual's actual duties and status'" and declared that "the test for distinguishing a partner from an employee requires consideration of all elements of the work relationship."[29]

Judge Sweet concentrated on three characteristics, which he denominated "the *Caruso* test":

1. the purported partner's ability to control and operate the business (Sweet quoted the court in *Caruso* and stated that "the title 'partner' is not normally applied to an individual whose employment duties are unilaterally dictated by another member of a business");
2. whether the purported partner received his or her compensation as a percentage of the firm's profits, rather than in the form of a fixed hourly wage or weekly salary; and
3. whether the purported partner has a "relatively high level of job security."

28. Ehrlich v. Howe, 848 F. Supp. 842 (S.D.N.Y. 1994).

29. Caruso v. Peat, Marwick, Mitchell & Co., 664 F. Supp. 144 (S.D.N.Y. 1987).

Sann & Howe had a written partnership agreement that provided for compensation to the partners, including Ehrlich, as a percentage of profits, subject to certain minimum adjustments. Concerning the third element of the *Caruso* test, Judge Sweet considered whether Ehrlich had greater job security than an employee. The law firm required the *unanimous* vote of all other partners to terminate Ehrlich. Under these circumstances, Judge Sweet held that Ehrlich was, in fact, a partner of the law firm and, therefore, had no cause of action under ERISA for wrongful termination.

The fact that the title of "partner" does not control one's destiny is apparent from an Ohio decision that preceded *Ehrlich*.[30] In the Ohio case, an accountant in a certified public accounting firm sued the firm, claiming various acts of discrimination against him under ADEA and ERISA. The Ohio federal court, noting that the case would turn on the accountant's status, held that general principles of partnership law would determine the outcome. Although the accountant was called a partner by Ernst & Young, the firm, he did not share in profits (he was paid a salary), had no right to examine the books and records of the firm, had very little authority to hire, and had no fiduciary relationship with the firm's management committee. Therefore, the Ohio federal court held the accountant was an employee and not a partner.

One thing a lawyer who has practiced for any significant length of time will learn is that things are not always as they appear to be.

For example, Harry Heller was a lawyer maintaining the Washington office for the New York–based firm of Simpson, Thacher & Bartlett. He represented the firm's clients in the District of Columbia, for which he was paid an annual fixed compensation, and he retained 60 percent of the fees he generated. He was denominated a partner of the firm in the Martindale-Hubbell directory and the firm's personnel directory, but he never signed the firm's partnership agreement, shared in the firm's profits, or was liable for the firm's losses. Heller evidently did not think he was a partner because he did not file any New York State income tax returns for 1965 and 1966. He must have been surprised when in 1968 he was assessed income taxes by the New York State Tax

30. Simpson v. Ernst & Young, 850 F. Supp. 648, 656 (S.D. Ohio 1994).

Commission. Whether he was a partner was not decided. In 1985, the assessment was annulled by the Appellate Division of the New York State Supreme Court because it "took the Tax Commission twelve years to schedule and hold a hearing and to file an answer" to the taxpayer's complaint.[31]

You may think you are dealing with a professional corporation when, in fact, your dealings are with a partnership. So found a trial court in Virginia, and the Virginia Supreme Court affirmed.[32] Mr. Boyd and others formed a professional corporation in 1977, another lawyer joined the original group, and then that lawyer and some of the original members left that practice and formed their own professional corporation, Payne P.C. In a series of motions and cross-motions, Payne P.C. argued that the professional corporation was a tax device only and that the lawyers had conducted themselves as a partnership. The ultimate question was whether Boyd P.C. owned certain assets or whether ownership of the assets was to be settled in accordance with partnership law. No formal partnership agreement ever existed during the life of the Boyd firm; after the professional corporation was formed, the firm continued to operate the way it had always operated. No physical assets were transferred to the corporation. However, the corporation's board of directors elected officers at an annual meeting and conducted other essential business through unanimous consent resolutions. The Virginia Supreme Court wrote that "[b]ecause Boyd P.C. was a close corporation and its shareholders validly conduct the internal affairs of their law practice as a partnership, we hold that the trial court properly settled their rights and liabilities according to partnership law."[33]

Boyd teaches that partners seeking to incorporate and obtain the advantages of incorporation "across the board," and not merely in the tax realm, must be careful to conduct business with all the trappings of a corporation and not those of a partnership.

Effect of a Partnership Agreement

Perhaps the most important element in the establishment of a lawyer's rights in relation to his or her colleagues in a law firm is the

---

31. Heller v. Chu, 111 A.D.2d 1007, 490 N.Y.S.2d 326 (App. Div. 1985).
32. Boyd P.C. v. Payne P.C., 244 Va. 418, 422 S.E.2d 784 (1992).
33. *Id.*, 244 Va. at 430, 422 S.E.2d at 790.

partnership agreement—or, in the case of a professional corporation, the articles of incorporation and bylaws. Although the factors that determine whether a person is a partner can be gleaned from an oral agreement, there is always the possibility, when a dispute is litigated, that testimony will differ. Moreover, as one court has held, if a lawyer accepts benefits suggesting that he or she has a particular status, that person may be estopped from claiming some greater status, absent any written agreement so stating.[34] As lawyers know, the best way to avoid controversy is to reduce the agreement to writing.[35]

Consequences of Partnership—Specific Situations

There are times in the life of a lawyer when it is better not to be a partner in the law firm. Partnership often means that the lawyer is left without legal protection he or she might otherwise have.

Collecting Retirement Benefits

The fact that you were a partner may inhibit your ability to collect retirement benefits you believe are owed to you by your former firm.

In *Bane v. Ferguson*,[36] Bane had been a partner with Isham, Lincoln & Beale, which had awarded him a pension. The Isham firm then had a disastrous merger and Bane's pension was terminated. He sued his former partners. The court said that because Bane had been a partner, he could not claim under ERISA, nor was he protected under the Illinois Uniform Partnership Act because he was no longer a partner; and because he was no longer a partner, his former partners owed no fiduciary duty to him and had no tort liability for the dissolution of the firm that ended his benefits. Mr. Bane was "up the creek without a paddle."

Later, we will consider retirement benefits in some detail. For now, suffice it to say that if a retirement benefit is tied to the

---

34. Reid v. Bickel & Brewer, 1990 U.S. Dist. LEXIS 11589 (S.D.N.Y. 1990).

35. In this chapter we will discuss those discrete aspects of the partnership agreement particularly affecting a partner's rights and responsibilities. In a subsequent chapter, we will consider the necessary and desirable elements of an effective agreement.

36. 890 F.2d 11 (7th Cir. 1989).

amount of legal fees the firm may derive from your client or clients, and you are no longer a partner, you will probably be unable to collect from your former firm should it cease paying you the benefits. In *Garfield v. Greenbaum*,[37] the New York Appellate Division held that a retirement benefit that is dependent on legal fees continuing from a former client is a division of fees without regard to services actually rendered. Therefore, the benefit in that form is against public policy and a violation of Disciplinary Rule 2-207, Division of Fees Among Lawyers. The lesson here is not to make your retirement benefit contingent upon the legal fees subsequently earned by the firm from your clients.

Claims for Age Discrimination

A partner may also have a problem asserting a claim for age discrimination under ADEA. In *Fountain v. Metcalf*,[38] one of the partners in a four-partner accounting firm, organized as a professional association, brought suit for wrongful discharge. The court said it would not honor form over substance and would treat the association as a partnership. After focusing on the plaintiff's role in operations, in management control, and in ownership functions, he was determined to be a partner-in-fact in the firm and not covered by ADEA.

In a 1994 case, a federal district court in Ohio reached a similar result in a case brought by an accounting firm partner under ADEA.[39] The court noted that the definition of the persons covered under Title VII and ADEA was virtually the same; it noted that Title VII had been held inapplicable to partners or shareholders in a professional corporation. The court said that to decide whether a plaintiff is a partner, "all factors should be considered with no one factor being decisive."[40]

As previously noted in the *Ehrlich* case, a partner seeking to hold his former partners responsible for a wrongful termination under ERISA will find that status as a partner has eliminated application of that statute to his or her situation.

---

37. 103 A.D.2d 709, 477 N.Y.S.2d 983 (App. Div. 1984).
38. 925 F.2d 1398 (11th Cir. 1991).
39. Simpson v. Ernst & Young, 850 F. Supp. 648 (S.D. Ohio 1994).
40. *Id.* at 659.

Workers' Compensation Claims

The partner who is injured in the course of partnership business may believe that there is the opportunity to recover for the injuries under workers' compensation laws. Wrong. See the comment of the court in *Wheeler v. Hurdman*.[41] In *Wheeler*, the issue was whether the plaintiff-partner in an accounting firm was entitled to recover in an action under Title VII. The court held that because the partner was an employee, she was not entitled to bring suit under Title VII. Judge Anderson, writing for the Tenth Circuit Court of Appeals, said that

> [c]onsidering the many exceptions in the law we must agree with Wheeler and the EEOC that categorical absolutes are difficult to sustain in this area. However, there is no discernable trend to erase the traditional line between partners and employees. For instance, state courts defining "employee" for purposes of workmen's compensation laws have usually refused to classify partners as employees absent express statutory authority. "With the exception of Oklahoma and Louisiana, every state that has dealt judicially with the status of 'working partners' or joint venturers has held that they cannot be employees."[42]

The Sexual Harassment Situation

As more and more women join law firms, claims for sexual harassment are bound to increase. If you are a law firm partner, male or female, it is important, to help avoid liability, that you take immediate remedial action should an instance of claimed sexual harassment come to your attention. Similarly, comments by other lawyers in your firm that may defame third persons are not chargeable to you unless you knew of them and failed to stop them. In *Frederick v. Shaw*,[43] a female associate in a large law firm claimed sexual harassment by one partner, and defamatory comments by him, in a suit against all the partners of the law firm. The court held that knowledge of the harassing partner is not imputed

---

41. 825 F. 2d 257, 268 (10th Cir.), *cert. denied*, 484 U.S. 986 (1987).
42. *Id.* (citation omitted).
43. 1994 U.S. Dist. LEXIS 1809, 63 Empl. Prac. Dec. (CCH) ¶ 42,864 (E.D. Pa. 1994).

to the law firm and defamatory statements by one partner do not make the partnership liable unless that partner is acting "in the ordinary course of business or [the statements were] made with the authority of the co-partners." Thus, the partners were not liable, the plaintiff was not entitled to injunctive relief, and the partnership was not required to apologize and retract the defamatory statements of the guilty partner.

I think most lawyers will agree that the members of the profession, with few exceptions, are honest and honorable people. The occasions when partnership in a law firm is detrimental are infrequent or even rare. But they do occur.

Malpractice: Liability for the Errant Partner

Most partners are concerned about their potential liability in the event of a successful malpractice claim—not against themselves, of course, but against one or more of their partners. Unfortunately, the issue is not a simple one.

Many differing circumstances can present themselves and each will produce a different result concerning the vicarious liability of a law firm partner.

All partners are generally liable if the errant partner's activity giving rise to the malpractice claim was within the scope of the partnership business; this is so, even if the other partners did not know of, participate in, or ratify the conduct of the errant partner. If the errant partner is guilty of conversion or misapplication of funds, all partners are liable if the funds came into possession of the errant partner as part of the partnership business, notwithstanding that he or she may have subsequently absconded with, or misapplied, these funds. However, a different rule exists in the case of misappropriation or embezzlement. If the errant partner receives funds in some capacity other than as a lawyer, his or her partners are not liable. In this latter case, the intent of the client in transmitting the funds—not the concept of the lawyer—controls; the issue is whether the client believed that the errant partner was acting as a lawyer or in some other capacity, such as in connection with a business deal.[44]

However, if one of your partners converts clients' funds in the ordinary course of business of the partnership, and you are one of

44. Note, J.R. Kemper, *Vicarious Liability of Attorney for Tort of Partner in Law Firm*, 70 A.L.R. 3d 1298 (1994).

the partners, you may find yourself facing a judgment. In *Majer v. Schmidt*,[45] the former partner of a dissolved law firm was held responsible for the dissolved firm's obligations, including the debts of a partner who had converted clients' funds in the course of winding up the partnership affairs. Not all courts follow the same rule as the New York court in *Majer*. In *Gibson v. Talley*, a Georgia case, a lawyer was held not liable for the alleged malpractice of a former partner when the partnership was dissolved before the alleged malpractice, despite the fact that the plaintiff had retained the errant copartner while the partnership was still in existence.[46]

Similarly, in a case decided under the Illinois Uniform Partnership Act, individual partners were held jointly liable for certain computer lease obligations of a dissolved law firm. The court held that dissolution of a law partnership does not discharge the existing liability of any partner.[47]

Suppose that your partner—your real estate expert who regularly signs title certificates on behalf of your firm—borrows from the bank. Unbeknownst to you, he negligently signs a title certificate on property securing the loan; there is a default on the loan, the title company pays the investors, and then sues your firm. Do the partners have any liability? This was the question in a North Carolina case. The trial court granted summary judgment for the law firm and the plaintiff appealed.

The North Carolina Supreme Court reversed. It held that the errant partner was a general agent of the firm and the plaintiff had no notice of any restriction on the partner's authority. The law firm was not entitled to summary judgment because a question of fact existed about whether the issuance of the title certificate was in the business of the partnership.[48]

Moreover, whether your partner has authority depends not on what you have told your partner, but on what you have held out to those who deal with your firm. When push comes to shove, the

---

45. 169 A.D.2d 501, 564 N.Y.S.2d 722 (App. Div. 1991).

46. Gibson v. Talley, 156 Ga. App. 593, 275 S.E.2d 154 (Ct. App. 1980); *aff'd*, 162 Ga. App. 303, 291 S.E.2d 72 (Ct. App. 1982).

47. Pacificorp Credit, Inc. v. Antonow & Fink, 1990 U.S. Dist. LEXIS 7733 (N.D. Ill. 1990).

48. Investors Title Ins. Co. v. Herzig, 320 N.C. 770, 360 S.E.2d 786 (1987).

crucial issue is what you told the plaintiff who is now suing your firm. There will be authority in your partner, unless you told the plaintiff otherwise or the activity was not in the normal business of the firm. What is even more significant is that you have no duty to supervise your partners. This issue is illustrated by another North Carolina case.[49] In *McGarity*, the law firm was sued when a partner, Clarkson, solicited investments for a mining operation. Clarkson never accounted for the monies. Clarkson was caused to resign from the firm and he ultimately went bankrupt. The defendants, other partners in the firm, moved for summary judgment, which was granted by the trial court. The plaintiff appealed.

The North Carolina Court of Appeals held that the motion was properly granted. It said there was no evidence that Clarkson had been authorized, or had apparent authority, to act as an agent of the firm in soliciting the money for investment. Also, the defendant-partners had no duty to supervise Clarkson and consequently their failure to exercise supervision over his activities that were outside the practice of law would not constitute negligence.[50]

Activities outside the Legal Realm

If you withdraw or retire from your firm before your partner engages in wrongdoing or malpractice, you will not be liable. But, there is a caveat; if you and the guilty one were associated as cotrustees in your firm's trust account and there is a deficiency in the trust account, the situation involves trust business and you can be liable. In a California case, this happened to Mr. Lee, when Mr. Adams absconded with trust funds after Lee had left the firm in which they were partners. The trial court let Lee "off the hook" when the depositor sought return of his deposit.

The California Supreme Court reversed, saying that Lee was obliged to render an accounting and "in the absence of such an accounting, however, Lee has not absolved himself of liability for the unaccounted-for balance."[51]

This does not mean that a partner is always responsible for the misdeeds of another partner. Whether the miscreant was acting in

---

49. McGarity v. Craighill, Rendleman, Ingle & Blythe, P.A., 83 N.C. App. 106, 349 S.E.2d 311 (Ct. App. 1986).

50. *McGarity*, 83 N.C. App. at 110–11, 349 S.E.2d at 313.

51. Blackmon v. Hale, 1 Cal. 3d 548, 463 P.2d 418, 83 Cal. Rptr. 194 (1970).

the business of the law firm is often a factual question. For example, in *Sheinkopf v. Stone*,[52] Saltiel was a law partner in Nutter, McLennan & Fish, a Boston firm. He organized a real estate venture that went sour, and he declared bankruptcy. Sheinkopf, a participant in the venture, then sued the firm. The law firm obtained summary judgment and dismissal, and the plaintiff appealed.

The First Circuit reversed, holding that a question existed about whether there had been an attorney-client relationship between the firm and Sheinkopf. The court observed that

> [h]uman beings routinely wear a multitude of hats. The fact that a person is a lawyer, or a physician, or a plumber, or a lion-tamer, does not mean that every relationship he undertakes is, or can reasonably be perceived as being, in his professional capacity. Lawyers/physicians/plumbers/lion-tamers sometimes act as husbands, or wives, or fathers, or daughters, or sports fans, or investors, or businessmen. The list is nearly infinite. To imply an attorney-client relationship, therefore, the law requires more than an individuals's objective, unspoken belief that the person with whom he is dealing, who happens to be a lawyer, has become his lawyer. If any such belief is to form a foundation for the implication of a relationship of trust and confidence, it must be objectively reasonable under the totality of the circumstances. . . .[53]

Take a rather usual situation: You are a partner in a law firm, and one of your partners practices a considerable amount of probate law. A client of the firm decides that your partner or you should be the executor of the estate. The client dies. There is mismanagement of the affairs of the estate, perhaps even conversion. The estate sues the firm. Are you vicariously liable for the wrong?

Not all courts agree and the result in such a case will vary. The Supreme Court of Indiana decided that in a case of a partner's conversion that did not benefit the firm, the partnership was not liable.[54] The court noted that a number of other states had reached a similar result. The Court of Appeals of North Carolina was somewhat more circumspect in a case involving an estate that sued a law firm for mismanagement by one of its partners who had served as executor. The court decided that it would be up to a jury

---

52. 927 F.2d 1259 (1st Cir. 1991).
53. *Id.* at 1265.
54. Husted v. McCloud, 450 N.E.2d 491 (Ind. 1983).

to determine which actions of the partner had been in his capacity as lawyer for the estate and which were in his capacity as executor. The court said that the indirect benefit to the firm from the partner's service as executor would not be enough to impose vicarious liability on the firm. The court also held that the firm would not be liable for punitive damages.[55]

In the view of the Supreme Court of Kansas, whether a lawyer is acting in the business of the law firm when he or she becomes involved in a business deal for a client is a factual question to be presented to a jury. You may find yourself in this situation: For years, one of your partners has been very friendly with a couple, Mr. and Mrs. Phillips. Mr. Phillips dies. His widow retains your firm to handle the estate of her husband. Your firm collects $80,000 in fees and Mrs. Phillips is told this amount will take care of all her legal business until the estate is closed. Another lawyer in the office prepares Mrs. Phillips's income tax returns. Meanwhile, your partner, Carson, is taking care of details of several important transactions for Mrs. Phillips. He finds himself in financial difficulty and she lends him several hundred thousand dollars. Although he was supposed to secure the loan with a recorded mortgage, he fails to do that. Carson files for bankruptcy. Ultimately, Mrs. Phillips sues not only your partner, Carson, but you and his other partners as well. Extended litigation ensues. The trial court enters judgment in favor of the partnership and the partners individually, except Carson. Mrs. Phillips appeals the decision to release the partnership.

In an actual case involving these facts, the trial court made twenty-nine findings of fact about whether Carson's activities were conducted on behalf of the law firm. The trial court then issued conclusions of law, based on those facts. Most important, it found that in giving advice to Mrs. Phillips about the loan transaction, Carson "was not acting as a matter of law within the scope of his actual, apparent and/or implied authority and [sic] were not as a matter of law acts engaged in by the defendant Carson for apparently carrying on the business of the law firm partnership in the usual way."[56] The trial court then entered judgment that, in part, was in favor of the defendant partnership and the individual partners, except Carson, on the ground that "as a matter of law said

55. Shelton v. Fairley, 86 N.C. App. 147, 356 S.E.2d 917 (Ct. App. 1987), *rev. denied*, 320 N.C. 634, 360 S.E.2d 94 (1987).

56. Phillips v. Carson, 240 Kan. 462, 471, 731 P.2d 820, 829 (1987).

defendants are not vicariously liable to plaintiff for the breach of duty and negligence of defendant Carson in light of the above and foregoing findings of fact and conclusions of law."[57]

From this judgment, Mrs. Phillips appealed to the Supreme Court of Kansas. The court's opinion states that

> [a]dvising a client on the propriety of making loans, the legality and sufficiency of proposed security, the method of ascertaining the value of the security, the method of recording security documents and the like are all matters well within the scope of the general practice of law. Had Mrs. Phillips been considering a loan to a third person and had a member of the partnership advised her as Carson did (or as he failed to advise her), there would be little question of the firm's responsibility in the event that she sustained damages as a result of that action or omission. Similarly, the preparation of notes and mortgages, and the filing of mortgages for record, are matters well within the scope of the general practice of law handled daily by lawyers throughout this state.[58]

Mrs. Phillips argued that a factual question remained about whether the transactions involved had been apparently authorized by the partnership. The partnership asserted that the indication of authority must come from the principal. The Kansas Supreme Court noted that no partner in the firm told Mrs. Phillips that Carson's actions were within his authority as a partner and no one told her that his actions were not within his authority as a member of the firm. Nonetheless, Carson's letters were written on firm stationery and mailed in firm envelopes, and firm employees had assisted Carson in his work for Mrs. Phillips. The Court then said:

> Under all of the facts and circumstances, we hold that the trial court erred in entering summary judgment on behalf of the partnership and the individual partners thereof, there being substantial competent evidence from which a trier of fact could find that Carson had apparent authority to prepare the notes and mortgages, and to advise Mrs. Phillips in the matters, as a part of the regular practice of law of the firm. On the record before the trial court, we cannot say as a matter of

57. *Id.*, 240 Kan. at 472, 731 P.2d at 829.
58. *Id.*, 240 Kan. at 480, 731 P.2d at 834.

law that Carson was not acting within the scope of his actual or apparent authority as a member of the firm.[59]

You, as a law firm partner, must vigilantly observe relationships between your firm and its clients as your clients view these relationships. This is particularly true when you or your clients may be performing services that you do not regard as being in the legal realm—services more in the nature of friendly business advice, or the like. If the client believes a lawyer-client relationship exists in the situation, the firm—and not solely the lawyer—may be liable.

A case in point follows. A partner in Coudert Brothers allegedly told the plaintiff's decedent that a certain diversion of assets was necessary for tax purposes. The plaintiff sought to hold the law firm liable for the improper activity as committed in the ordinary course of the partnership business. The law firm moved to dismiss, and the judge in the Southern District of New York granted the motion. He noted that the New York Partnership Statute does not exclude fraud as a wrongful act giving rise to vicarious liability of the firm. However, the plaintiff-estate had not pled that the law firm (or one of its partners) had been retained by the estate, and the complaint failed to allege that the errant lawyer had acted as a lawyer for the estate. Consequently, the court ruled that the complaint did not state a cause of action.[60]

Partnership and Vicarious Liability

When the Firm Signs a Lease

There is probably no circumstance in the life of a law firm partner giving more cause for concern than entrance into a new, extensive lease for expensive office space. You ask yourself, "Am I liable?" Under almost any combination of circumstances, the answer is yes.

A case in federal court in the Southern District of New York tells us that you do not even need a partnership agreement; if you are working with other lawyers under arrangements that indicate a partnership and a lease is made, then you are liable on the lease—whether you signed it or not.

---

59. *Id.*, 240 Kan. at 483, 731 P.2d at 836.

60. Bingham v. Zolt, 683 F. Supp. 965 (S.D.N.Y. 1988). Subsequent proceedings in this case did not relate to Coudert Brothers.

Stuart Matlins sued several partners of the firm of Sargent, Ahearn and van Heemstra when the firm failed to satisfy a judgment for nonpayment of lease rental. The individual lawyers defended on the ground that they were not partners in a firm but merely participants in an "expense sharing agreement."[61] As a footnote in the decision put it, "[n]o evidence of a written partnership agreement was presented to the court in this case."[62] The district court said that four factors were to be considered in determining whether a partnership existed:

1. Pro rata sharing of profits and losses
2. Pro rata contribution to capital of the enterprise's assets
3. Intention of the parties that they be partners
4. Participation in the management of the enterprise[63]

The court noted that one defendant, lawyer Murray Sargent, had filed certain tax forms (K-1) for years he assumed a loss. In response to the lawyer's claim that he did not assume a loss in the year the lease was signed, the court held that "not having accepted losses for the year of the lease signing does not signify that Murray Sargent was not in fact sharing in the losses of the partnership."[64] The court found that the tax forms evidenced Sargent's bearing of losses and participation in capital contribution. As for Sargent's intent to be a partner, the facts that he signed a business certificate for partnership, signed an application as a "general partner" for a safe-deposit box, and deposited payments he received for legal services in an account held by Sargent, Ahearn and van Heemstra satisfied the court that the requisite intent was present.[65] As for participation in the management of the enterprise, the court said that Murray Sargent had signed not only the Matlin lease, but another lease on other premises occupied by the group, as well as other documents; these were all in the name of Sargent, Ahearn and van Heemstra. "It is clear," the court said, that "Murray Sargent had a voice in the management of the . . . partnership."[66] Thus, Murray Sargent was "de facto" a partner in Sargent, Ahearn

61. Matlins v. Sargent, 1991 U.S. Dist. LEXIS 6093, at *2 (S.D.N.Y. 1991).
62. *Id.* at *6, n.7.
63. *Id.* at *8.
64. *Id.* at *10.
65. *Id.* at *13–14.
66. *Id.* at *15.

and van Heemstra and could be sued for the liabilities incurred by the partnership.

In the presence of a partnership agreement, it is even clearer that individual partners are liable under a lease made by the firm.[67] Borod & Huggins, a firm in Memphis, Tennessee, entered into a lease for offices in a building to be renovated by its client, Joseph Larkey/Memphis Associates, a developer. The developer was to construct a parking garage adjacent to the building. The parking garage was not completed on time and the law firm then failed to pay the rent, whereupon the developer sued the law firm and its individual partners. Among the defenses raised by the individual partners was "lack of privity."[68] Moreover, two partners who withdrew from Borod & Huggins before the litigation commenced defended on the ground that there was no default on the lease and no rents were owed when they withdrew and, consequently, they should have no legal obligation for future rents or after-acquired obligations of the reconstituted law firm.[69] The trial court dismissed the developer's suit for rent and, in the firm's counterclaim for rescission, held that the firm was justified in cancellation of the lease agreement. The law firm had continued to represent the developer as its lawyer during the dispute and had also counterclaimed for unpaid attorneys' fees. This claim the trial court dismissed for lack of proof. The parties appealed.

Regarding the issue of the liability of the individual partners of Borod & Huggins, the court held:

> Nothing appears in this record that would release any partner who was a partner at the time that the lease was entered into from personal liability under the lease. None of the discharge scenarios set out in [the Tennessee enactment of section 36 of the Uniform Partnership Act relating to discharge of liabilities] were proved. Of course, rights and obligations between and among the partners undoubtedly exist. One of the partners has filed for indemnity, but because of the prior ruling of the trial court that claim was not reached. We reverse the dismissal of the lessor's complaint for rent against the individual partners who had left the firm; but this is without prejudice to their rights to rely upon matters of personal

---

67. Larkey v. Borod & Huggins, 1990 Tenn. App. LEXIS 335 (Tenn. Ct. App. 1990).

68. *Id.* at *4.

69. *Id.* at *5.

> defenses in further proceedings should such defenses exist. The mere fact that they left the law firm partnership after the execution of the lease does not discharge their liability.[70]

So the *Larkey* case is a warning: it holds that the mere fact that a partner leaves a law firm does not release that partner from liability on a lease executed before his or her departure. One must review the facts in light of the provisions of the Uniform Partnership Act to determine whether there has been a discharge. The Revised Uniform Partnership Act, adopted in Connecticut and Florida and under review in a number of other states, appears to make clear that a partner who has withdrawn ("dissociated") from a firm is liable for firm obligations for a period of two years after his or her departure, but only if the firm continues in business and does not dissolve, and the other party to the transaction with the firm reasonably believed, when entering into the transaction, that the dissociated partner was then a partner.[71]

Be wary of signing a lease for office space before there is a clear understanding with your partners and a written partnership agreement; otherwise, you may find yourself wholly responsible for the lease. In one New York case, Herbert Katz and another lawyer agreed to form a law partnership and Katz signed a lease for office space. The partnership was not formed and Katz moved out. The landlord brought suit for damages, and the trial court awarded summary judgment to him on the issue of liability. Katz appealed.[72] In a brief opinion, the court held that

> [o]ne who signs an agreement on behalf of a nonexistent principal may himself be held liable on that agreement. The customary indices of partnership are not prerequisites for liability. On a search of the record it is determined that plaintiffs are entitled to damages consequent on defendant's breach of his obligation as a signator to the lease, which damages plaintiffs have mitigated by subletting. Plaintiffs may prove the quantum of their damages on remand.[73]

We have considered the scenario of a partner departing from the firm that subsequently defaults on a lease (*Larkey*) and the scenario of an individual lawyer's liability on a partnership lease

---

70. *Id.* at *23.
71. *See* Rev. Unif. Partnership Act § 35 (1994).
72. Grutman v. Katz, 202 A.D.2d 293, 608 N.Y.S.2d 663 (App. Div. 1994).
73. *Id.*, 202 A.D.2d at 293, 608 N.Y.S.2d at 664 (citation omitted).

when the partnership fails to materialize. What about the liability of a lawyer who joins a partnership after the firm has been committed to a lease and then the firm defaults?

This was the situation in a Connecticut case.[74] The defendant law firm, Davidson & Naylor, and its individual partners, including Peter Leepson, were sued by the landlord for nonpayment of rent. The lease with the developer had been signed on July 15, 1988, and the law firm took possession of the premises on November 23, 1988. Leepson joined the firm approximately one week later. The court affirmed the findings of a trial referee that Leepson "was liable to the plaintiff, but only to the extent of his interest in the partnership, pursuant to [section 17 of the Uniform Partnership Act as then in effect in Connecticut]."[75]

The Revised Uniform Partnership Act, recently adopted by Connecticut, would shrink the new partner's liabilities still further. Section 18(b) of that act provides that

> [a] person admitted as a partner into an existing partnership is not personally liable for any partnership obligation incurred before the person's admission as a partner.

Consequently, *Norwalk Twin Towers, Inc.* would not be decided against Leepson in the same way today. His liability would be nonexistent, regardless of whether he had any interest in the partnership. That result is at least one very clear reason for urging the adoption of the Revised Uniform Partnership Act in your state.

Procedural Issues

Issues relating to vicarious liability sometimes take an unusual procedural twist, as demonstrated in the following case.

The Chicago firm of Sidley & Austin was sued in Connecticut by Steven Biro, who alleged that Sidley & Austin had managed to persuade Thomas Hill Jr., Biro's then-partner, to become a partner with Sidley & Austin. The latter then took over the Oman office where the Biro firm was situated, and ousted Biro. When Biro brought suit (this was another Connecticut case), Hill was not made a party. Sidley & Austin moved to dismiss the complaint under a Connecticut rule governing "necessary parties."

---

74. Norwalk Twin Towers, Inc. v. Davidson & Naylor, 1993 Conn. Super. LEXIS 2691 (Conn. Super. Ct. 1993).

75. *Id.* at *9–10.

The Connecticut Supreme Court considered an appeal from an order dismissing the Biro complaint. It held that the action was brought before enactment of the Connecticut Tort Reform Act, when the law provided for joint and several liability for joint tortfeasors. Consequently, Sidley & Austin would be liable and it would be unnecessary to join Hill in the lawsuit.[76]

An appellate court in Illinois has decided that lawyers cannot form a corporation for the purpose of insulating themselves from liability if "substantial justice" requires a different result.[77] Warren Strom was a partner in a partnership with Clarence Wittenstrom Jr. and H. Greg Meyer. Each of the partners had executed a note in the amount of $23,000 to the First National Bank of Elgin in 1983. Before the note became due, Strom withdrew from the partnership and Wittenstrom and Meyer formed a corporation, known as Gromer, Wittenstrom & Meyer, P.C. These two gentlemen then withdrew $2,300 from the old partnership account and sent it to First National Bank in partial payment of debt service on the note.

Subsequently, the corporation paid off the balance of the note and it was assigned to Gromer, Wittenstrom & Meyer, P.C. The corporation then obtained a judgment against Strom for $15,084.49, representing the balance due after payments by the corporation to the bank plus interest and attorney fees. Strom appealed.

Strom asserted several defenses, noting that a cosigner who has paid a note could not, under Illinois law, obtain judgment against another cosigner. Strom further contended that because the old partnership accounts had never been settled, Wittenstrom and Meyer could not have their judgment; under Illinois law, Strom said, one partner may not maintain an action against another partner until a settlement of partnership affairs has occurred.[78]

In a struggle to relieve Strom of the burden of the judgment, the court finally found a way:

> [D]efendant also set forth facts which indicated that his ex-partners were the sole shareholders of plaintiff corporation, and that the law establishes that cosigners of a note may not after payment or assignment of the note obtain a judgment by confession against another cosigner. We believe that these facts and arguments sufficiently indicate that to recognize

76. Biro v. Hill, 214 Conn. 1, 570 A.2d 182 (1990).

77. Gromer, Wittenstrom & Meyer, P.C. v. Strom, 140 Ill. App. 3d 349, 489 N.E.2d 370 (App. Ct. 1986).

78. *Id.*, 140 Ill. App. 3d at 351–52, 489 N.E.2d at 372.

> plaintiff corporation as an entity separate from its shareholders would be to sanction an injustice.[79]

Regarding the act of taking the sum of $2,300 from the old partnership account to use in partial payment of the note, the court said:

> This act . . . took place many months after Meyer and Wittenstrom had formed a professional corporation. Thus, we believe that this additional fact indicates there was no clear separation of the corporation and the shareholders in the handling of this entire matter. In our opinion, the facts presented to the trial court indicated that *substantial justice* would be denied the defendant if the judgment were not vacated. Thus, we conclude that the trial court erred in denying defendant's motion to vacate the confession judgment.[80]

The Problem of the Incompetent Partner

Your duties to your clients deserve first consideration, and your obligations to your partners come next. An Iowa decision illustrates the point.

The plaintiff's decedent, Daniel Cutler, had been a partner in his firm. He suffered from severe depression, became incompetent to practice law, and was hospitalized. After several weeks, believing himself cured, he wanted to return to the office, and asked one of his partners about coming back on a part-time basis. The response was that the request would have to be considered by the partners after conferring with Cutler's doctors. A group of the partners then met and concluded that Cutler should not be allowed to return until the matter had been considered by the full partnership.

One of the partners wrote to Cutler, explaining the firm's position and saying that "a complete review and discussion should be held before a final decision is made. . . . Meanwhile I am glad you are doing better and hope you continue to make good progress." Cutler was informed that the letter was coming, but, concerned that Cutler might think the letter meant he was being expelled from the firm, another firm member reassured Cutler's wife that the letter was not a notice of expulsion. Nonetheless, Cut-

79. *Id.*, 140 Ill. App. 3d at 354, 489 N.E.2d at 374.

80. *Id.*, 140 Ill. App. 3d at 354–55, 489 N.E.2d at 374 (emphasis added).

ler then purchased a shotgun and killed himself. His estate sued the firm for negligent infliction of emotional distress.

In holding that the trial court correctly entered summary judgment for the defendant firm, the Supreme Court of Iowa said, in part:

> The firm cannot be faulted for delaying Cutler's return to active practice; indeed the firm was bound to take that position. Even though the ethical considerations and disciplinary rules do not specifically state that members of a law firm must terminate the practice of a mentally ill partner, the firm must take steps to ensure that the public is not provided incompetent service. Several cases point out this ethical duty.[81]

Concerning the letter, the court said it was "a message that, under the facts alleged, the firm was required to send. Under the facts alleged the firm had to send the message."[82]

Partnership from the Tax Collector's View

As usual, the Internal Revenue Service (IRS) may take a somewhat strained view of what constitutes a partner for purposes of paying federal income tax. Consider this situation: you are a law associate in Firm A, which agrees to pay you a salary plus a percentage of the business you bring to the firm. You leave the firm to become a partner in Firm B, and you have an understanding with Firm A that you will consult on matters relating to clients you had introduced to the firm. Your understanding with Firm B is that you will turn over to the partnership all income from the law practice from the date you joined the firm. Firm A makes payments to you in accordance with the agreement with you, and you turn the monies over to Firm B, which reports these sums in the partnership return. However, the IRS asserts a deficiency against you for your failure to report these sums in your return. You go to the Tax Court. What result?

It took a very long opinion (forty-three pages on LEXIS) for the Tax Court to decide that you were correct. You could not have foreseen that the commissioner would argue that when you made

81. Cutler v. Klass, Whicher & Mishne, 473 N.W.2d 178, 182 (Iowa 1991)(citations omitted).

82. *Id.* at 181.

the arrangement with Firm B, you made an "anticipatory assignment" of income you had already earned by virtue of the clients you brought to Firm A. However, the Tax Court would accept your position that the income was not earned until after you left Firm A and joined Firm B. Moreover, the Tax Court said that the type of partnership agreement to which you were a party in Firm B provided, in effect, for a redistribution of the monies earned by you in Firm A, and had previously been approved by the IRS. The Tax Court, despite a vigorous dissent, but with several, separate concurring opinions, held that your return and that of Firm B were correctly filed.[83]

The moral here seems to be that as a law firm partner, you need to assure yourself that you and your firm are provided with sound tax advice, either from your tax partner (if you are not a tax lawyer) or your accounting firm. This is certainly the case when a partner is about to receive a substantial sum from a law firm that has dissolved.

In all probability, Milton Tolmach would confirm that. He was a partner in a law firm dissolved in 1976. The firm had no written partnership agreement. With some rancor, the partnership was dissolved, and legal action followed. Ultimately the lawsuit was settled and Tolmach was to be paid $1.7 million (in monthly installments) for his share of unrealized receivables at the time of dissolution, plus $155,000 for fixed assets and goodwill. The settlement included certain other benefits to Tolmach. Sums paid to him in 1983 and 1984 were reported by him to the IRS as resulting from the sale of his interest in the partnership and, therefore, as capital gain under section 741 of the Internal Revenue Code. The commissioner claimed deficiencies in Tolmach's returns, contending that the payments to him were guaranteed payments made in liquidation of his interest in the partnership, were taxable under section 736 of the Internal Revenue Code and, therefore, were ordinary income.

The *Tolmach* decision[84] is a thorough examination of the principles underlying the difference between section 736 and section 741. Particularly, the opinion notes the distinction between liquidation and dissolution. The Tax Court said:

---

83. Schneer v. Commissioner, 97 T.C. 643 (1991).

84. Tolmach v. Commissioner, 1991 Tax Ct. Memo LEXIS 592, 62 T.C.M. (CCH) No. 1991-538, ¶ 910538, at 1102 (1991).

> The dissolution of a partnership no more terminates the partnership for Federal income tax purposes than it does for State law purposes. . . . On dissolution the partnership is not terminated, but continues until the winding up of partnership affairs is completed. . . . Although liquidation of the partnership often follows dissolution, it is not required. . . . Indeed, after dissolution of the partnership, the partners may continue the business of the partnership indefinitely, so that winding up occurs, if at all, only in the technical sense of paying off the outgoing partner (or his estate). . . . If the business of the partnership is carried on by any of its partners in partnership form, the partnership is deemed not to terminate at all for Federal income tax purposes. . . .
>
> If, following dissolution, the business of the partnership is carried on by any of the partners in partnership form, and if the withdrawing partner is paid off out of the assets of the continued business by way of a liquidating distribution to him, section 736 will apply to such payment. If, on the other hand, his interest is purchased by the continuing partners, section 741 will apply.[85]

The court quoted *Cooney v. Commissioner*,[86] which said:

> The critical distinction between a sale of a partnership interest under section 741 and a liquidation of such an interest under section 736 is that a sale is a transaction between a third party or the continuing partners individually and the withdrawing partner, where a liquidation is a transaction between the partnership as such and the withdrawing partner.

Finding that Tolmach made an arrangement with the firm rather than with his former partners individually, the Tax Court decided that the payment was in liquidation of Tolmach's interest and was taxable under section 736 of the Internal Revenue Code. The Tax Court then proceeded to analyze in detail the several aspects of the payment to Tolmach for various assets and goodwill, including provisions in the partnership agreement concerning allocations to goodwill. The additional assessments of the commissioner were sustained.

---

85. *Id.* (citations and footnote omitted).

86. 65 T.C. 101, 109 (1975).

Had Tolmach and his firm considered the tax implications of the partnership agreement provisions related to goodwill and the arrangements to make payments to a withdrawing partner, the result might have been different.

Just as there are federal income tax implications regarding payments a retired partner receives from his or her law firm, the state taxing authorities also get into the act. Fortunately (for the taxpayer) judges are also lawyers, and they may feel the unpleasant burden of the revenue collectors. Hence, opinions in tax cases are sometimes curt and pithy, as in the *Pidot* case.[87]

Mr. Pidot, after retirement from his New York City law firm, moved to Florida. Upon retirement, the firm paid him in full for his share of the firm's capital. Thereafter, he received annual retirement benefits according to a formula prescribed by the firm's partnership agreement. When Pidot filed a New York State income tax return, he reported, and paid tax on, the amount received from the law firm. He asserted that the amount was a pension in the form of an annuity and was nontaxable by New York. He claimed a refund. The commissioner denied the claim on the basis that the payments to Pidot were his distributive share of partnership income.

The New York Supreme Court, Appellate Division, found that according to the partnership agreement, Pidot had no interest in the partnership and received no distributive share of partnership income. The court declined to make a distinction between tax treatment of annuities paid to former employees and those paid to former partners who retain no interest in the partnership and do not share in partnership profits or losses. Pidot won in the trial court and in the appellate division, and his case went before the New York Court of Appeals. In a summary decision, the court affirmed "for the reasons stated [by] . . . the Appellate Division." The court noted that the appellate division found that, regarding certain sums reported as "other income," the "petitioner failed to sustain his burden of proving that such amount constituted retirement benefits paid by the partnership."[88]

This is a warning that, when it comes to taxes, the burden is usually on the taxpayer to prove that the tax is not due; seldom is the tax collector required to prove the tax is owed. It is in the part-

---

87. Pidot v. State Tax Comm'n, 69 N.Y.2d 837, 506 N.E.2d 536, 513 N.Y.S.2d 965 (1987).

88. *Id.*

ner's best interest to structure retirement arrangements carefully to avoid unanticipated taxes.

As a partner, what do you do about your tax return if one of your partners has "his hand in the till"—as the expression goes—and puts your firm in a precarious financial position? This was the dilemma facing Theo Pinson when his partner was guilty of excessive draws that were funded by firm borrowings. Pinson claimed either a "theft loss" or "bad debt" deduction regarding his inability to receive his proper share of firm distributive income. The Tax Court ruled that he was not entitled to either deduction, because he neither received the income nor added to basis with respect to it.

Nonetheless, the court held that Pinson was entitled to a loss deduction under section 731(a)(2) of the Internal Revenue Code. That section, said the court, provides for loss recognition in the case of liquidation of a partnership interest "where no property other than money, unrealized receivables . . . or inventory . . . is distributed; the amount of such loss is measured by the difference between the adjusted basis of a partner's partnership interest upon liquidation and the sum of any money distributed and the adjusted basis to that partner in uncollected receivables or inventory distributed in liquidation."[89] The court noted that "[u]nder the circumstances of this case, loss recognized upon liquidation of petitioner's partnership interest is considered loss from the sale or exchange of a partnership interest, and as such is a capital loss."[90]

This outcome is not of great moment in an era when capital gains are taxed at the same rate as ordinary income and capital losses are limited. However, one can plan for the day when capital gains will be taxed favorably and use of capital losses will be treated more generously.

Of significant interest to many lawyers faced with divorce is the value to be attributed to his or her interest as a partner in a law firm. This issue arose in a case in which the Commissioner of Internal Revenue assessed deficiencies against William Borror, a lawyer.[91] He had agreed to make, and was making, payments to his ex-wife and the issue was whether those payments were in

89. Pinson v. Commissioner, 1990 Tax Ct. Memo LEXIS 241, 59 T.C.M. (CCH) No. 1990-234, ¶ 900234, at 554 (1990).

90. *Id.*

91. Borror v. Commissioner, 1989 Tax Ct. Memo LEXIS 565, 58 T.C.M. (CCH) No. 1989-579, ¶ 890579, at 499 (1989).

exchange for an interest in property or for her support. In the latter instance, Borror's deduction of them on his tax return was proper. In deciding that the payments were not made in exchange for property, and hence that the deductions were allowable, the Tax Court wrote:

> William was a partner in the Fort Wayne, Indiana, law firm known as Hunt, Suedhoff, Borror, Eilbacher and Lee during the time period relevant in this case. The partnership agreement stated that if a partner withdrew from the firm and engaged in litigation within 60 miles of the City of Fort Wayne for certain listed clients, the partner would forfeit his entire interest in the law firm. If a partner withdrew and chose not to so compete, the partner would be entitled to his percentage share of partnership assets less the total of all accrued and contingent liabilities of the partnership. Under Indiana law, the proper method to value an attorney's interest in a partnership, in the event of a dissolution of marriage, is to treat the law partner's interest as if the attorney withdrew from the partnership on the date of the marital separation. The court may value the partnership interest as if the partner withdrew and competed or did not compete, provided that there is no direct evidence that the court's choice is an abuse of discretion.
>
> We find that William's partnership interest is to be valued as if he voluntarily withdrew and competed with the firm as described in the partnership agreement. No evidence in the record suggests that this method of valuation is inappropriate. Accordingly, we find that William's partnership interest retained no value which Gertrude could have surrendered in exchange for the monthly payments. We find credible and accept William's testimony as a fact that Gertrude agreed that William's partnership interest was essentially worthless.[92]

---

92. *Id.*, 1989 Tax Ct. Memo LEXIS 565 at *27, 58 T.C.M. (CCH) ¶ 890579, at 499.

Irrelevant to a consideration of the rights of a partner in a law firm is a comment, nonetheless interesting, by the court:

> The original draft of the Agreement (of separation) stated that the monthly payments would terminate upon Gertrude's death or remarriage. Gertrude requested that the language "or remarriage" be removed from the draft of the Agreement, tearfully stating that it insulted her. Gertrude stated at the time that William had poisoned her against all men. William granted her request and removed the language. Gertrude remarried within 6 weeks of the dissolution decree.

Partners sometimes believe that tax authorities show little mercy toward members of the bar. That is not always true. Consider Harry Heller's joust with the taxing authorities. The facts of his case are described above (page 13). You will recall that he was a Washington, D.C., resident, associated with the office there of New York's Simpson, Thacher & Bartlett. He was held out as a partner and was listed as a partner in *Martindale-Hubbell* but hadn't signed a partnership agreement. He didn't share in firm profits but received a percentage of fees generated. In 1984, when the New York State Tax Commissioner upheld a notice of deficiency following a 1980 hearing on a 1968 assessment, Heller went to court.

Said the Appellate Division of the Supreme Court of New York:

> We annul. We are deeply disturbed by the delay which has characterized this matter. Without explanation, it took the Tax Commission 12 years to schedule and hold a hearing and to file an answer. It took another four years before the Tax Commission issued a determination following the hearing. Such inordinate, unexplained delay cannot pass scrutiny. . . .[93]

Score one for the taxpayer.

Heller's case was procedurally outrageous but the facts suggest how the confrontation with the taxing authorities in New York might have been avoided. He should not have been listed as a partner in directories, but, perhaps, as of counsel. Fixed compensation, adjusted annually, could replace fee-sharing. These matters could have been written into an of counsel agreement.

However, there are other procedural obstacles for the partner to overcome when dealing with the IRS. For example, although IRS rules prohibit more than one inspection of a taxpayer's books within a single year, the inspection of the books of a partnership is not counted in determining whether the Service may inspect the books of one of its partners in the same year,[94] unless, as in the case of a two-person partnership, it was "merely an extension of the persons of the taxpayers themselves."[95]

---

93. Heller v. Chu, 111 A.D.2d 1007, 490 N.Y.S.2d 326 (App. Div. 1985).
94. Curtis v. Commissioner, 84 T.C. 1349 (1985).
95. *Id.* (citing Moloney v. United States, 521 F.2d 491, 501 (6th Cir. 1975)).

Avoidance of Financial Disaster

In this era when partners move about far more frequently than in days of yore, there are two groups of lawyers who need to consider how best to protect themselves against financial disaster. The first group comprises the lawyers who are pulling up stakes and moving to a new firm: they must consider how to avoid answering for hidden obligations of a new partnership. The second group is represented by the lawyers who remain in a firm, saddled with whatever burdens it may have, after other partners have withdrawn. The obituary list of law firms in the late 1980s and early 1990s presents a warning to the profession to think about the problems and how to solve them in the best interests of both sides.

If you are in the group making a change, you certainly want to know whether you are joining a firm that is already in trouble or one with a truly "clean" balance sheet. That suggests you will want to review—and have your own accountant examine—*audited* financial statements. If, down the road, you find there are obligations predating your joining the partnership, you will be relieved of responsibility for them under provisions of the Uniform Partnership Act. But do not let that lull you into a false sense of security. Should the firm get into serious financial trouble—perhaps a bankruptcy or reorganization—the creditors will come after everyone and the Uniform Partnership Act will be of scant comfort.

Moreover, if you joined your new firm as a nonequity partner (counsel, special partner, contract partner, or whatever) you might say to yourself, "I do not have any liability." That is a very risky supposition. Remember, you wanted the world to think you were a real partner and the firm held you out as a partner; now, when receipt of payment from the firm may be in doubt, creditors will want to hold you liable in whole or in part for the firm's obligations—on the ground that they were told you were a partner. That indemnity you sought and obtained from the equity partners will be of little avail. After all, the equity partners, in our hypothetical, are already in serious financial difficulty.

Remote as these problems may be in most cases, there are things you can do to avoid a total disaster when such problems do exist. You might incorporate yourself as a professional corporation in your state. There is also the possibility that your state has recently enacted legislation allowing for limited liability companies or limited liability partnerships. These three devices may help to insulate you, to some degree, from creditors' claims.

Also, in today's world, there are many husbands and wives who are both breadwinners and who amass considerable amounts in their respective estates: either may be a lawyer, exposed to these risks. Therefore, it is prudent for the lawyer in the family to decide that joint ownership of the family assets should be eliminated and that each spouse hold his or her own property separately.

But suppose you are a continuing partner in a firm where there is risk that one or more partners may withdraw. How do you protect yourself from "holding the bag" of responsibility for discharging the firm's obligations, when the necessary revenues may have walked out the door?

It may not be possible to provide for every eventuality, but you can take some protective measures. First, you can provide in the partnership agreement that a withdrawing partner will be responsible for an appropriate portion of the firm's debt, as of the date of his or her departure. Assuming that a withdrawing partner, in the usual situation, will receive a percentage interest in the earned but unbilled inventory of the firm, he or she might be held liable to the firm in an amount at least equal to the amount representing the distribution of inventory.

Because there are so many permutations and combinations of financial debacles possible, one can only generalize about the proper course to avoid them all. Suffice it to say that prospective partners and those who expect to remain continuing partners need to face up to the issues realistically. With a little give-and-take, a fair compromise should result.

Partnership amidst Divorce

There are times when partnership is a decided advantage, aside from the fact that partners are usually ahead financially. One lawyer found that the debt incurred in buying out his two law partners was taken into consideration by the court when the financial settlement of a divorce action was appealed. Although he wound up paying his spouse additional alimony, it was only after the court recognized, among other items, that he was "in the process of buying out his two former partners in the law firm so that the law firm is actually a liability of $30,000 to him."[96]

96. Meredith v. Meredith, 1988 Tenn. App. LEXIS 737, at *9 (Tenn. Ct. App. 1989).

We have already seen in the *Borror* case (discussed previously in the "Partnership from the Tax Collector's View" section) that the IRS found no value in a partnership interest in a law firm. However, in the divorce area, there is substantial disagreement about the value that should be attributed to a law firm partnership interest. For example, consider the problem of J. Grant McCabe III, a lawyer. He and his wife obtained a no-fault divorce. The Pennsylvania Superior Court had ordered equitable distribution of the couple's property and had valued Mr. McCabe's interest in the law firm of Rawle & Henderson at $18,900. Mrs. McCabe appealed to the Pennsylvania Supreme Court, contending that the superior court should have approved the award granted by the Pennsylvania Court of Common Pleas. This court utilized the formula in the partnership agreement for computing the sum subject to withdrawal when a partner terminates association with the firm ($286,276 in McCabe's case). In a carefully reasoned opinion, the supreme court affirmed the decision of the superior court, which approved the lower number.[97] The court said in part:

> Furthermore, Rawle & Henderson is not an entity with shares that can be traded publicly or privately. There is no market to which a partner can refer to ascertain the value of his partnership interest. Nor can the firm be sold or liquidated at the behest of a partner.
>
> . . . Further, a partner is not permitted to sell his partnership interest to another individual. Nor does a partner have a right to retire from the firm and continue to receive a share of the firm's profits. Under these circumstances, it would be inequitable to apply a "going concern" value to the partner's share.
>
> Granted, a "going concern" value would better reflect the future income that Mr. McCabe might earn as a result of holding a partnership interest. However, future income is not marital property because it has not been acquired during the marriage. It is not, therefore, subject to equitable distribution.
>
> The substantive rights of a partner consist only of those specified in the partnership agreement, and, in appraising this bundle of rights, the agreement cannot be disregarded. Indeed, the agreement must be viewed as the preeminent factor in valuing a partner's rights. The present agreement sets

97. McCabe v. McCabe, 525 Pa. 25, 575 A.2d 87 (1990).

forth a method for determining the realizable value of a partner's share, and the value determined in accordance with that method, $18,900, must be regarded as controlling.[98]

But *McCabe* has not convinced all the judges in Pennsylvania that the decision applies universally. In *Butler v. Butler*,[99] virtually the same question arose when one of two partners in a certified public accounting firm was divorced. The shareholders' agreement of the professional corporation had a provision for a buyout of one shareholder by the other for $2,450; if one shareholder died, the agreement provided for the other shareholder to purchase the deceased shareholder's shares from the estate for $100,000. The trial court had placed the value of the divorcing shareholder's shares at $2,450 for purposes of equitable distribution in the divorce. On appeal, the Pennsylvania Superior Court reversed, finding *McCabe* distinguishable and declining to follow it. The court noted that McCabe had been a partner in a large law firm, while the husband in *Butler* was one of only two shareholders; in *McCabe*, there was no difference between the amount due upon McCabe's leaving and upon his death, and in *Butler*, the difference in amounts in those two circumstances did "not give a clear valuation for the husband's interest."[100] The case was remanded to the Pennsylvania Court of Common Pleas.

When a dispute exists about financial matters in a lawyer's divorce, one of the central issues is whether there is any goodwill to be valued in the lawyer's practice. The New Jersey Supreme Court discussed this issue at some length in the *Dugan* case.[101] The Dugans obtained a no-fault divorce. In a distribution of property, the trial court determined that the marital estate had a value of $606,966, with $182,725 attributable to goodwill. Mr. Dugan, the lawyer, appealed, and the appellate court affirmed. The case then went before New Jersey's high court.

In its opinion, the supreme court reviewed the definitions of goodwill advanced by Justices Cardozo and Story, Lord Eldon, Chief Justice Summers, accountants (including the Accounting Principles Board), and other writers of legal and accounting treatises. In a succinct statement, the court observed that

98. *Id.*, 525 Pa. at 28, 575 A.2d at 87 (footnote and citation omitted).

99. 423 Pa. Super. 530, 621 A.2d 659 (Super. Ct. 1993).

100. *Id.*, 423 Pa. Super. at 541, 621 A.2d at 665.

101. Dugan v. Dugan, 92 N.J. 423, 457 A.2d 1 (1983).

> [g]oodwill is generally regarded as the summation of all the special advantages, not otherwise identifiable, related to a going concern. It includes such items as a good name, capable staff and personnel, high credit standing, reputation for superior products and services, and favorable location.[102]

The opinion also noted that goodwill can be translated into prospective earnings. It said that variances in the form of an enterprise do not eliminate goodwill, "though they may affect its worth," and that "the calculation of goodwill may depend upon the purpose for which the measurement is being made."[103] The court noted that its Advisory Committee on Professional Ethics had accepted and announced a rule that a lawyer's practice and goodwill may not be offered for sale.[104] Notwithstanding this principle, the court held that goodwill has a determinable value and it set forth a formula for making the determination.[105] After mentioning a number of adjustments to the formula, the court remanded the case to the trial court to determine the value of Dugan's law practice with respect to goodwill.

In New York, as in New Jersey, an amount for goodwill has been included in the formula for determining the value of a spouse's interest in a law firm for purposes of a financial settlement in a divorce.[106] In the *Harmon* case, the issue was whether the husband's interest in his law firm should be determined by the partnership agreement's specification of the amount due a withdrawing partner, or its death benefit provision. The trial court chose the latter and applied a formula that established a value equal to the capital account, plus an amount equal to 175 percent of earnings for the past three years; this would compensate for the husband's share of work in process, uncollected accounts, assets,

102. *Id.*, 92 N.J. at 430, 457 A.2d at 4.

103. *Id.*, 92 N.J. at 431, 457 A.2d at 5.

104. *Id.*, 92 N.J. at 437, 457 A.2d at 8.

105. The court said that the determining court should first ascertain the earning power, after taxes, of a lawyer of comparable experience, for a year of normal billable hours, and compare this figure with the average net income, over five years, of the lawyer being evaluated. Any excess of the latter's net income over the former's would be capitalized, generally perceived as the number of years of excess earnings a purchaser would be willing to pay, in advance, to acquire the goodwill.

106. Harmon v. Harmon, 173 A.D.2d 98, 578 N.Y.S.2d 897 (App. Div. 1992).

and goodwill. On appeal, the court affirmed the trial court. (The decision directed some modifications not relevant to the inclusion of goodwill in a valuation formula.)

A later decision of the appellate court expands and clarifies the *Harmon* ruling.[107] In *Dawson,* the court said that the proposition that a law practice has no goodwill is a "consequence of ethical concerns that the sale of a law practice would necessarily involve the disclosure of client confidences."[108] The court said such concerns do not come into play in contexts other than a sale, and specifically distinguished the *Harmon* case.

The rules applied to partnerships[109] are also applied to a sale of shares in a professional association. This is good news for the partner involved in a divorce proceeding, whose spouse may be seeking additional financial resources on the basis of the partner's shareholding. In the *Thompson* case, the Florida court dealt with the issue in this way:

> Nevertheless, inasmuch as this is an issue herein, we certify the following question as being one of great public importance:
>
> In marriage dissolution proceedings to which an owner of a professional association is a party, may the value of the professional association's good will be factored in determining the professional association's value?
>
> Attention of bench and bar is called to Miller, *Professional Goodwill, The Phantom Asset?*, 14 The Family Law Commentator (1989). The article discussed the above issue in light of the Florida Supreme Court's declination of jurisdiction to review *Moebus v. Moebus,* 529 So. 2d 1163 (Fla. 3d DCA 1989), *rev. denied,* 539 So. 2d 475 (Fla. 1989), which opinion answers this question in the negative.[110]

Given the variations in views among the highest courts in several states, it is important that, if you as a law partner should be involved in a personal divorce, you review your partnership or shareholders' agreement, as well as the decisions in your jurisdic-

107. Dawson v. White, 1995 N.Y. App. Div. LEXIS 1228 (N.Y. App. Div. 1995).

108. *Id.* at *1.

109. Jacob A. Stein, The Law of Law Firms § 13.31 (1994).

110. Thompson v. Thompson, 576 So.2d 267, 268 (Fla. 1991).

tion. For example, some states make a clear distinction between the rules applicable to commercial and law partnerships. As the Wisconsin Court of Appeals stated:

> In *Holbrook,*[111] the husband appealed from a trial court determination that his partnership interest in a large law firm was worth $23,790, the amount of his capital account, plus $161,330, the value that the trial court assigned to the husband's share of his firm's goodwill. This court noted that while the goodwill of a commercial business is salable, "a partner's theoretical share of a law firm's goodwill cannot be exchanged on an open market." We held that professional goodwill is not divisible as a marital asset where the value of the goodwill can only be set by judicial determination and can never be "realized by a sale or another method of liquidating value." We concluded that only the value of the husband's capital account, a sum that he would receive pursuant to the partnership agreement were he to leave the firm, should have been assigned as a marital asset.[112]

Claiming Against the Miscreant Partner

Unless you are a partner in a firm, you may feel frustrated if you are aware of a partner's wrongdoing that only the partnership can redress by claiming against the wrongdoer. In my home state of Connecticut, a firm can recover damages against an errant partner. The recovery can include the cost of defending suits brought against the firm by any clients who had been wronged, as well as attorney and accounting fees and the amount of any insurance deductible.[113]

Eisenberg & Anderson is an interesting case. There the firm sued its former partner, Mylnarski, who had been guilty of several breaches of trust while a partner in the firm. The firm had paid various amounts to settle claims against it, and the suit sought to recover these amounts as well as other claimed damages. Mylnar-

---

111. Holbrook v. Holbrook, 103 Wis. 2d 327, 309 N.W.2d 343 (Ct. App. 1981).

112. Lewis v. Lewis, 113 Wis. 2d 172, 178, 336 N.W.2d 171, 174 (Ct. App. 1983) (footnote added, citations omitted). *Lewis* involved the sale of a veterinarian's practice.

113. *See* Eisenberg & Anderson v. Mylnarski, 1992 Conn. Super. LEXIS 3349 (Conn. Super. Ct. 1992).

ski claimed that a provision of the partnership agreement barred the suit. That provision read:

> Negligence: Except to the extent that the partnership is insured against liability, a partner guilty of negligence or wrongdoing shall reimburse the partnership for damages sustained as a result of such negligence or wrongdoing.

The court held that this provision was inapplicable to intentional wrongs, such as those committed by defendant Mylnarski, and the court said:

> Even if the Court concluded that [the relevent partnership agreement provision] applied to the intentional misconduct or wrongdoing perpetrated by the defendant, that paragraph would not bar the plaintiffs' recovery. This is so because [that paragraph] relieves the defendant of the duty to reimburse the partnership only to the extent that the loss is covered by insurance. However, as indicated in the plaintiffs' brief, the only coverage provided by the policy insuring the firm was excess coverage for the "innocent insured," i.e. the remaining partners.[114]

This result followed because the malpractice policy covering the partnership contained exclusions making the policy inapplicable (1) to any claim arising out of a criminal act, error, or omission of any insured, and (2) to any claim arising out of a dishonest, fraudulent, or malicious act, or an error or omission of any insured committed with actual dishonest, fraudulent, or malicious intent. As a result, there was no malpractice coverage for the "innocent partners" until after the assets of the guilty partner had been exhausted. The court allowed the partnership to recover against the guilty partner.

There is a lesson here. Your firm's malpractice policy may be inoperative should there be claims against the firm for the intentional wrong of one of your partners; the firm must first pursue the errant partner's assets. Should those assets be inadequate to satisfy the claims against the firm, only then will there be a viable chance for the firm to recover against the malpractice insurance carrier.

One partner going astray can cause a whole series of "headaches" for a law firm; it behooves all partners to choose their partners carefully and to be aware of their partners' activities. You may

---

114. *Id.* at *3.

want to be a partner in many situations, but at the same time you must be an astute and observant person.

The Obligation to Supervise

Partnership carries with it obligations other than those already discussed. For instance, it seems clear that a partnership has the obligation to supervise the activities of retained local counsel.[115] Partners also have the duty to supervise nonlegal employees and a duty to make restitution should the nonlegal staff cause client loss.[116] In *Galbasino,* a lawyer had contracted with a collection agency to effect collections on behalf of the lawyer's clients. The agency proceeded to write to debtors of these clients, using the lawyer's letterhead. Monies were collected but the agency failed to remit them to the clients. The lawyer did not even discover the problem until the state bar received a complaint and contacted him. He was charged with violation of the Model Rules of Professional Conduct, particularly Model Rule 5.3 relating to "reasonable" supervisory efforts. The court quoted Professors Hazard and Hodes:

> An attorney who supervises a nonlawyer associate is not required to guarantee that the associate will never engage in "incompatible" conduct, for that would be tantamount to vicarious liability. On the other hand, if a supervising lawyer takes no precautionary steps at all, he or she violates Rule 5.3 whether or not their nonlegal associates misbehave.
>
> Circumstances will dictate what constitutes a "reasonable effort" to instill in nonlawyer personnel an appropriate respect for their duties. Certainly new personnel must be carefully screened and given at least some instruction in the fundamentals of professional responsibility.[117]

The legal relationships between lawyer and paralegal, and between paralegal and client, are well analyzed in a recent Illinois

---

115. Ingemi v. Pelino & Lentz, 855 F. Supp. 156 (D.N.J. 1994).

116. *In re* Galbasino, 163 Ariz. 120, 786 P.2d 971 (1990).

117. *Id.,* 163 Ariz. at 124, 786 P.2d at 975 (citing G. HAZARD JR. & W. HODES, THE LAW OF LAWYERING: A HANDBOOK ON THE MODEL RULES OF PROFESSIONAL CONDUCT, 464 (1989)).

case.[118] In *Divine*, Mr. Poznanovich, a lawyer, hired Ms. Giancola as a legal assistant in his probate law office. She befriended a long-time client of the lawyer and the client subsequently turned over two bank accounts to her. When the client died, the estate sued the legal assistant. The plaintiff did not sue the lawyer, contending that because Giancola was a paralegal and an employee of the lawyer, who was a fiduciary as a matter of law, so also was Giancola a fiduciary as a matter of law.

In affirming the trial court's finding of no impropriety on the part of Giancola, the appellate court found "no reported case in the United States involving a paralegal's fiduciary responsibility, as a paralegal, to the attorney's client."[119] The court went on to say that in Illinois and elsewhere, "the idea that an attorney is liable, in malpractice or as an ethical violation, for his paralegal's acts is well-supported." It noted that courts in other jurisdictions held divergent views about whether a paralegal could be sued for legal malpractice. The court concluded that

> [n]onetheless, holding Giancola liable as if she were an attorney is not consistent with general respondeat superior law or with the decisions discussed above treating paralegals as subordinate employees of attorneys. The theme running through all these cases is that paralegals do not independently practice law, but simply serve as assistants to lawyers. They are not equal or autonomous partners. Thus, while supervisors properly are held liable for paralegals' actions, the subordinate paralegals should not be liable for the actions of these supervisors. Therefore, we refuse to find that Giancola owed [the client] a fiduciary duty simply because she worked for [the client's] attorney, and we refuse to hold that paralegals are fiduciaries to their employers' clients as a matter of law.[120]

Practice as a Professional Corporation

Many law firms and some individual partners have formed professional corporations under state law. The practice of law in the corporate form is a relatively recent development. The use of the corporation was adopted to provide lawyers with some of the tax

---

118. Estate of Divine v. Giancola, 263 Ill. App. 3d 799, 635 N.E.2d 581 (App. Ct. 1994).

119. *Id.*, 263 Ill. App. 3d at 808, 635 N.E.2d at 587.

120. *Id.*, 263 Ill. App. 3d at 809, 635 N.E.2d at 588.

advantages available to the management and shareholders of corporations: the ability to defer taxation of earnings, to accumulate funds for expansion of the business, and so on. Another object, but not a principal one originally, was to shield the partners' individual assets from the reach of judgment creditors.

The question then arises—against which sorts of creditors is the shield effective? Is the shareholder in a professional corporation responsible for satisfying claims of malpractice against fellow shareholders? Suppose the claims pertain to matters not involving the provision of professional services? Are the assets of the individual stockholders in the professional corporation (in addition to the assets of the corporation itself) available to satisfy a judgment against the corporation?

Those states that have enacted statutes permitting lawyers to practice in a corporate form generally have required that a number of conditions be satisfied. In California, for example, the corporation must be registered with the state bar and must maintain security by obtaining insurance (or otherwise) for malpractice claims brought against it by clients. The state bar then requires each shareholder to sign an agreement guaranteeing the corporation's payment of all malpractice claims brought against it by its clients, subject to certain limits and offsets.[121] Other states have similar rules.[122]

Suppose that you are a shareholder in a professional corporation, and a fellow shareholder, with whom you are practicing, issues checks and withdraws funds from the corporate checking account. Then, at real estate closings, he issues additional checks that are dishonored. You and the firm are sued. Are you liable? The Georgia Supreme Court has held that if you are a shareholder in a professional corporation in Georgia, you are.[123] The court said

---

121. Beane v. Paulsen, 21 Cal. App. 4th 89, 26 Cal. Rptr. 2d 486 (Ct. App. 1993).

122. Florida, Georgia, Hawaii, and North Carolina; in Rhode Island, the corporation is liable to the extent of its assets, but not the individual shareholders. Annotation, 39 A.L.R.4th 556 (1994). "In allowing lawyers to practice as professional corporations, the Supreme Court of New Jersey was careful to protect the public by requiring professional liability insurance in significant amounts, see N.J. Court Rule R. 1:21-1A. It has also established a pioneering Clients' Security Fund to provide a means for reimbursement of losses caused by a dishonest lawyer. N.J. Court Rule R. 1:28." Davis v. Bd. of Medical Examiners, 497 F. Supp. 525, 530 (D.N.J. 1980).

123. First Bank & Trust Co. v. Zagoria, 250 Ga. 844, 302 S.E.2d 674 (1983).

it did not need to interpret the statute governing professional corporations, because the court had inherent power to regulate the law practice. The court described the professional corporation in the following way:

> By enacting the professional corporation statute the legislature performed a useful and constitutional act. A professional corporation has numerous and legitimate business purposes. By conducting a law practice through the structure of a professional corporation, its shareholders realize the advantages of more orderly business operations, greater ease in acquiring, holding and transferring property, and more continuity of its existence. Additionally, a professional corporation affords to its shareholders insulation against liability for obligations which do not arise as a result of a breach of a lawyer's obligation to his client or an act of professional malpractice. The shareholders of a professional corporation have the same insulation from liability as shareholders of other corporations with respect to obligations of a purely business and nonprofessional nature. However, the influence of the statute upon the professional corporation cannot extend to the regulation of the law practice so as to impose a limitation of liability for acts of malpractice or obligations incurred because of a breach of a duty to a client.[124]

However, some states hold that a shareholder in a professional corporation is not vicariously liable for another shareholder's acts or omissions in the performance of professional service unless he or she had participated in the acts giving rise to the liability.[125]

If a shareholder in a professional corporation sells his or her shares and leaves the corporation, he or she is nonetheless vicariously liable for malpractice claims concerning matters that arise thereafter, including those that arise following the disposition of the shares. This liability will remain unless the client has been notified of the change in ownership of the professional corporation and has given consent to the nonrepresentation by the removing shareholder.[126] Consequently, if there is a change in the stockhold-

---

124. *Id.*, 250 Ga. at 845, 302 S.E.2d at 675.

125. Stewart v. Coffman, 748 P.2d 579 (Utah Ct. App. 1988).

126. Beane v. Paulsen, 21 Cal. App. 4th 89, 26 Cal. Rptr. 2d 486 (Ct. App. 1993).

ing of a professional corporation in which you are a shareholder, be sure to take the same precautions regarding notifying clients of the change and securing their consent as you would if you were practicing with a partnership.

The imposition of liability in the case of a professional corporation works in reverse. That is, if an officer of a professional corporation is guilty of legal malpractice while acting in his or her capacity as an officer, then the professional corporation will be held liable.[127]

There are a number of interesting "wrinkles" to practicing as a professional corporation. For example, just as a partner is not an employee of a law firm organized as a partnership, a shareholder in a professional corporation is not counted as an employee for purposes of determining whether the corporation has the minimum number of fifteen employees needed to provide jurisdiction in a Title VII case.[128]

If a plaintiff sues a professional corporation for malpractice, the plaintiff is entitled to consider the attorney-client privilege waived regarding any matters that the corporation needs to disclose to defend itself; the privilege is not waived only as to those lawyers owning, or employed by, the corporation that actually provided the legal services.[129]

Lawyers who are employed by, but not shareholders of, a professional corporation are not vicariously liable for professional malpractice committed by members of the corporation, unless the employed lawyers were participants in the improper activities.[130] An Arizona court so held despite the appellant's contention that "since no distinction was made on the firm's letterhead between owners and employees, all lawyers listed on the letterhead and practicing under a common name were vicariously liable for [appellee's] alleged malpractice." Said the court, "this argument is so specious as to be ludicrous."[131]

Moreover, sanctions may not be imposed against a professional corporation but only against the individuals whose conduct

---

127. Fox v. Wilson, 85 N.C. App. 292, 354 S.E.2d 737 (Ct. App. 1987).

128. EEOC v. Dowd & Dowd, Ltd., 736 F.2d 1177 (7th Cir. 1984).

129. Surovec v. LaCouture, 82 Ohio App. 3d 416, 612 N.E.2d 501 (Ct. App. 1992).

130. Standage v. Jaburg & Wilk, P. C., 866 P.2d 889 (Ct. App. 1993), 1993 Ariz. App. LEXIS 160.

131. *Id.*, 866 P.2d at 896, 1993 Ariz. App. LEXIS 160 at *22.

merited the sanctions. This holding was announced by the Oklahoma Supreme Court in a case that arose under a statute providing for sanctions whenever a pleading (or other court document) is signed in violation of a rule passed by the state legislature. The statute requires the court to "impose upon the person who signed it, a represented party, or both" an appropriate sanction. Because the Oklahoma decision[132] dealt with the narrow issue of sanctions concerning a specific rule, the holding may not necessarily be followed should sanctions be imposed on a professional corporation due to improper activity of the corporation's lawyers other than the activity specified in the statute.

The existence of a professional corporation will not prevent an adversary from discovering client documents placed in the hands of a lawyer who is a member of the corporation. That is, the papers are in the safeguard of the lawyer and do not pass to the corporation. Moreover, any lien that attaches to the documents inures to the benefit of the individual lawyer and not to the corporation.[133] In *State ex rel. Wise,* a professional corporation sued the court (Judge Basinger) in an attempt to prohibit the production of documents by a lawyer-member of the corporation. The corporation contended that the materials sought to be obtained, upon which the corporation claimed an attorney's lien, were its personal property. Because the judge had already ordered the individual lawyer to produce the documents, the appellate court considered the appeal as it related to enforcement of Judge Basinger's order. The court denied the writ. After quoting from several appellate opinions in Ohio and other jurisdictions, the court observed:

> It is obvious from the foregoing that there was no intent in authorizing attorneys to incorporate to insulate the individual attorney from his professional relationship with his client. If those papers and documents came into the possession of the legal professional corporation it was only through the individual attorney.
>
> Likewise any lien which attaches to the papers and documents is in favor of the attorney to secure payment for his legal services and not in favor of the legal professional association, which had no professional relationship with the client.[134]

---

132. Unit Petroleum Co. v. Nuex Corp., 807 P.2d 251 (Okla. 1991).

133. State *ex rel.* Wise, Childs & Rice Co., L.P.A. v. Basinger, 54 Ohio App. 3d 107, 561 N.E.2d 559 (Ct. App. 1988).

134. *Id.*, 54 Ohio App. 3d at 109, 561 N.E.2d at 562–63.

If a lawyer is practicing as an individual and then forms a professional corporation, his service to his clients is considered to be continuous—there is no difference in providing service as an individual practitioner or as a professional corporation. Consequently, the formation of the corporation will not serve to time bar an action that was timely brought against an individual. Robert Weed, a lawyer, had incorporated his practice in 1977; subsequently, in 1984, he was discharged by the plaintiff as his counsel. In 1986, the plaintiff sued Weed for malpractice in both his individual capacity and as a professional corporation. Weed contended that the suit against him should be dismissed because he had ceased practicing as an individual in 1977; because the lawsuit had not been filed until 1986, it was time-barred under a statute of limitation that required suit to be brought within two years from the date the lawyer "discontinued servicing" the client. The trial court accepted the lawyer's argument and dismissed the claim. On appeal, that decision was reversed. The appellate court said:

> In the present case, Weed was not retained to perform any specific legal service. Instead, Weed, either as an attorney practicing individually or as the sole shareholder of Robert G. Weed, P.C., continuously handled [the client's] various legal and investment affairs from 1971 until March of 1984, at which time [the client] discharged him. The only change that occurred during the entire period of Weed's representation was the legal form of his practice, a fact which the trial court found to be dispositive.
>
> We do not believe that plaintiff's claim against Weed should be cut short merely because Weed changed his legal form of doing business. Therefore, we conclude that since Weed never "discontinued servicing" [the client] until March of 1984, plaintiff's March, 1986, lawsuit, which was timely against the professional corporation was timely against Weed, individually.[135]

The distinct nature of the attorney-client relationship, and the separation that exists between that relationship and others, becomes apparent when there is a dispute between the professional corporation and a third party that does not involve the provision of legal services. In *We're Associates Co. v. Cohen, Stracher &*

---

135. Nugent v. Weed, 183 Mich. App. 791, 796, 455 N.W.2d 409, 411 (Ct. App. 1990).

Bloom, P.C., the shareholders of a legal professional service corporation were sued in their individual capacities for rents due under a lease executed solely in the name of the corporation by one of its members acting as an officer of the corporation.[136] The shareholders moved to dismiss as neither necessary nor proper parties. The court below granted the motions and the appellate division affirmed, stating that a

> review [of the legislation providing for professional corporations] discloses no indication whatever that . . . the Legislature intended to exempt them from the general rule of limited liability attendant to an enterprise conducted in the corporate form. Moreover, while the provisions of [the aforementioned legislation] are tailored to address the unique problem of a professional corporation, it is nonetheless specifically provided . . . that, except to the extent that its provisions are in conflict with those of [the aforementioned legislation] the Business Corporation Law (with certain exceptions not relevant here) shall be applicable to professional corporations. Thus, rather than evidencing an intent that professional corporations be treated differently than other corporations, the statute evidences an explicit intent that the statutory rules regarding corporations be applied as well to professional corporations, except where a contrary rule is explicitly set forth.[137]

The court then discussed several other decisions holding a contrary position; that is, that the law setting up professional corporations had purely a tax purpose and should not shield the individual members from liability for the corporate debts. The court said this approach would require reading into the law establishing corporations generally a special exception for professional corporations involving lawyers. This the court declined to do. On the appeal to the New York Court of Appeals, the state's highest court agreed with the analysis by the appellate division. The chief judge wrote:

> Plaintiff contends the statute should be liberally construed to apply to debts incurred ancillary to the rendering of

136. 103 A.D.2d 130, 478 N.Y.S.2d 670 (App. Div. 1984), *aff'd*, 65 N.Y.2d 148, 480 N.E.2d 357, 490 N.Y.S.2d 743 (1985).

137. *Id.*, 103 A.D.2d at 133, 478 N.Y.S.2d at 673.

> professional services; that the rationale underlying the limitation of shareholder liability, i.e., the inability of shareholders to participate in the management of the corporation, does not apply to professional service corporations, which are run by their shareholders; and that affording limited liability to the shareholders of a legal professional services corporation would contravene the Code of Professional Responsibility. Finding none of these contentions meritorious, we affirm.[138]

The foregoing review, brief though it may be, points out that there are many variations from state to state in the rules governing the personal liability of shareholders of professional corporations or associations. Some states follow the rules applicable to business corporations generally, and others look specifically to the language of the enabling statute regarding the professional corporation or association. Very often there are discrete rules applicable to liability for torts or business debts of the corporation or association. A good collection of cases is found in the annotation entitled *Professional Corporation Stockholders' Nonmalpractice Liability,* at 50 A.L.R. 4th 1276.

If you, as a partner, are considering incorporating your own practice, or the practice of your firm, it is important that you look carefully at the statute in your own state and any decisions thereunder. Should there be no decisions in your state—a distinct possibility because, as yet, the professional corporation or association has not had a long lifespan—then it would be wise to look at other state statutes after which yours is patterned or that have a similar philosophy. Perhaps you will find decisions in those states that provide some guidance about the consequences you can expect.

Appearance of the Limited Liability Partnership

The newest arrival on the scene as a legal entity by which to practice law is the limited liability partnership. A creature of the late 1980s, it was engendered by the plethora of lawsuits against law and accounting firms that had been players in the savings and loan crisis.

When implementing legislation has been adopted, the establishment of a limited liability partnership is a relatively simple

---

138. We're Assocs. Co. v. Cohen, Stracher & Bloom, P.C., 65 N.Y.2d 148, 149, 480 N.E.2d 357, 359, 490 N.Y.S.2d 743, 745 (1985).

procedure. The partnership need only file a certificate with the designated state official, pay the required fee, and add to the firm letterhead the initials "L.L.P." or a legend "limited liability partnership" or "registered limited liability partnership," as the statute may specify. In some jurisdictions, the law firm must provide evidence of insurance and must file an annual report.

Let use suppose that you establish your law firm as a limited liability partnership. You are no longer responsible for certain firm obligations created by your partners; that is, your personal assets are not reachable by creditors. In my home state of Connecticut, the state's code section 34-53(2) provides that

> a partner in a registered limited liability partnership is not liable directly or indirectly, including by way of indemnification, contribution or otherwise, for debts, obligations and liabilities of or chargeable to the partnership arising from negligence, wrongful acts or misconduct committed while the partnership is a registered limited liability partnership and in the course of the partnership business by another partner or an employee, agent or representative of the partnership.

But the statute, which becomes effective January 1, 1996, in section 34-53(3), adds the provision that

> [t]he provisions of [the section quoted above] shall not affect the liability of a partner in a registered limited liability partnership for his own negligence, wrongful acts, or misconduct, or that of any person under his direct supervision and control.

Delaware has a similar provision. In other states, the statutory language may vary but the effect is the same.

Legislation allowing limited liability partnerships has not been universally enacted. As of the end of 1994, some twenty states and the District of Columbia had passed implementing statutes that either permit domestic limited liability partnerships or recognize limited liability partnerships organized in other states. Those jurisdictions are: Arizona, Connecticut, Delaware, District of Columbia, Georgia, Illinois, Iowa, Kansas, Kentucky, Louisiana, Maryland, Minnesota, Mississippi, New Jersey, New York, North Carolina, Ohio, South Carolina, Texas, Utah, and Virginia.

By mid-1995, no case that tested the viability of the limited liability partnership appears to have been decided. Certain problems are apparent. For example, suppose your firm has its principal office in state A, but has large branch offices, with significant partner presence, in states B and C. Suppose further that state A has a limited liability partnership statute, but states B and C do not. If a partner in the principal office has committed some major malpractice, it would seem that the personal assets of his or her partners residing in state A are protected. But must the partners residing in states B and C pick up the tab from their personal resources? What happens if state B passes a "shield law" but state C does nothing? Must the partners in state C put their personal assets on the line? These, and other questions, remain to be answered.

The emergence of the limited liability partnership received special attention in the federal Bankruptcy Reform Act of 1994. The provisions of section 212 of the act were explained by Representative Brooks on the floor of the U.S. House of Representatives (140 CONG. REC. H10752, H10757) on October 4, 1994:

> Section 723 of the Bankruptcy Code addresses the personal liability of general partners for the debts of the partnership. Section 723 grants the trustee a claim against "any general partner" for the full partnership deficiency owing to creditors to the extent the partner would be personally liable for claims against the partnership. It is unclear how this provision would be construed to apply with regard to registered limited liability partnerships which have been authorized by a number of states since the advent of the 1978 Bankruptcy Code. [Section 212] clarifies that a partner of a registered limited liability partnership would only be liable in bankruptcy to the extent a partner would be personally liable for a deficiency according to the registered limited liability statute under which the partnership was formed.

To be able to take advantage of section 212 would seem a major benefit of being a partner in a registered limited liability partnership.

However, note that section 212 does not relieve you as a partner in a registered limited liability partnership from *all* personal liability, but only from debts from which you are relieved by the applicable limited liability partnership statute. If that statute gives relief from debts unrelated to malpractice of your partner, so also does the bankruptcy statute; but if the limited liability partnership statute is confined to debts arising out of a partner's legal malpractice, so also is the trustee limited.

Some partners have been reluctant to vote to have their firms become registered limited liability partnerships. Their thought is that without personal assets at risk, partners will be less observant of, and less concerned about, their partners' activities, and thus the firm will suffer a diminution in the quality of work and an increase in the potential for malpractice. Others argue that when a client brings a successful malpractice action against a law firm, the image and reputation of that firm is tarnished; the incentive to avoid such a consequence is sufficient to maintain partners' concerns about the activities and quality of work of their colleagues.

The issue of the effect of the limited liability partnership on clients and client relations must also be considered. Law firms generally have few hard assets of any significant value. Even though the firm assets are at risk (regardless of whether there is a limited liability partnership) the protection to the client seeking to recover on a judgment for professional malpractice is greatly reduced when the firm is a limited liability partnership. The client must look to the firm's malpractice insurance coverage, and the client is seldom made aware of the size of the firm's policy and very rarely inquires when the firm is retained. The client takes a significant risk should a substantial malpractice claim arise when the law firm is a limited liability partnership. That risk can be alleviated if the limited liability partnership carries adequate malpractice insurance and, discreetly, lets its important clients know that the coverage is there.

Strangely, little has been written about the limited liability partnership. Information about the extent of developments in the area has come, principally, from occasional articles in national publications such as *The National Law Journal* or *The American Lawyer*. Each carries one or two articles a year.

According to *The National Law Journal,* during 1994 "there was an unprecedented rush" to cut off the risk of judgments because of claims made as a result of the savings and loan industry collapse. The newspaper reported in its December 26, 1994–January 2, 1995, issue that in New York, thirty-five firms filed for registration as a limited liability partnership in the first five weeks after the state's limited liability partnership law became effective. The newspaper noted that since 1991, when Texas inaugurated the limited liability partnership format, "more than 800 firms, including nearly all the state's largest, have switched."

Why is the limited liability partnership more attractive than the limited liability company or the professional corporation? Several reasons come to mind. Aside from the work involved in drafting the necessary documents, there is a shift in the firm's ambiance when it adopts a company or corporate form. In a partnership, every equity partner owns "a piece of the action" and is a manager as well as a proprietor. When a corporation is organized, it must have a board of directors and officers. In a large partnership, not everyone can be a director and not all former partners can become officers (except, perhaps, "vice presidents" in name only). The limited liability partnership also allows the owners to retain the benefits of being taxed as partners, and not suffer the exposure to dual taxation present in the professional corporation and limited liability company.

The registered limited liability partnership is certain to grow in popularity among law firms. Accounting firms have lobbied state governments extensively to secure passage of the necessary legislation, and they are succeeding. As law practice moves more toward being a business, and not merely a profession, the individual partner does not want to see his or her personal assets garnished to pay a judgment against a partner—particularly if that partner is in another department, another city, or a distant state. To protect clients, it may be preferable to pay the premiums for additional malpractice coverage than to leave one's own home and belongings at risk.

If you are in one of the thirty states that have not yet passed legislation allowing limited liability partnerships, you should remind yourself to watch for this development.

The Mantle of Partnership

In the era in which lawyers live and practice today, it is difficult to think of lawyering as a profession.

There are pressures to control costs, which may mean insisting upon longer hours for one's self, associates, and support staff—and just when the idea of allowing people more time for family is gaining increasing acceptance. These two concepts are in conflict.

There is pressure to raise revenues. This may mean billing for items on which little or no time was actually spent, justifying the charge on the ground the research was accomplished on a previous matter and is now part of "inventory." It may mean boosting the charges for ancillary services, such as secretarial overtime, word processing, photocopying, and messenger delivery, to a level that may include an unconscionable markup.

As a result of these pressures, partners may find themselves in conflict with their fellow partners, and may discover there is no time for social contact with other partners and that serving as a law firm partner is not a great joy at all.

You are a partner—you can change all that. The practice of law is a profession, not a business. Your first obligation is to your clients; you must do the best you can in their behalf. But you also have an obligation to your partners; you must do what *you* can to restore life in your office to what it might have been before the "age of pressure." Try to go to lunch with your partners occasionally, and not only with prospective clients. Arrange to invite your partners and their spouses to dinner and get to know their families, as they come to know yours. Granted, you may not be able to spend a large amount of time in pursuit of a different atmosphere in your office, but every effort will bring an even greater reward.

Why Aspire to Partnership?

With so many problems, roadblocks, and crises to confront, why should any lawyer aspire to partnership?

If you are a lawyer, probably no one needs to tell you why most lawyers place a high value on partnership. But oftentimes it is useful to put down on paper why that is so. As I attempt to recite some of the reasons, perhaps you will relate to them—and even think of others.

Needless to say, whether one is working as a lawyer in a small firm or a large one, there is usually a significant difference between the earnings of the partners and the salaries of the associates. One of the principal reasons for surviving the cut and being invited into the firm is to earn more *money*. Is that crass? Indeed not. Lawyers with more money are in a position to help, not only themselves, but their families and the community in general. Charity—whether of time, of service, or of money—usually requires that the givers first sustain themselves. The partner is entitled to earn more than his or her employees because of the risk factor. It is the partners, and not those who are employed by the partnership, who assume the risk that clients will come in the door and that revenues will be there to satisfy the landlord and meet the payroll. Partners earn their keep, and there is nothing irreverent in the quest for a reasonable degree of largesse.

Next, partnership provides a great sense of personal accomplishment. Partners own the firm. Each partner, quite properly, can feel that he or she has a "piece of the action." A part of the entity called the partnership or the corporation belongs to him or her. To be a partner is to be as much an owner as the proprietor of any other form of business enterprise. It is the "American way"—own your own business.

Power may be another incentive to partnership. While lawyer-bashing may remain a favorite indoor sport in the United States, society nevertheless recognizes that the legal profession wields tremendous influence over everyone's life. We are a nation of "law and order" and we are constantly striving to improve the way we administer it. Partners in law firms—and the more prominent the law firm, the more power to the partner—have tremendous influence in their communities and in the ways the legal system operates in them. This sense of power translates into a great feeling of satisfaction, and is another reason for the aspiration to partnership.

Then, there is prestige. When the lawyer goes through a crucible of education, examination, and apprenticeship, culminating in partnership, he or she has shown the world that here is a person of greater intellect and ability than many others. Here is a person who has earned admiration and respect. Society generally responds, and the prestige associated with partnership is a prize to be won.

Partnership also brings opportunity. Partners are in demand to fill—and have an obligation to assume—leadership positions in government and in professional associations. As most lawyers are aware, the development of business stems from becoming known in one's community. Partnership in a law firm that has a fine reputation in the community brings a degree of distinction to the individual partner. That partner then has the obligation to respond and to accept responsibility when called upon to serve. The service itself, in turn, enhances the stature of the partner and is a marketing opportunity for the lawyer and the partnership. Opportunity met is a reward of partnership.

When some of the difficulties encountered by partners seem burdensome, think of those great advantages of partnership. Do they not, unquestionably, outweigh the burdens?

* * *

And what about the associates? We turn next to the partner-associate relationship and what it means to the partner.

CHAPTER II

The Relationship of Partners to Associates

Hiring of Associates

Today, most law firms and lawyers—even single practitioners—employ an associate or associates. But, note that I said "most," because some law offices have *no* associates. Several acquaintances of mine recently formed a boutique law firm in New England. In commenting on the firm's lack of associates, one partner told me:

> This is significant in that I believe that our firm represents a new approach to law practice that bypasses reliance on the traditional leverage system. . . . Quite frankly, we find that corporate in-house counsel are fed up with the leverage system. While that system has its place, considerable rethinking of the system is warranted in corporate practice firms.

This book is not about the organization and structure of law firms, but about partners. Nonetheless, in a discussion of associates, the thought expressed in the paragraph above is worth noting.

Should a Firm Employ Associates?

A law firm partner has several important considerations always in mind: improving the economic vitality of the firm and avoiding situations that may present opportunity for firm liability. How do these objectives tie in with the decision about whether to employ associates?

The conventional wisdom is that partners make money from the work of associates; the billing rate for associates includes all the costs related to their employment plus a profit for the firm. Thus, the problem for the partner is to be sure that (1) sufficient work exists to provide an adequate number of billable hours for the associates and (2) the associates have the level of knowledge and experience appropriate for the work assigned. In larger firms, the ratio of associates to partners is an important consideration as well. The firm can advance only so many associates to partnership; should the firm hire too many associates, the partners will have the unpleasant task of denying partnership to some, often very promising, lawyers. Even when the procedure for partnership selection is put in place with extreme care, the opportunity exists for litigation from, and possible liability to, an associate who lost in the partnership selection process.

These factors suggest that the firm must determine, as best it can, how many new partners it will need some seven or eight years *after* the year it recruits its new associates. Should it hire too many in the first year, it will have to pare its number of lawyers in the seventh or eighth year; hire too few, and the firm will lack the number of experienced supervising lawyers it will need in its partnership ranks. If the partners have exercised perfect judgment, the ratio of associates to partners will be one-to-one and every associate will be elevated to partner.

But not all firms are content with such an even ratio. Some are willing to take the risk that not every new associate will become a partner and see a higher associate-to-partner ratio as an opportunity to increase profits. In any event, firms hiring newly graduated lawyers realize that over the years there will be normal attrition; associates will leave the firm for various reasons, sometimes at the suggestion of the firm. It is essential that careful records be maintained to ensure that one can predict, out of a given number of recruits each year, the percentage who will survive to become candidates for partnership. When economic conditions are favorable, the number of associates leaving a firm for "greener pastures" will rise, but in a recessionary period, fewer will abandon the fort.

When the number of candidates for partnership exceeds the number of available slots, a firm must consider whether it can afford to lose any of its lawyers, even though not all can be advanced. Those who are excellent lawyers, but who may lack other requisites for partnership—such as "rainmaking" ability—can be considered for permanent positions in the firm under some other category.

Some law firms have created a distinction between "equity" partners and "contract" partners. Often this distinction serves only limited internal purposes of the law firm. As we have seen from the discussion of the *Caruso* case in Chapter I, the obligation to pay a lawyer a portion of the firm's profits may be avoided, but that lawyer may enjoy rights against the firm appropriate to his or her status as an employee. Having been held out to the world as a partner, that person has the apparent authority to bind the firm—and hence, all its "equity" partners.

Classifying the lawyer who will not achieve partnership status as a "senior attorney" has the disadvantage of announcing to the world that the person is not a partner. On the other hand, it also makes clear that the lawyer lacks a partner's authority to bind the firm in matters generally requiring the act of a partner.

If a lawyer is to be retained but not advanced to partnership, the choice between "contract" partner status and the title of "senior attorney" requires consideration of all these factors, weighing the advantages against the risks.

The Hiring Process

Any study of a partner's rights must include his or her rights in the process of hiring associates. The associates in a law firm are, indeed, its most valuable assets. They must be chosen carefully, nurtured fully, and compensated adequately, to assure that the investment of the firm in them will be worthwhile. In the zeal to acquire only the best associates and the most qualified candidates for partnership, law firm partners often fail to counsel themselves properly; some ask improper and embarrassing questions at interviews and create situations that put every partner (not only the one conducting the interview) at great risk. Consequently, it behooves every partner to have an interest in ensuring that interviewers are soundly instructed and that interviews are properly conducted.

In recent years, the focus of society on equal employment opportunity and the avoidance of discrimination have changed the rules on the search for associates. The law firm that fails to open its doors to women and minority applicants at law school interviews, and that does not hire a reasonable cadre of aspirants from these groups, runs the risk of suit under equal employment opportunity and antidiscrimination laws. It is no defense to the partnership, nor to the partners who have no part in the activities of the firm's hiring committee, that they were not involved in such endeavors. They have the obligation—and the right—to review the firm's procedures in making hiring decisions.

Recruiting in the last decade of the twentieth century is no longer a task for amateurs. Seemingly innocuous questions can become the foundation of a lawsuit. Those entering law school campuses in search of new associates must be extremely vigilant in choosing interview subjects and framing questions. While conversation to "break the ice" in an interview might include an otherwise innocent question such as "Are the kids glad that you have finished law school?" or something along those lines, that can be a dangerous question in today's world. The interviewee may think that having, or not having, children is somehow related to job qualification. There are dozens of other areas of interrogation equally fraught with peril. As a partner, you have a duty to assure that everyone from your firm who conducts interviews—including your own partners—has been thoroughly instructed about what may be said and what is taboo.

To be ready to defend the firm should litigation arise, those operating the firm's hiring process should keep detailed records. Of particular significance are entries in the applicant's or interviewee's record that demonstrate the person (1) does not meet the firm's legitimate criteria (such as the required level of grades, experience, or communication skills) or (2) fails to provide any permissible and required documentation (such as grade transcripts or employer references).

An applicant does not have the same privilege of access to the firm's employment records as does an associate or other employee of the firm. Consequently, there is no reason for the firm to release any information to the applicant about the reason why he or she might have been denied employment. Should an applicant question the reason, the firm should merely state that it is not the firm's policy to discuss its selection procedures.[1]

The potential problems related to the hiring and firing of associates are well known to the law firm of Baker & McKenzie. An article in the *National Law Journal* for March 6, 1995,[2] under the byline of Ann Davis, a *National Law Journal* staff reporter, relates the problems of a partner who, in 1988, asked an African-American candidate during an interview at the University of Chicago Law

---

1. An excellent discussion of the subjects of associate selection and interview techniques appears in Chapter 9 and Chapter 11, respectively, of *Your New Lawyer*, published by the ABA's Section of Law Practice Management.

2. Ann Davis, *Baker Drops N.Y. AIDS Appeal*, NAT'L L.J., Mar. 6, 1995 at A6; NEXIS, load date March 17, 1995.

School about how the applicant would react to racial epithets. According to the *Journal,* this resulted in the firm's being banned from recruiting at several law schools for a year. Then, in 1993, the story goes, the New York State Division of Human Rights assessed compensatory damages of $500,000 against the firm for firing an associate after he contracted AIDS. The firm appealed, contending that the associate was fired for other reasons. Thereafter, the *Journal* reports, a settlement on undisclosed terms was reached and the appeal was withdrawn.

As a partner, it will be your objective to do whatever is possible to avoid such controversies.

Steps to Avoid Litigation

In the area of employment discrimination, the risk to the employer that a claim will be filed is exceedingly great. The perception that discrimination exists comes easier than the fact. A firm that looks upon itself as exhibiting the essence of fairness and equity to all may not be seen in that light by applicants. If the expense of defending a lawsuit is to be avoided, the policies and process involved in hiring lawyers and staff must be subject to close scrutiny by the partners.

The hiring process begins with a determination by the firm management that one or more associates must be hired. The firm risks claims if the discussion revolves around numbers of any groups who are to be preferred. The firm must be careful to assure there is no suggestion that the staff includes "too many women" or "more than a sufficient number of Hispanics," for example. The selection of a number to be hired should be entirely without regard to such standards.

Over time, the firm has probably had its sources of new lawyers from particular law schools. In some cases, local institutions (those within the state or city) might have been the primary source; in others, law schools of national prominence might have provided the recruits. The law firm that suddenly makes a change in its traditional sources must be careful to justify its new choices. Failure to record the specific reasons may make it difficult to defend against a charge that the firm was motivated by an effort to eliminate a particular group of applicants.

Similarly, the firm that finds it lacks a significant number of minorities among its lawyers and staff may decide that it should broaden the scope of its recruiting effort and seek students from a wider number of institutions. If the firm makes that choice, hires from these institutions, finds that it is dissatisfied with the employees, and wants to return to its former policy, it may face trouble. The perception, again, will be that the return to the traditional sources was not made because the recruits could not measure up, but because the firm wanted to reduce the number of minority hires. Consequently, the firm should review the qualifications and postgraduation records of the graduates of each law school before it decides from which institutions to recruit. Only in this manner will the firm have some assurance that it will be able to find the people it needs at any particular law school.

Many firms are fortunate to have one or more lawyers qualified in employment law. The partner who is not knowledgeable in this area may decide that he or she may safely rely upon the firm's internal experts. But if the firm has no fully qualified employment lawyer, it may be prudent to have an outside lawyer well versed in employment law review the firm's hiring procedures.

In many offices, particularly among the larger firms, the hiring committee serves on a rotating basis; both partners and associates are placed on the committee without regard to their knowledge of employment law, or the lack thereof. The hiring committee sallies forth to conduct hiring interviews at various law schools without any instructions or coaching on the vagaries and vicissitudes of employment law. Committee members can inadvertently pose a question to an applicant, or make a comment on results of the interview, with implications for liability. It is risky business for the partnership—for all partners—to send uninstructed lawyers on recruiting expeditions.

The firm should insist that every lawyer sent forth to conduct interviews on behalf of the firm be thoroughly briefed, before departure, by a lawyer well versed in employment law so that there are no lapses, deliberate or inadvertent, that could expose the firm (and thus, all its partners) to liability. Should the firm not have anyone on its staff qualified in employment law, it should retain outside counsel to provide the requisite advice. Partners should also require that associate application forms be subjected to scrutiny by a lawyer versed in employment law, to avoid any embarrassing or possibly incriminating questions. In fact, it would be prudent to issue the same instructions to staff members charged with hiring support personnel, and to make the same review of applications for employment of support staff.

Personnel Policy and Associates

Evaluation of Associates

In an era when lawyers often take umbrage at the willingness of clients to rush into litigation, scant attention is given to the fact that associates left behind in the race for partnership often file a lawsuit against their former firm as their first act after departure. In the ensuing battle, the law firm usually contends that such an associate did not pass muster, failing to meet the law firm's standards for partnership. When these standards are vague and the criteria that the associate failed to satisfy are unspecified, the outcome of the lawsuit may well be a defeat for the law firm and an award of damages to the associate.

With such prospects in mind, law firm partners are well advised to spend some time setting the yardstick by which candidates for partnership will be measured. This is no easy task, as the test cannot be so vague as to be meaningless, nor so precise as to eliminate virtually all but a discrete candidate. Obviously, some factors will require a subjective judgment regarding their presence or absence. An example is a lawyer's rapport with clients. Partners cannot always agree about whether a lawyer possesses the personality traits sought by the firm; being attracted to a personality, or not, is a subjective thing. The firm's criteria in this area must necessarily be less than precise. On the other hand, there are other tangible factors that can be set out in a firm policy statement or memorandum and applied more or less uniformly. For example, knowledge in a particular area of practice, ability to draft legal documents, facility in writing clearly and cogently, and skill in the spoken word are all capable of measurement in a relatively objective fashion. Because these factors are measurable, it is important for partners to assure that the firm maintains constant observance of them in each of its associates, and that the observations are recorded accurately and completely. The importance of these chronicles suggests they not be reduced to answers to multiple choice questions; it is far better to require partners to enlarge upon their thoughts in a narrative that states, with some specificity, how the associates are dealing with these factors.

If a candidate is passed over for partnership because of a lack of ability in the communications area, and he or she files lawsuit, the firm can point to particular instances of failure that support its decision.

In the *Hishon* case,[3] the U.S. Supreme Court held that a woman denied partnership may have a claim on the basis of sex discrimination under Title VII of the Civil Rights Act of 1967 (Title VII) if she can show that a partnership opportunity was a condition of employment. The burden then shifts to the law firm to establish by the "preponderance of the evidence"[4] that she would not have been elected to partnership even if she had not been a woman. Thus, it is incumbent upon the law firm to maintain complete and accurate evaluations of *all* associates.

Accurate evaluations and maintenance of records are not enough, however, to preserve your freedom from risk that an associate may prevail against the partnership. It is imperative that those who make the evaluations and maintain the records make the results known to all the partners. A failure to do so was significant in producing adverse results when an associate sued a Pennsylvania firm.[5]

In that case, Ellen Masterson sued La Brum & Doak on the grounds of sex discrimination when she was passed over for partnership. The case was tried to the court before a 1991 amendment that permits a jury trial, and Judge Newcomer made seventy-four findings of fact. Among them, he noted that Masterson "had developed business prior to the partnership election in 1991. This fact was not revealed to the partnership at any meeting prior to the election. Virtually no partners were aware of this fact, nor did any partner make any effort to discover this fact."[6] Judge Newcomer also observed that "Masterson had tried several cases to jury verdicts prior to the 1991 partnership election. This fact was not revealed to the partnership at any meeting prior to the election, virtually no partners were aware of this fact, nor did any partner make any effort to discover this fact."[7] Judge Newcomer found that this pattern was not followed with male candidates for partnership. The court also reached twenty-three conclusions of law, stating, in part, that Masterson had established a prima facie case of discrimination and that the burden had shifted to La Brum & Doak to "produce evidence of a legitimate, nondiscriminatory rea-

---

3. Hishon v. King & Spalding, 467 U.S. 69 (1984).
4. Price Waterhouse v. Hopkins, 490 U.S. 228 (1989).
5. Masterson v. La Brum & Doak, 846 F. Supp. 1224 (E.D. Pa. 1993).
6. *Id.* at 1228 (Finding No. 45).
7. *Id.* at 1229 (Finding No. 51).

son for its decision."[8] The Court concluded that the firm failed to do that.

The case demonstrates that whatever records of associates the firm may possess, they are certain to be educed at trial. Partners who want to avoid litigation and potential liability should assure themselves, before voting the election of associates to partnership, that the full record of the associates has been made available to the partnership.

While a few law firms make all of an associate's evaluations available to that associate, the usual practice is to provide access only to the associate's final evaluation made by the partners before the partnership vote. This is more a matter of policy than of litigation management; there is little prospect that the firm will be able to protect any of the personnel file from discovery in the event of litigation.

The Importance of Records

Perhaps no case illustrates more dramatically the importance of complete and accurate records of associate evaluations than *Ezold v. Wolf, Block, Schorr & Solis-Cohen.*[9] Ms. Ezold had been denied partnership by the Pennsylvania firm of Wolf, Block, Schorr & Solis-Cohen. She sued on a Title VII claim and won her liability case after an extended bench trial in the district court. The case returned to the district court on the issue of damages. The court decided that a trial would be necessary to determine whether Ezold should receive back pay, instatement, or front pay. The law firm appealed.

The review in the Third Circuit resulted in a thirty-nine page opinion by Judge Hutchinson, after twenty-five advocacy groups appeared as amicus curiae, largely on behalf of various women's rights groups. Their pleas were to no avail. The Third Circuit reversed the district court.

Before embarking upon its detailed analysis of the evidence, the court set out its decision and the philosophy that dictated it:

> This case raises important issues that cut across the spectrum of discrimination law. It is also the first in which allega-

---

8. *Id.* at 1231 (Conclusion of Law No. 7).

9. Ezold v. Wolf, Block, Schorr & Solis-Cohen, 983 F.2d 509 (3d Cir. 1992), *reh'g denied,* 1993 U.S. App. LEXIS 2193 (3d Cir.), *cert. denied,* 114 S. Ct. 88 (1993).

> tions of discrimination arising from a law firm partnership admission decision require appellate review after trial. Accordingly, we have given it our closest attention and, after an exhaustive examination of the record and analysis of the applicable law, have concluded that the district court made two related errors whose combined effect require us to reverse the judgment in favor of Ezold. The district court first impermissibly substituted its own subjective judgment for that of Wolf in determining that Ezold met the firm's partnership standards. Then, with its view improperly influenced by its own judgment of what Wolf should have done, it failed to see that the evidence could not support a finding that Wolf's decision to deny Ezold admission to the partnership was based upon a sexually discriminatory motive rather than the firm's assessment of her legal qualifications. Accordingly, we hold not only that the district court analyzed the evidence improperly and that its resulting finding of pretext is clearly erroneous, but also that the evidence, properly analyzed, is insufficient to support that finding and therefore its ultimate conclusion of discrimination cannot stand. We will therefore reverse and remand for entry of judgment in favor of Wolf. This disposition makes it unnecessary to address the issues raised in Wolf's appeal concerning the remedy the district court awarded to Ezold or those in Ezold's cross-appeal concerning her claim of constructive discharge.[10]

Wolf had a thorough system of associate evaluation in place, which was used during Ezold's tenure at the firm. Associates within two years of partnership consideration were evaluated annually, and nonsenior associates semiannually. An "Associates Committee," comprising ten partners representing each of the firm's ten departments, reviewed the evaluations and made recommendations for admission to partnership to the "Executive Committee," which included five partners. The Executive Committee then reviewed these recommendations and made its own recommendations to the full partnership.

In evaluating associates, partners completed an extensive form, which provided various grade levels to be assigned by the reviewing partner. Each partner was also expected to provide a written critique of the associates, with legal analysis skills always

---

10. *Id.* at 512 (footnote omitted).

listed as the first criterion to be evaluated. Illustrative of the extent to which Wolf went in appraising the merits of its associates is the Third Circuit's statement that "in 1988, ninety-one partners submitted evaluations of Ezold."[11] The matter then went to the Associates Committee, which voted not to recommend her for partnership. The Executive Committee decided to make an independent review of the Associates Committee's recommendation regarding Ezold and a similar negative recommendation regarding a male associate. A former Executive Committee Chair then interviewed four litigation partners (Ezold had been assigned to that department). He reported that the Executive Committee should not recommend Ezold's admission unless it was prepared to reduce the firm's partnership standards. The Executive Committee then reviewed the matter again and decided not to recommend Ezold for partnership.

In the language of employment discrimination law, the Third Circuit found the Ezold matter to be a "pretext case" as distinguished from a "mixed motive case." In a pretext case, the issue is "whether illegal or legal motives, but not both, were the 'true' motives behind the [partnership] decision."[12] The court then set forth the legal challenge a plaintiff must meet to prevail, and described the burden on the defendant—the law firm and its partners in this case—if it is to overcome the plaintiff's case. Judge Hutchinson wrote that the plaintiff must first establish, by a preponderance of the evidence, a prima facie case of discrimination.[13] If the plaintiff does so, the burden shifts to the defendant to produce evidence of a legitimate, nondiscriminatory reason for the employee's rejection.[14] If the defendant's evidence creates a genuine issue of fact, the presumption of discrimination drops from the case. Then the plaintiff—because she retains the ultimate burden of persuasion—must prove, by a preponderance of the evidence, that the defendant's proffered reasons are a pretext for discrimination.[15]

The court noted that the law firm's articulated reason for denying Ezold admission to the partnership was that she did not possess sufficient legal analytical skills to handle the responsibili-

---

11. *Id.* at 520.
12. *Id.* at 522 (citation omitted).
13. *Id.*
14. *Id.*
15. *Id.*

ties of a partner in the firm's complex litigation practice. The opinion then devotes the next twenty-three pages to analyzing the views expressed by individual partners to determine whether the articulated reason had validity.

What is important from the law firm management viewpoint is that the court announced that the firm "reserves for itself the power to decide, by consensus, whether an associate possesses sufficient analytical ability to handle complex matters independently after becoming a partner. It is Wolf's prerogative to utilize such a standard."[16]

The Third Circuit found error in the district court's application of proper legal principles to the evidence in the case. The district court noted that the Wolf firm's complex litigation practice might require a senior partner, a "junior" partner, and an associate to be assigned to a case. Accordingly, it believed that requiring Ezold to have the ability to handle, on her own, any complex litigation within the firm before she was eligible to be a partner was a pretext. As for that view, the Third Circuit declared that the district court "is not a member of Wolf's Associates Committee or Executive Committee. Its belief that Wolf's high standard of analytical ability was unwise in light of the staffing of senior partners on complex cases does not make Wolf's standard a pretext for discrimination."[17]

As the Third Circuit saw it, the evaluations that the district court relied on in making its finding of pretext praised Ezold for skills other than legal analysis. The Third Circuit held that "[i]t was not for the district court to determine that Ezold's skills in areas other than legal analysis made her sufficiently qualified for admission to the partnership."[18]

For the law firm anxious to establish a system that demonstrates the firm's fairness in associate evaluation, *Ezold* provides another lesson. It is not enough to create a record of the credits and debits applicable to the women and minority associates in the firm. It is essential to have the same full and complete record for *each and every* associate. The Third Circuit opinion in *Ezold* contains a detailed analysis of the evaluations of eight male associates who were considered for partnership at the same time as Ezold. Significantly, the court found that two of the male associates "who were

16. *Id.* at 527.
17. *Id.* at 528.
18. *Id.*

comparable to Ezold in the category of legal analysis, were also rejected for regular partnership."[19]

In addition to partner evaluations of associates, a firm must maintain other records to avoid charges of discrimination. One of Ezold's claims was that illegal discriminatory treatment based on sex deprived her of equal opportunities to work on significant cases, or with a wide variety of partners. Hence, it is vital that a firm maintain detailed records of the cases on which an associate worked and the identity of the partner or partners who were supervising the associate. The records should provide a concise description of the matter and of the issues involved, together with an explanation of the tasks assigned to the associate. This record will be useful not only in establishing the nature and complexity of assignments, but also in refreshing the partner's recollection regarding the associate's duties and performance in the matter.

Partners need to be circumspect in their speech concerning their opinions of women and minorities in the profession. Innocent comments, perhaps made in an effort to be funny or particularly astute, can be misinterpreted and cause all sorts of problems for the firm. The fact that one Wolf partner made certain comments over a five-year period was cited by Ezold as indicating a bias against women by the law firm. During the selection process, this partner allegedly made a statement that "it would not be easy for her at Wolf, Block because she did not fit the Wolf, Block mold since she was a woman." On another occasion, after instructing Ezold in the hallway of the firm, he allegedly asked her whether she had any romantic encounters the night before. Ezold also claimed that this same partner, at a litigation associates' breakfast, had recounted a judge's comments about a murder case in which a man killed a woman and had sex with her afterwards; and that the partner also told Ezold not to refer a talented female lawyer to the firm for employment because he did not want the problems caused by another female lawyer working in the litigation department.

Because there was an issue about whether all these statements had been made by the partner, the Third Circuit found it obliged to decide "whether these six alleged comments by [the partner] over a period of five years are sufficient to sustain the district court's finding that Wolf's reason for denying Ezold admission to the partnership—her legal analytical ability—was just a pretext to

19. *Id.* at 538.

cover up sex discrimination."[20] The court held that the partner was not involved in the decision to deny Ezold partnership because he had previously left the firm, and that although the comments were "crude and unprofessional" and "reflected unfavorably on [the partner's] personality or his views," they were not sufficient to prove "that Wolf's associate evaluation and partnership admission process were so infected with discriminatory bias that such bias more likely motivated Wolf's promotion decision than its articulated legitimate reason."[21]

You must watch your language in these matters. You can get yourself and your law firm into as much trouble with careless speech in this area as if you jokingly announce to the airport metal detector attendant that you are carrying an AK-47! It can cost your firm a significant amount just to prove that you did not mean what you said.

Potential Damages for Denial of Partnership

As a law firm partner, you have to be concerned not only with the fact of liability, but with the amount of damages that can be assessed against your firm (and yourself) should your firm discriminate in selection for partnership.

As discussed, Nancy Ezold had initially won her case on liability against the firm of Wolf, Block, Schorr & Solis-Cohen. In the district court, the firm had been found guilty of sex discrimination under Title VII in electing not to admit her to partnership. The case then came before the district court on the question of damages. As explained, her victory was for nought, because the judgment was reversed on appeal on the liability issue; hence, the Third Circuit did not review the award of damages. However, the result in the district court is interesting.

Ezold sought back pay, and either instatement as a member of the partnership or front pay. The firm asserted that Ezold had not been constructively discharged because she had voluntarily resigned; consequently, she was entitled to back pay only from the date on which she would have become a partner to the date of her voluntary resignation from her associate position.

---

20. *Id.* at 546.
21. *Id.*

The court discussed at great length the application of the "constructive discharge rule" in Title VII cases. When this rule applies and no constructive discharge has occurred, the plaintiff is limited to the collection of back pay, the relief claimed applicable by Wolf. In its decision, the court reviewed the positions taken by the various circuits. Some approved of only limited back pay (that is, pay from the date of the discriminatory act to the date of resignation) while others awarded back pay past that date when a constructive discharge had occurred. The court noted that the Third Circuit had not taken any position on the issue, and that the Eastern District of Pennsylvania had recognized that the restriction of a remedy to back pay was inconsistent with Title VII's remedial objectives.

The court noted that there was precedent for broad discretion in the award of damages. It observed that Ezold's decision to resign from the firm "was not a knee-jerk reaction to a one-time discriminatory act by Wolf" and that "as it is for any senior associate in a large law firm, the partnership decision regarding Ms. Ezold was a culmination of her entire career theretofore at the firm, most likely encompassing 10,000 or more hours billed. . . . In Ms. Ezold's case, however, the adverse partnership decision also represented a culmination of the numerous elements of discriminatory treatment she had received throughout her years at the firm."[22]

The court did not criticize Ezold's decision to resign from the firm, and recognized that her career opportunities would be far greater elsewhere. Therefore, it declined to rule out application of the constructive discharge doctrine to Ezold's situation. The court ordered that trial on the issue of damages should proceed regarding:

> (1) back pay;
>
> (2) the instatement of the plaintiff, Nancy O'Mara Ezold, as a Partner within the defendant Firm, Wolf, Block, Schorr & Solis-Cohen, or in the alternative, front pay; and
>
> (3) proper mitigation of damages by the plaintiff.[23]

---

22. Ezold v. Wolf, Block, Schorr & Solis-Cohen, 758 F. Supp. 303, 311 (E.D. Pa. 1991).

23. *Id.* at 312.

The reasoning of the district court may well apply in a proper case, when the liability of the law firm is sustained. The case demonstrates that when discrimination is present and proven, the potential for damages against the offending firm is significant.

There are at least two lessons to be drawn from the *Ezold* case, if you are a law firm partner. First, you may not take gender into consideration when deciding whether to invite someone into the partnership. Second, to avoid any charge that you have violated this principle, you must carefully maintain accurate and detailed records regarding associates' performance. If you do not wish to promote a person to partnership, you must be able to demonstrate that the reasons had nothing to do with factors that would violate Title VII.

In a Title VII case, the result can be disastrous for the law firm guilty of discrimination on the basis of gender. You could find yourself with a partner you do not wish to have should you deny partnership to that person because she is a woman—even though there would have been another legitimate, but unrecorded, basis for the firm's action.

Up-or-Out Policy

Should a firm adopt an "up-or-out" policy? Such a policy usually means that an associate who reaches the point when a vote for partnership is usually taken must receive the partners' invitation to join the firm and, if not, the associate must leave the firm.

From the viewpoint of the partners, adoption of such a policy probably has little effect on increasing the risk of liability from a disaffected associate. The associate who is not elected to partnership would have a claim against the partnership if it failed to disclose to the associate, when he or she was hired, that the firm had such a policy. The associate would also have a claim, even if the policy were disclosed, if the partnership had not applied the policy fairly and evenly to those associates eligible for consideration and the claimant was denied partnership while others less qualified were invited into the firm. It is for this reason that the establishment and maintenance of complete and accurate performance records for the associates is important for the protection of the partners.

Law firms that do not have an up-or-out policy may decide to retain some associates in the capacity of senior lawyers, special counsel, or some other category. The existence of these special classes of lawyers within the firm does not lessen the risk of liability for the partners; the same obligation to choose fairly and equitably among the associates exists, and the same hazard exists if the choices are improperly made.

Rather, whether a firm should have an up-or-out policy probably depends on the ambiance that the partners wish to have. In firms where the policy exists, so does the likelihood that associates having a higher degree of aggressiveness, scholarship, and legal skill will be attracted; law school graduates with lesser ability will be unwilling to take the gamble that they can succeed in a "win-or-lose-all" situation. Those who do succeed and become partners find themselves in a group of highly qualified individuals, and chances are reduced that some partners will look upon others as less able.

Lawyers in Transition

In a moral sense, if not a legal one, the existence of an up-or-out policy places a special burden on the partnership. Once an associate has been advised that he or she has no real chance of becoming a partner and should seek a career elsewhere, that person is a "lawyer in transition." (The phrase was coined by the Association of the Bar of the City of New York, which, in 1990, established the Special Committee on Lawyers in Transition to provide guidance and mentoring for lawyers facing a career crisis.) Persons outside the firm who are aware of the up-or-out policy may stigmatize any associate who fails to become a partner.

Wisely, many firms have taken cognizance of this unfortunate tendency. They attempt, early in an associate's career, to advise the associate if there is little chance for partnership. They then provide what help they can to assist this "lawyer in transition" in finding another career opportunity.

If a firm is careful in its recruiting efforts, then only infrequently will a lawyer be turned down for partnership because of incompetence. In almost every case, there are other reasons for denial of partnership. Consequently, the firm can honestly recommend the "lawyer in transition" to another prospective employer. Also, by assisting firm alumni in securing placement in corporate law departments, for example, the firm will maintain the goodwill of the alumni and lay the groundwork for future business relationships.

These two elements—early notification to the associate that partnership is not in his or her future, and assistance in finding alternative employment—leave the associate with the option of explaining his or her change of position as a search for a new career opportunity, dislike for the work at the previous firm, or other face-saving "excuses" for what might otherwise be an embarrassing move. Given the law firm's assistance, the associate is not likely to comment negatively about the firm to outsiders. Too often, in the haste to rid the partnership of the expense of an associate who is not going to "make it," the law firm terminates the relationship abruptly. This may make for short-term savings, but long-term folly. Good partners will take the long view.

The Employment Contract (Short and Long Forms)

There are as many forms of employment contracts with associates, it seems, as there are law firms. Some firms write a very short letter to applicants who have been accepted, while other firms expound at great length to tell the associate about what is being offered. A few examples of the language from representative letters[24] are set forth in Appendix A.

Subjects covered in letters offering employment to new associates include:

- Congratulations on the applicant's performance, as a law student, as an interviewee, or as a summer associate
- An offer of a specific salary or a salary at some unspecified amount, usually related to competition in the location involved
- A statement that the position offered is that of an associate
- An indication of the office and/or the department of the firm to which the associate will be assigned
- The date on which the salary will commence, perhaps tied to successful passage of the state bar (some firms offer a stipend from the date of hire until the date the "real salary" commences, to provide income while the new graduate is studying for the bar)
- Assurance that the applicant will be considered for partnership in a specified number of years
- A listing of the benefits that are provided to new associates in the firm, including such items as health, life, and disability insurance, payment of dues to bar associations and

24. The author has revised some language to protect the anonymity of the firm supplying the example.

social clubs, contributions by the firm to pension plans (Keogh and 401(k) plans), and vacations and holidays
- A statement that employment is contingent upon any one or more of a number of factors, such as a conflicts-of-interest check (particularly if the applicant was employed by another firm during law school), successful passage of the bar examination, acceptance of the offer by a specified date, or arrival at the firm by a specified date

Some of these provisions are essential to the existence of an agreement between the firm and the associate, while others are in the nature of terms in a "selling document." The issue for the partner in the law firm is to assure that he or she agrees with the terms of the offer. If the firm has provided a condition of employment by making a promise—with which a partner disagrees—the firm may nevertheless be committed and unable to rescind the term without breaching the contract with the associate.

For example, one thorny problem turns on the question of when an associate will be considered for partnership. In the past, the larger firms often stated, either during the course of interviews with applicants or in offer letters, that associates were voted upon for partnership at the end of their seventh year with the firm. Many firms discovered, when the halcyon days of the 1980s came to an end, that election to partnership at the end of the traditional seventh year was no longer a viable option. If the firm did not need a new partner or partners, and failed to elect any at the end of a seven-year period, it might elect to reconsider a class in the following year. This had the effect of delaying all partnership consideration until the end of an eight-year period. Those associates who had been promised that their partnership would be voted upon at the end of their seventh year might well have a claim for breach of contract, unless the original letter of employment indicated that partnership consideration was not unequivocal. If the original letter of employment was silent about conditions for partnership consideration, it would have been important to advise the associate that factors other than those directly related to the associate would be weighed by the firm in deciding the partnership issue.

The importance, not only of the original hiring letter, but of changes in the arrangements with an associate after the original hiring, cannot be overestimated—not only for the protection of the firm but for the associate as well. Wallace Stalnaker Jr. was an associate in a Florida law firm. He was brought up on disciplinary charges by the Florida bar on the ground that he diverted firm funds to his own use. Stalnaker contended that he considered leaving the firm because he was generating about twice the fees of the two partners, but all three lawyers were receiving the same compensation. He brought this up, he alleged, with one of the partners who decided, after realizing Stalnaker would take valuable clients with him should he leave the firm, that the arrangement with Stalnaker should be amended as follows: he should be allowed to retain a portion of the fees he earned as long as he forwarded to the firm an amount comparable to the fees he had earned in the past. At the hearing, the partner denied making any such commitment to Stalnaker. The hearing officer decided the credibility issue in favor of the partner and Stalnaker was disciplined. On appeal to the Florida Supreme Court, the decision below was affirmed, with a strong dissent.[25]

There is a lesson here. Had there been a record of Stalnaker's demand and a record of the partner's action—whether the partner approved or disapproved—both the firm and Stalnaker would have been spared embarrassment and expense incident to the disciplinary proceeding.

Compensation Policy

There is probably no problem more vexing to law firm partners than the establishment of a policy for compensating associates, particularly in the multioffice firm. Often, the large, financial center law firm will have a very high salary scale for its associates. It then decides to open an office in a smaller city, where traditional salary scales are lower than in the financial center city. If it establishes salary scales in the new office below the level of its principal office, the associates in the new location will consider themselves as somewhat inferior lawyers—"second class citizens." Should the firm wish to induce associates—particularly experienced associates—to move from its principal office to the new office, it will have the difficult task of persuading those individuals to accept less money or, more realistically, forego some or all of a salary increase. On the other hand, if the firm establishes the salary scales in the new office at the same level as in the principal office, the new office will not be competitive with other law offices in the area, as the firm's billing rates would be above those of other firms in the new location. The office would not be a financial success.

---

25. Florida Bar v. Stalnaker, 485 So. 2d 815 (Fla. 1986).

This problem has been presented in reverse to some local and regional firms in smaller cities near major metropolitan centers, such as New York, Chicago, and San Francisco. Firms from these centers have elected to open offices in suburban cities, and often choose to offer associate salaries on the same scale as the firms pay in the metropolitan center. This factor presents the suburban firm with a major obstacle in recruiting the best lawyers from the top-ranked law schools. When the pros and cons of the salary issue are weighed, the answer seems to be that the suburban firm should not try to compete with the firms in the metropolitan center on a salary basis. Lawyers who prefer the quality of life available in the suburban location will accept a somewhat lower income as an acceptable trade-off. Metropolitan center firms will find that clients accustomed to suburban billing rates from their legal service providers will be unwilling to pay higher rates, just because they are dealing with a metro-center firm.

Another source of friction within a firm is the compensation policy related to salary increases for associates. A firm has a choice: adjust salaries of all associates equally each year by class, or make the adjustment on the basis of merit. Often a firm believes that a merit-based increase will work, because it can be kept confidential between the firm and the individual associate. Seldom is this possible. If the firm is dedicated to the merit-based system, it must be prepared to defend the system and the salary adjustments it dictates. When a careful and serious effort is made to compensate associates on the basis of individual performance and ability, there should be little grumbling from the lawyers. The risk is that some personal favoritism and subjective judgments will replace objective measurements. When favoritism and subjectivity are avoided, a merit-based system will induce hard work and accomplishment, and bring out the best from the associate staff.

Many firms have a dual system for adjusting salaries of associates. All associates in the same class receive an annual salary increase in equal amounts, and a bonus may be added to this increase, based on individual performance during the preceding year. In most firms, each associate is evaluated by a number of partners, usually those with whom the associate had any significant contact during the year. These evaluations are then reviewed by a committee charged with administering the salary adjustment program, and an appropriate bonus is determined. Several of the evaluators meet with the associate and discuss his or her contributions or shortcomings, suggest areas for improvement, and inform the associate about the "bottom line" for the ensuing year. Few law firms expect associates to be "rainmakers" and business contribution is seldom a criterion for salary adjustment. However, associates are encouraged to become active in the community and to bring business to the firm whenever they can. Even though not a primary factor in salary evaluation as an associate, the potential to produce business will ultimately be a major consideration when the associate is a candidate for partnership.

In a very competitive situation, each law firm attempts to keep its salary adjustments in line with other firms in the city or county in which it practices. Finding out what your competitor is doing, while at the same time not violating the antitrust laws, is no mean trick. Your own associates are your best source of information, but you must be careful to sift rumor from fact and the reliable from the spurious.

Although there is pressure on law firms to enlarge the number of minority associates, there appears to be no significant attempt to attract minority applicants by offering them higher salaries or larger bonuses than are offered to other associates. The lack of a strong minority presence in the partner ranks of many law firms seems due to the relatively small pool of minority graduates in the top ranks of the leading law schools. This small pool is recruited by a few of the very large, elite firms, and by the clerks' offices of federal judges and state appellate courts. There are few competent minority candidates left to supply the demand of the many firms seeking them. Without the ability to hire and retain excellent minority associates, law firms lack the opportunity to elect minority partners.

Partners' Liability for Associates' Actions

While associates, in their capacity as lawyers for a client, may have direct liability to the client for legal malpractice, it is also clear (at least in New York) that the firm's partners also have liability to clients for damages due to the legal malpractice of the firm's associates.[26] Suppose an associate in your office accepts client funds for investment, fails to invest the funds, and does not return them to the client. This was the situation in the *Haight* case. You, as a partner, may not have a direct attorney-client relationship with this particular client because his affairs were handled by an associate, but you are liable to the client for the negligence of the associate.

---

26. Haight v. Grund, 1990 U.S. Dist. LEXIS 5600 (S.D.N.Y. 1990).

Your law firm will not be vicariously liable for your associates' improper activity that may cause damage to a third party who is not a client of the firm.[27] Thus, Sullivan & Cromwell was not liable for its support personnel's theft and sale of confidential information to outside parties. The outside parties had made illegal trades, which damaged the plaintiff. However, because the plaintiff was not a Sullivan & Cromwell client, the firm had no duty to him regarding the hiring and supervision of firm employees.

The issue of vicarious liability is not always clear when an attorney-client relationship is present. Geraldine Logan sued Hyatt Legal Services, Inc., which had a contract with her employer, AT&T, to provide her with legal services. When she sought a divorce, she was sent to Mr. Lebovitz, a lawyer. Lebovitz employed an associate, Ms. Doliner. At a meeting among Logan, her spouse, and Doliner, romantic "sparks" evidently flew and Logan claimed that Doliner and Logan's then husband allegedly had "a sexual relationship" that continued during Doliner's representation of Logan. The trial court dismissed Logan's complaint.

An appellate court in Missouri reversed.[28] The court stated: "However, we cannot say that it is impossible to imagine a set of facts in which . . . Lebovitz could hypothetically have involved [himself] in this matter to such a degree that vicarious liability is appropriate."[29] Ms. Logan was allowed to replead.

As we have seen from the discussion of partners' obligation to supervise, failure to carry out that obligation can have grave consequences to the delinquent partner. In the *Galbasino* case,[30] Galbasino's failure to supervise earned him a six-month suspension of his license to practice from the Arizona Supreme Court, even though he had made restitution of all sums that had to be repaid to his clients.

If an associate performs negligently, courts will sometimes impose liability almost summarily upon the law firm that employs the associate. Ellen Fowler was employed by the law firm of Johnson, Blakely, Pope, Bokor & Ruppel, P.A. The plaintiff's com-

---

27. Gottlieb v. Sullivan & Cromwell, 203 A.D.2d 241, 609 N.Y.S.2d 344 (App. Div. 1994).

28. Logan v. Hyatt Legal Services, Inc., 874 S.W.2d 548 (Mo. Ct. App. 1984).

29. *Id.* at 552.

30. *In re* Galbasino, 163 Ariz. 120, 786 P.2d 871 (1990).

plaint alleged that Fowler was negligent in her performance. Count II of the complaint charged the employing law firm with responsibility, and damages, for her conduct. In one sentence, a motion to dismiss Count II was set aside by the court:

> The Court heard argument of counsel for Ellen Fowler and the Law Firm and response by PMI [the client] and is satisfied that the Motion is not well taken and the claims set forth in Counts I and II do set forth a claim for which relief could be granted; therefore, the Motion to Dismiss addressed to Counts I and II shall be denied.[31]

Rapport between Associates and Partners

Law firms expecting to survive through years of both prosperity and adversity need to establish a good rapport between partners and associates. The firm that has developed a sense of loyalty among all its lawyers, partners and associates alike, will overcome the vicissitudes of declines and advances in business. Without it, when revenues decline and expenses rise, the partners will begin to battle among themselves over the remaining profits; the tensions among the partners will filter down to the associates. The result will be erosion of morale, poor legal performance and, eventually, further deterioration in the client base.

Loyalty can be built up if, at the commencement of their relationships with the firm, associates are treated with dignity and respect. This does not mean there should be any lack of good discipline in the office. It does mean that partners and associates should meet socially on a regular basis, in small groups, and in an informal setting. Associates should get to know the partners as human beings, and not only as overbearing tyrants. Partners should learn that associates are people with families and problems and, as older and more senior lawyers, the partners can often serve as surrogate parents and provide support and solutions to the associates.

Unfortunately, the practice of law has changed dramatically over the years. The small firm, with only a tiny coterie of associates, is a great rarity in the cities, although many small firms continue to exist successfully in smaller communities and rural areas. The "big city" firms have grown larger and larger, so that a partner

---

31. *In re* Property Management & Inv., 20 B.R. 319 (Bankr. M.D. Fla. 1982).

may not even know all his fellow partners. In these circumstances, it is difficult to build rapport among partners, let alone among partners and associates. But the effort is well worth it. A strong sense of loyalty and camaraderie will prevent dissention and even litigation, should things become too contentious. Most important of all, that sense of loyalty and camaraderie will make going to work a real pleasure.

There is no gainsaying that over time things change. Partners are, almost by definition, older people. Unless there is an opportunity for off-the-record exchange of ideas between the older group (the partners) and the younger generation (the associates), the partners will suffer the most. Without knowing the associates' views on matters such as hiring policy, compensation, evaluation, promotion, and expectations of the firm on billable hours—matters of moment to the entire firm—the partners will not be able to administer partnership affairs properly. For example, you may believe that associates in your office are "lazy" and complaining about long hours of work; they will not work the long hours that you did when you were young. This is a typical attitude of a senior partner in many offices. The fact may be that the associates are disgruntled, not because they are unwilling to put in the hours, but because the firm does not adequately reward those lawyers who do give exemplary performance with high billable hours and outstanding work. You will find that out only if you spend some time away from the office with your associates, under circumstances that will put them at ease to express themselves openly.

Those associates who perform well, get along with the clients of the firm, attract business, and improve the ambiance of the office are indeed valuable to the success of the firm, both professionally and financially. They deserve "tender loving care."

CHAPTER III

The Construction of a Partnership Agreement

Constitutional Aspects of the Partnership Agreement

It may be trite to say that in a law partnership, your rights as a partner are governed by the partnership agreement. However, if you think about it for more than a minute, you realize how important it is to examine the partnership agreement in your own firm. You may find it needs a complete redrafting, or you may conclude that preparing an amendment to change certain provisions will be sufficient.

Should you decide to go the amendment route, bear in mind the lesson of the *Hinshaw* case.[1] There a law firm had adopted a partnership agreement in 1983, which specified certain payments to be made to a withdrawing partner. In 1986, the firm entered into a withdrawal agreement with Mr. Hinshaw. The latter agreement contained a merger clause. Under the partnership agreement, Hinshaw would receive (1) a payment for his capital account (representing his interest in partnership property) plus (2) 50 percent of taxable income for the last three years he was with the firm, taxable to him and deductible to the firm, as payment for receivables and work in progress. Under the withdrawal agreement, he would receive a specified sum in payment for his partnership interest and would assign to the firm all his interest in work in progress. Litigation ensued over the failure of the firm to make payments. Hinshaw

1. Hinshaw v. Wright, 105 N.C. App. 158, 412 S.E.2d 138 (Ct. App. 1992).

sought a declaratory judgment that the withdrawal agreement neither superseded the partnership agreement nor altered or modified the terms of the latter.

On appeal, the court referred to general principles of contract law regarding a novation. It cited the North Carolina Supreme Court's decision in the *Daniel* case: "If the second contract deals with the subject matter of the first so comprehensively as to be complete within itself or if the two contracts are so inconsistent that the two cannot stand together a novation occurs."[2] The court decided that the withdrawal agreement dealt comprehensively with the payments due upon termination and contained a merger clause. It held that the 1986 agreement effectively superseded the 1983 partnership agreement.

Should you amend your partnership agreement, make sure it is clear whether the entire agreement is amended or only portions and, if the latter, to what extent the amendatory document governs.

It is also important to keep in mind, as you contemplate drafting a partnership agreement, the interplay between the agreement and the Uniform Partnership Act. There is a line of cases noting that when a partnership is dissolved, the partners' fiduciary duties continue until the windup is completed, and that the partners are entitled to receive their partnership interest in the profits from this work.[3] In *Kelly*, the partnership agreement provided for payments to a withdrawing partner that valued his capital account and interest in receivables and contingent fees. It did not address the withdrawing partner's obligation to the firm regarding matters that followed him.

The court noted that when the partnership agreement does not cover the matter, the Uniform Partnership Act will govern. The court decided it would be inequitable to give Kelly the benefit of the partnership agreement as far as payments were concerned, and not impose upon him the obligations of the Uniform Partnership Act to account for fees earned by matters taken from the firm upon his departure. "To impose the agreement on one half of the equation and the [Uniform Partnership Act] on the other half of the

---

2. *Id.*, 105 N.C. App. at 160, 412 S.E.2d at 140 (citing Wittaker General Medical Corp. v. Daniel, 324 N.C. 523, 379 S.E.2d 824, *reh'g denied*, 325 N.C. 277, 384 S.E.2d 531 (1989)).

3. Kelly v. Smith, 611 N.E.2d 118, 120 (Ind. 1993).

equation leads to an inequitable result and defeats the intent of the parties in creating the agreement."[4]

Thus, the drafter of the partnership agreement must be aware of the necessity to cover all angles, or face the consequences of a result governed by the Uniform Partnership Act. A significant issue to keep in mind when drafting a partnership agreement (or the certificate of incorporation and bylaws of a professional corporation) is that the document is in the nature of a constitution. It is not an instrument to govern the details of daily operation of the law firm, but one that sets the tone and policy to guide fundamental decisions. It is a living document that must survive over time and be amended only infrequently.

What should this document contain?

Usual Introductory Features

Name

PARTNERSHIP IDENTIFICATION

When you think about preparing a partnership agreement, one of the first questions you will ask yourself is, "What is our firm to be called?" As long as you remain with the prosaic, and use the names only of living persons who will be practicing law with you, there is no problem. However, stray from the straight and narrow, and you can run into some sticky issues. Before you know it, you may be facing an inquiry from the state grievance authority or a complaint from a disgruntled competitor.

You may also have in mind that it would be a good idea to provide for the transfer of your partnership interest, including the use of your name—especially if you have been the rainmaker in the firm. You may consider writing a side agreement to the partnership agreement to take care of that eventuality. You may also want to assure yourself that if any partner in the firm is disciplined for malpractice or an ethical violation, you will be able to rescind the right of the firm to any further use of your name.

How does this play out in the scheme of things?

Perhaps there is a respected lawyer in your town who is a little older than you. He is thinking of retiring and you would like to form a partnership with him and use his name in the future. No

---

4. *Id.* at 121.

problem. You can do that, and if the "Esteemed Counselor" should die, you may continue to use the partnership name that you used during his lifetime.

THE NONEXISTENT PARTNER

But consider a little variation on that scenario. You, John Q. Lawyer, form a professional corporation, which in turn forms a partnership with the "Esteemed Counselor." You then decide to retreat from active law practice. Your daughter is a lawyer and you transfer the shares in your corporation to her. May your daughter practice law, using the name "John Q. Lawyer, P.C." in connection with her practice?

An appellate court in New York, examining a slightly more complicated fact situation, determined that your daughter would be unable to do that. In the *Klein* case,[5] two professional corporations, Lawrence A. Klein, P.C. and Wagner & Morris, P.C., formed a third law partnership—Klein, Wagner & Morris—in March, 1983. In late 1989, Mr. Klein (the sole shareholder in his professional corporation) transferred his shares to his daughter, Susan Klein Elicks. A short time later, in January, 1990, Klein died. His daughter continued to use "Lawrence A. Klein" and "Lawrence A. Klein, P.C." in her law practice. Meanwhile, the firm of Klein, Wagner & Morris continued its law practice. It sought an injunction regarding the use of the name "Lawrence A. Klein" or "Lawrence A. Klein, P.C." by Elicks. The trial court granted the injunction. Elicks (as "Lawrence A. Klein, P.C.") appealed. The appellate court noted that the partnership agreement between Lawrence A. Klein, P.C. and Wagner & Morris, P.C. provided that the death of any of the partners would not terminate the partnership and that the partnership would be continued by the remaining partners. It further provided that the name of the deceased partner would be continued as part of the firm name.

The court stated that the Code of Professional Responsibility provides that the letterhead of a law firm may give names and dates relating to deceased members, and that a firm may include in its name a deceased member of the firm in a continuing line of succession if the public is not misled. It said also that the Code of Professional Responsibility contains a prohibition against the use of a firm name by an associate when all the partners are dead,

5. Klein, Wagner & Morris v. Lawrence A. Klein, P.C., 186 A.D.2d 631, 588 N.Y.S.2d 424 (App. Div. 1992).

except to wind up partnership affairs. The court observed that Susan Klein Elicks was never a partner in Klein, Wagner & Morris and never had "any legitimate shareholder interest" in Lawrence A. Klein, P.C.[6] The appellate court affirmed the trial court and remanded the case to the trial court to determine the amount of an undertaking.

YOUR NAME AFTER DEATH

As you proceed with drafting a partnership agreement, it may occur to you or your partners that should any of you die, it might be well to pass on the rights to your names to the survivors. Such a situation arose in a Tennessee case.[7] In *Gracey*, the widow and executrix of Hugh Gracey Sr. obtained an injunction in chancery court against the use of her husband's name by his former law firm. The partnership appealed to the Tennessee Court of Appeals.

The court's opinion reveals that in 1974, Gracey had entered into a partnership agreement with a partnership known as Gracey, Maddin, Cowan & Bird. At the same time, Gracey made a side agreement with the partnership. Because Gracey decided to reduce his activity, it was agreed in 1977 (as amended in 1978) that his participation in partnership income would be fixed at declining percentages through the year 1982. It was further understood that the arrangement represented a buyout of all interests that Gracey had in the firm, leaving no residual partnership income to his estate should he die within the time period covered by the agreement. The agreement provided that "the arrangements between Mr. Gracey and the firm for the calendar years 1983 and beyond are to be determined and decided by and between him and the then partners in the firm."[8] The 1978 amendment further provided that Gracey agreed to sell to the partnership all interest he had in the firm. The general partnership agreement provided that the death of a partner would not terminate the agreement and upon such death, the remaining partners would reconstitute themselves as a continuing partnership.

The opinion recites numerous changes in the roster of partners between 1974 and 1987. Gracey Sr. died in 1984, Cowan and Bird left in 1987, Binkley died in 1980, Gracey's son Hugh Jr. was admitted as a partner in 1980 but left in 1986, and four other changes occurred.

6. *Id.*, 186 A.D.2d at 633, 588 N.Y.S.2d at 426.
7. Gracey v. Maddin, 769 S.W.2d 497 (Ct. App. 1989).
8. *Id.* at 498.

In an extended discussion, the court concluded that related to the question about whether the remaining partners have a right to continue to use the name of a retired or deceased partner is the more fundamental matter concerning ownership by the partnership of the name as part of the goodwill of the partnership. The court noted Judge Cardozo's "distinction between names purely personal or individual, and names that had acquired, through the incrustations of time, a veneer of associations, artificial and impersonal."[9] The court said that Gracey's name had not gone through that metamorphosis and hence had not been transformed into part of the partnership's goodwill. Consequently, in the absence of a voluntary agreement between Gracey or his estate and the partnership, the firm did not have the right to the use of his name.

The court then turned to the obvious question concerning whether Gracey had a property right in his name that he could sell or assign. After a wide-ranging discussion, the court concluded that Gracey had a property right in his own name.

Then there remained the ultimate question—whether Gracey had the right, under the agreements between himself and the partners, to assign to the remaining partners his right to use his name after his retirement and/or death. The court held that Gracey had assigned the use of his name through 1982; for the years 1983 and after, the parties had agreed they would enter into further negotiations. The court held that although the parties had agreed on provisions in the event of retirement, there were no comparable provisions in the event of death. Therefore, because 1982 had passed, the estate was entitled to its injunction.

The partnership agreement you draft must, therefore, make clear (1) whether surviving partners are entitled to use the name of a retiring or deceased partner, and (2) the consideration due the retiring partner or his or her estate in those respective events. When deciding whether it is permissible to include goodwill in computing the value of a partner's interest in a law firm, bear in mind that courts have distinguished between transfers of an intervivos or continuing interest and an interest related to death or retirement.

THE "TRADE NAME"

Should you elect to practice law under a trade name, you may do so. However, the highest court in New York has held that you

---

9. *Id.* at 499 (citing *In re* Brown, 242 N.Y. 1, 150 N.E. 581, 583 (1926)).

must make sure to include with the trade name the identities of those lawyers through which the practice will be carried on. In that case, Eric von Wiegen was seeking business arising out of the Hyatt Regency Hotel disaster in Kansas City, Missouri, and he used direct mail solicitations of families of accident victims. He appealed from an order suspending him from practice on the ground, among others, that disciplinary rules prohibited the use of the phrase "The Country Lawyer" as von Wiegen's trade name. The court said:

> The purpose of the prohibition against trade names embodied in [Disciplinary Rule] 2-102 (B) is to prevent the public from being deceived about the identity, responsibility and status of those who use the name. The use of the motto "The Country Lawyer" in respondent's flyer did not deceive in that way because the lawyer's name was inserted apart from the motto. The case relied upon by the Appellate Division, *Matter of Shephard* (92 A.D.2d 978), is distinguishable. In *Shephard*, the court found that the corporate name "The People's Law Firm of Jan L. Shephard, Attorney, P.C." constituted a trade name because it suggested that the firm was controlled by the public, received public funding or provided legal services on a nonprofit basis. No such potential for deception is present in the use of the term, "The Country Lawyer."[10]

The court held that, as to this portion of the lower court's order, the charge should be dismissed.

Another example of a court's approval of a trade name in which the name of the lawyer is associated with the trade term is found in an Oregon case.[11] There the Supreme Court of Oregon ruled that a law office operating under the names "Shannon and Johnson's Hollywood Law Center" and "Hollywood Law Center, a Branch of Shannon and Johnson" did not violate disciplinary rules.

Given unreasonable circumstances, however, use of a trade name will not be allowed. Louis Mezrano, a lawyer, found that out when he was suspended for practicing under the name "University Law Center." The court noted that Mezrano's office was located on University Boulevard in very close proximity to the University of Alabama in Birmingham, and that he was not affiliated with the

---

10. *In re* von Wiegen, 63 N.Y.2d 163, 470 N.E.2d 838, 481 N.Y.S.2d 40 (1984), *cert. denied*, 105 S. Ct. 2701 (1985) (citations omitted).

11. *In re* Complaint, 292 Or. 339, 638 P.2d 482 (1982).

university. The court indicated that the general public might associate Mezrano with the university due to the name of the legal center and its location, thus being misled about his identity. The court held "this use of the name is in violation of [Disciplinary Rule] 2-102(B)."[12]

PREPAID LEGAL SERVICES

The issue of firm identification has also arisen in the context of a group of lawyers, banded together for the purpose of providing the prepaid legal services required by a union's collective bargaining agreement. A union covering employees in New Jersey, New York, and Florida offered those services in Florida by a private law firm, and in New Jersey and New York with its own lawyers. The latter group of lawyers identified themselves as "1115 Legal Service Care." As described in the opinion of the New Jersey Supreme Court, the

> 1115 Legal Service Care attorneys are employed directly by the plan on a full-time basis and work exclusively on matters covered by the plan. The clients of the plan are employee members of 1115 Joint Board. The attorneys are not permitted to accept as clients persons not covered by the service, nor are they permitted to recommend other counsel to such persons. . . . They are not affiliated with any private law firm, and do not constitute a partnership or professional corporation. . . . All pleadings are signed in the name of the individual staff attorney assigned to a particular matter, with the name of the service's Legal Director also indicated, as well as the address of the program's office at which the matter is being handled. . . .[13]

The letterhead of the group also made clear that it was a "multi-employer funded legal service plan established through collective bargaining." The letterhead listed the group's offices in New Jersey and New York, and the names of the lawyers with an indication of which were licensed in New York, New Jersey, or both, as the case might be. The issue before the Supreme Court of New Jersey was whether the state's Advisory Committee on Advertising was correct in ruling that the letterhead violated the

---

12. Mezrano v. Alabama State Bar, 434 So. 2d 732 (Ala. 1983).
13. *In re* 1115 Legal Serv. Care, 110 N.J. 344, 347, 541 A.2d 673, 674 (1988).

Rules of Professional Conduct. The court also considered "the more fundamental question about the ability of a staff-operated prepaid legal service plan to engage in the practice of law in New Jersey."[14]

The court first noted the general proposition that a lawyer may render legal service within an organizational framework if it is a partnership, professional corporation, or a nonprofit public interest law firm (which was extended to include one operated for charitable and benevolent purposes). Practice otherwise constitutes the unauthorized practice of law.[15]

Deciding that the legal service provided by 1115 Legal Service Care Center did not constitute unauthorized practice of law, the Court said:

> We believe that 1115 Legal Service Care is organized in such a manner as to prevent the abuses at which our Court's regulatory strictures over the profession are directed. It is a vehicle for making legal services available to persons who might not otherwise be able to obtain such services. It provides services to clients within the framework of conventional attorney-client relationships. Individual attorneys providing legal services remain professionally responsible and accountable for their conduct. No control over the rendition of legal services is retained or exerted by non-lawyers. No profits generated by the practice of law enure to the organization itself. The practice of law under the aegis of the plan, in terms of the matters handled and the client interests served, is in no way inconsistent with or inimical to the regulatory standards governing the legal profession.[16]

Should you and your colleagues decide that your law practice will, in fact, be on behalf of a legal service plan, then by following the precautions taken by 1115 Legal Service Care Center, you will probably avoid censure for unauthorized practice. However, if your group also wishes to serve clients outside the plan in a more traditional practice, you better stick to the partnership or professional corporation form of organization.

---

14. *Id.*, 110 N.J. at 348, 541 A.2d at 674.
15. *Id.*, 110 N.J. at 350, 541 A.2d at 675.
16. *Id.*, 110 N.J. at 352, 541 A.2d at 676.

USING YOUR OWN NAME

In conjuring up a name for your practice—and assuming you want a name with some marketing appeal—you might think about following the route taken by Joel Hyatt when he included his own name in the title of "Hyatt Legal Services." Whether you can do that and avoid litigation may well depend upon your name. Such an issue created a lawsuit for Mr. Hyatt.

Hyatt Corporation, an operator of numerous hotels across the United States, brought suit against Joel Hyatt and Hyatt Legal Services in Illinois federal court, alleging violations of the Lanham Act and the Illinois Anti-Dilution Act. The hotel company sought a preliminary injunction, which was denied by the district court. The Hyatt Corporation then appealed to the Seventh Circuit.

The court held that because the public was not likely to be confused between Hyatt Legal Services and Hyatt Hotels, the hotel company was unlikely to prevail on the merits.[17] Thus, there appeared to be no violation of the Lanham Act.

The Illinois Anti-Dilution Act provides a trademark owner injunctive relief against a person using a similar mark "if there exists a likelihood of injury to business reputation or of dilution of the distinctive quality of the mark."[18] Concerning harm to reputation, the Seventh Circuit decided that because Hyatt Legal Services was being operated in a circumspect manner, the fact that a few malpractice claims might be filed against it would not result in harm to the reputation of Hyatt Hotels. Concerning dilution of the Hyatt Hotels trademark, the court had more difficulty. It noted that Hyatt Legal Services had not been modified in any way to show that it was a personal name rather than a trademark (as would be the case, for example, had it been named "Joel Hyatt Legal Services"). Observing that Hyatt Legal Services spent millions of dollars in an extensive advertising campaign and had offices in a third of the states, the court found that Hyatt Hotels had shown a likelihood of success on the question about whether Hyatt Legal Services' use was a dilution of the mark. However, the court declined to enjoin Hyatt Legal Services from using the mark at all. It suggested that the name could be modified by incorporating Mr. Hyatt's first name or by adding the names of his two part-

---

17. Hyatt Corp. v. Hyatt Legal Services, 736 F.2d 1153 (7th Cir.), *cert. denied*, 469 U.S. 1019 (1984).

18. *Id.* at 1157.

ners to the name. The court remanded the case for a preliminary injunction and further proceedings.[19]

The case serves as notice that although you may have a right to use your name, it may not be used in a way that diminishes the value of another's trademark. If you and another lawyer or lawyers are thinking about practicing together under a trade name, be sure that your use will not clash with that of another.

NAMES OF THE NONADMITTED

You must also be careful about using the names of lawyers who are not admitted to practice in the jurisdiction. In New Jersey, the Advisory Committee on Professional Ethics opined that Jacoby & Meyers could not open an office in New Jersey under that name because its named partners were not, nor had they ever been, members of the New Jersey bar. Disciplinary Rule 2-102(C) forbade the use of law firm names "unless all those named are or were members of the bar in New Jersey." Jacoby & Meyers sought revision of the rule or an exemption. The New Jersey Supreme Court affirmed the advisory committee's opinion.[20]

During the same time frame, the same issue arose in New York under a slightly altered fact situation. The New York Criminal and Civil Courts Bar Association sought an injunction to restrain Jacoby & Meyers from practicing law in New York. Neither Mr. Jacoby nor Mr. Meyers was admitted in New York, but their partner, Gail Koff, was a member of the New York bar. After the action commenced, the firm changed its letterhead; Koff's name appeared first on the letterhead and an asterisk notation reading "California Bar Only" was placed after the names of Jacoby and Meyers. The appellate court said:

> This complies with [Disciplinary Rule] 2-102(D). Since there is no question but that Mr. Jacoby and Mr. Meyers do not and have not performed services in this State and that such legal services as are performed in this State by the firm of Jacoby & Meyers are performed by attorneys duly licensed and admitted to the Bar of this State, we hold that there has been no violation of the Judiciary Law nor of the Code of Professional Responsibility.[21]

---

19. *Id.* at 1160.

20. *In re* Advisory Comm. on Professional Ethics, 89 N.J. 74, 444 A.2d 1092 (1982).

21. New York Criminal and Civil Courts Bar Ass'n v. Jacoby, 92 A.D.2d 817, 808, 460 N.Y.S.2d 309, 310 (App. Div. 1983).

The complaint was dismissed. As disclosed in a footnote in the *Weiss* case, discussed below, the result was a revision of the New Jersey rule, which now reads "[w]here the name of an attorney not licensed to practice in this State is used in a firm name, any advertisement, letterhead or other communication containing the firm name must include the name of at least one licensed New Jersey attorney who is responsible for the firm's New Jersey practice or the local office thereof."[22]

If you and your colleagues want to adopt for your partnership identification a name that includes the names of nonadmitted lawyers, make sure that those who are not admitted do not provide legal services in your state and that the partnership includes one or more lawyers who are admitted and do provide the legal services.

THE "INSURANCE COMPANY FIRM"

There is still another possibility when it comes to choosing a name, particularly if several lawyers are providing legal services for a single employer (usually an insurance company). Some eight lawyers, all full-time employees of an insurance company, had their offices in the same building as the insurance company. They named their firm "Weiss, Healey & Rea." It so happened that Weiss, the "senior partner," was the insurance company's Regional Manager for Legal Services in New Jersey; he had numerous administrative duties and handled some trial work. Healey was the insurance company's senior trial lawyer and directed trial work in southern New Jersey. Rea was the supervisor of litigation and directed trial work in central New Jersey. The lawyers worked only on defending the company's insureds. They shared no profits or losses, and all their expenses were paid by the insurance company. The Advisory Committee on Professional Ethics held that the use of the name "Weiss, Healey & Rea" was proscribed by the Rules of Professional Conduct. The committee stated that lawyers who are not partners may not combine their names for an office designation that implies a partnership practice.

In its opinion on review, the court said the question was whether there is anything deceptive about the use of a name like "A, B & C" to describe the association of lawyer-employees of an insurance company. In affirming the finding of the committee, the court said:

---

22. *See In re* Weiss, Healey & Rea, 109 N.J. 246, 251, 536 A.2d 266, 268, n.3 (1988).

> We believe that the message conveyed by the firm name "A, B & C" is that the three persons designated are engaged in the general practice of law in New Jersey as partners. Such partnership implies the full financial and professional responsibility of a law firm that has pooled its resources of intellect and capital to serve a general clientele. The partnership arrangement implies much more than office space shared by representatives of a single insurer. Put differently, the designation "A, B & C" does not imply that the associated attorneys are in fact employees, with whatever inferences a client might draw about their ultimate interest and advice. The public, we believe, infers that the collective professional, ethical, and financial responsibility of a partnership-in-fact bespeaks the "kind and caliber of legal services rendered."[23]

In remanding the case, however, the court did not require the lawyers to cease use of the name, provided that adequate disclosure was made to clients, court, and counsel. In the absence of a genuine partnership agreement, you should not assume that another court would be as generous in the same situation.

Term

The term of a partnership, unless otherwise specified in the agreement, is indefinite. When it is indefinite, it can be dissolved by any partner at any time. The partnership is known as an "at will" partnership.[24] At times, this concept can be important in determining the rights of a partner. In *Clapp v. LeBoeuf,*[25] Alison Clapp, a former partner of LeBoeuf, Lamb, Leiby & MacRae, contended that she had continuing rights as a partner in the firm. She had been terminated and the partnership reformed without her. In denying her claim, the court stated:

> Clapp's interest in the LeBoeuf partnership was strictly a creature of statutory and contractual sources. Clapp admits that her partnership agreement with LeBoeuf was for an indefinite term. New York's courts have unambiguously held that a partnership agreement of an indefinite term is an at will

---

23. *Id.*, 109 N.J. at 251, 536 A.2d at 268.

24. Rosenfeld, Meyer & Susman v. Cohen, 191 Cal. App. 3d 1035, 1044, 237 Cal. Rptr. 14, 18 (Ct. App. 1987).

25. 1994 U.S. Dist. LEXIS 11792 (S.D.N.Y. 1994).

partnership which may be terminated by any partner at any time.[26]

Consequently, in drafting an agreement, it is necessary to decide whether to make dissolution of the partnership a simple process (that is, allowing the Uniform Partnership Act to govern) or whether partners would be better protected by establishing a term for the partnership and permitting earlier termination upon notice and partnership vote.

Dissolution; Incapacity

Because the Uniform Partnership Act calls for the automatic dissolution of a partnership in certain instances, some may believe there is no need to include provisions for dissolution of the partnership. However, there are extreme situations that can possibly arise and there should be a solution for those situations in the partnership document.

For example, *Raymond v. Vaughn*,[27] an 1889 case, involved a partnership of two sugar brokers in Chicago. A court adjudged Vaughn temporarily insane. Upon application, the other partner, Raymond, was appointed conservator of the ill partner's estate. In 1878, Raymond filed a final accounting and was discharged as conservator. Vaughn was discharged from the asylum the following year. Vaughn then sued, demanding an accounting and asserting that the partnership continued.

The Illinois Supreme Court reviewed the history of the law on the point, including discussion in Kent's *Commentaries* and in the English cases. It then said:

> No further citation or analysis of authorities will be necessary. The rule, supported by the decided weight of authority and announcing the correct doctrine, is, that the insanity of a partner does not, per se, work a dissolution of the partnership, but may constitute sufficient grounds to justify a court of equity in decreeing its dissolution. But this doctrine must be understood, and is applied by courts of equity with appropriate limitations and restrictions, for while curable, temporary insanity will be sufficient, upon an inquisition, to sustain an adjudication of insanity in the county court, the appointment

---

26. *Id.* at *18.
27. Raymond v. Vaughn, 128 Ill. 256, 21 N.E. 566 (1889).

> of a conservator and commitment of the ward to an insane asylum, yet it will not authorize a court of chancery to decree a dissolution of a partnership if the malady is temporary, only, with a fair prospect of recovery within a reasonable time. *Story on Partnership*, § 297.[28]

Thus, the court laid down the rule that a decree in equity is required to dissolve a partnership in cases of only temporary incapacity of a partner.

Although hardly a modern case, *Barclay v. Barrie*,[29] decided in the New York Court of Appeals in 1913, distinguishes *Raymond* and establishes a rule when the incapacity is permanent. In *Barclay*, two partners had worked together in the manufacturing business for years. They had entered into a series of partnership agreements and the last agreement, dated in February, 1908, was for five years, ending in January, 1913. One of the partners, Barrie, suffered a cerebral hemorrhage and resultant paralysis in May, 1908, and was disabled. In March, 1909, Barclay sent Barrie a notice explaining that Barrie was not able to perform his duties under the partnership agreement and stating that thirty days thereafter, the partnership would be terminated. A month later Barclay commenced suit for a dissolution of the partnership. The court below found for Barrie and Barclay appealed.

The high court stated that the case could be decided on general principles of equity, and so found it unnecessary to rule on Barclay's contention that the partnership agreement permitted dissolution on the ground that Barrie was unable to perform his duties. First, the court noted that a fair construction of the findings regarding Barrie's physical condition was that he continued wholly incapacitated for the discharge of his duties from May, 1908, until March, 1912, and that the most that could be expected in the future was that he would make a practical recovery within the time limited for the existence of the partnership. The court then observed that

> the cases and text writers as well as common sense make it apparent that "permanent" incapacity as a ground for dissolution does not and should not mean incurable and perpetual disability during the life of the partner. It means incapacity which is lasting rather than merely temporary, and the pros-

---

28. *Id.*
29. Barclay v. Barrie, 209 N.Y. 40, 102 N.E. 602 (1913).

> pect of recovery from which is remote; which has continued or is reasonably certain to continue during so substantial a portion of the partnership period as to defeat or materially affect and obstruct the purpose of the partnership.[30]

After noting the precedent for a distinction between a permanent disability or insanity, and one that is only temporary, the court held:

> Within these principles I think that the plaintiff on the facts as now found established his right as matter of law to a dissolution of the partnership.[31]

Whether dissolution is equitably available in cases of incapacity is fact-dependent. It behooves the drafter of the partnership agreement to include some carefully thought-out definitions of the conditions for dissolution, particularly with reference to the mental or physical incapacity of a partner and the right of the remaining partners to dissolve the partnership in that event.

Business of the Firm

In writing a partnership agreement for a law firm, some might believe it would suffice to say that the firm will provide legal services. However, in today's world, when some law firms are attempting to enter into many related (or unrelated) fields, it is wise to decide whether your firm will be restricted to the traditional practice of law. Taking on other types of work, such as economic consulting in the field of antitrust prosecution or defense or evidentiary review in technical fields for use in product liability or criminal cases, can prove financially rewarding to the firm. At the same time, such work will expose the partners to a broader scope of potential liability and will require a complete examination of the malpractice and other insurance coverages of the firm. Moreover, for the lawyers who wish to maintain a high standard of professionalism *as lawyers*, embarking upon nonlegal ventures adversely impacts that effort. Finally, in putting together a firm with a number of lawyers of partnership caliber, there is bound to be disagreement about whether to restrict the enterprise to the practice of law. Hence, the decision is fundamental and should be set out in the partnership agreement.

---

30. *Id.*, 209 N.Y. at 48, 102 N.E. at 604.
31. *Id.*, 209 N.Y. at 50, 102 N.E. at 605.

Headquarters

The location of the firm may be important to some partners, and of no concern to others. If the partnership is to be headquartered in a particular geographic location, it should be specified; the partnership agreement should provide that additional offices for the partnership are to be established only with the affirmative vote of a specific percentage—probably a very high percentage—of the partners.

Professional Standards

It would seem obvious that lawyers are to conform to the standards required by the Code of Professional Responsibility and other professional rules of conduct established by state and local bar associations. However, because the partnership agreement is a constitution, it should recite that all lawyers in the firm are to conform to these standards. When arriving at a formula for expelling a partner from the firm, or subjecting any lawyer in the firm to disciplinary action, it will greatly assist the effort if the basic partnership document sets out the required level of behavior.

Types of Partners

A half century ago, the existence of any but an equity partner was almost unthinkable. Today, there are all kinds of partners, including equity partners, salaried partners, contract partners, and special partners. When establishing the constitution for a law firm, it is important that the organizers decide the types of partners the firm will be permitted to have. Then, when it is time to vote for the admission of a candidate into a designated class of partnership, all who vote will be aware of the consequences of the admission. Even if the partnership contemplates that when the new partnership agreement becomes effective the firm will have only one class of partner—equity partner—it is advisable to provide for other classes. This will avoid the turmoil that can ensue when a new class is framed around a single individual, instead of establishing a concept acceptable to all partners.

Equity partners will have unlimited authority to bind the partnership and unlimited personal liability for the obligations of the partnership. Every other class of partners—merely by being designated as partners—will have apparent authority to bind the partnership. While this consequence follows as to third persons, it does not have to follow with respect to equity partners.

Most lawyers accepting a status less than equity partnership (a contract or salaried partnership, for example) will insist upon indemnity from the equity partners should the contract or salaried partner become a defendant in litigation against the partnership. The equity partners normally will provide such indemnity in any case in which the contract or salaried partner has not been a contributing party. The contract or salaried partner should lose that protection whenever he or she has been guilty of (1) any violation of the standards of behavior established in the partnership agreement, or (2) misfeasance or malpractice giving rise to the lawsuit. This would include action by the contract or salaried partner binding the partnership in an area prohibited to him or her and reserved to the equity partners in the partnership agreement.

To avoid cluttering the partnership agreement with excessive detail, the writing (letter or contract) between the firm and the contract or salaried partner should contain particulars about the extent of authority granted (with respect to issuing letters of opinion, signing checks and other orders for the payment of money, hiring, and incurring expenses for travel and entertainment, for example) and the limits upon that authority. The writing should make clear that violation of these limits is ground for disciplinary action or, in a serious matter, termination of the agreement.

Just as the contract or salaried partner may expect to be indemnified by the equity partners in appropriate cases, so also will the equity partner anticipate recovery against the contract or salaried partner who causes damage to the firm by reason of his or her malpractice or misfeasance. The writing between the firm and the contract or salaried partner should make clear that this result will follow when that situation arises.

Noncompetition Clauses

In drafting a partnership agreement, a question arises about whether it is legal and ethical to include a noncompetition clause. As in most situations, the answer is: it depends. The bottom line is that the clause must strike a fair balance between protection of the right of the individual to practice law for livelihood and the right of the firm to protect itself against predatory action by a former partner.

The California courts have given careful attention to the issue. For example, in the *Haight* case, the partnership agreement was drafted to provide:

> [E]ach Partner agrees that, if he withdraws or voluntarily retires from the Partnership, he will not engage in any area of the practice of law regularly practiced by the law firm and in so doing represent or become associated with any firm that represents any client represented by this law firm within a twelve (12) month period prior to said person leaving the firm, within the Counties of Los Angeles, Ventura, Orange, Riverside or San Bernardino nor within any City in such Counties for a period of three (3) years from the date of withdrawal or retirement, so long as continuing members of this firm engage in practice in the same areas of law.
>
> A Partner . . . may violate this [section]. However, by so doing, he forfeits any and all rights and interests, financial and otherwise, to which he would otherwise be thereafter entitled as a parting Partner under the terms of this agreement.[32]

Certain Haight, Brown & Bonesteel partners left the firm and set up practice in violation of the noncompetition clause. They also asserted rights that would contravene the forfeiture clause. The firm sought a declaratory judgment that the competing partners were not entitled to any financial interest in the firm, and the withdrawing partners filed a cross-motion attacking the enforceability of the noncompetition clause. The California Business and Professions Code contains a section authorizing any partner to agree not to carry on a similar business within a specified county or city where the partnership business is transacted, for as long as any other member of the partnership carries on a like business in the area. At the same time, under Rule 1-500 of the California State Bar, a lawyer licensed in California may not be a party to an agreement if the agreement restricts the right of the lawyer to practice law; however, such a restriction is not prohibited if it is part of a partnership agreement and the restriction does not survive termination of the partnership. The *Haight* court was faced with resolving the inconsistency between the Statute and the rule of the state bar.

The withdrawing partners argued that the forfeiture had the effect of dissuading departing partners from handling cases for clients in competition with the firm and from practicing law in com-

---

32. Haight, Brown & Bonesteel v. Superior Court of Los Angeles County, 234 Cal. App. 3d 963, 966, 285 Cal. Rptr. 845, 846 (Ct. App. 1991).

petition with the firm. Thus, they said, it was an impermissible restriction on the practice of law in violation of the public policy behind Rule 1-500.

The *Haight* court said:

> We do not construe rule 1-500 in such a narrow fashion. In our opinion, the rule simply provides that an attorney may not enter into an agreement to refrain altogether from the practice of law. The rule does not, however, prohibit a withdrawing partner from agreeing to compensate his former partners in the event he chooses to represent clients previously represented by the firm from which he has withdrawn.[33]

The court also observed:

> We recognize the personal and confidential relationship which exists between lawyers and their clients. We do not, however, believe that such a relationship places lawyers in a class apart from other business and professional partnerships. We find no reason to treat attorneys any differently from professionals such as physicians or certified public accountants, for example, by holding that lawyers may not enter into noncompetition agreements in accordance with [the Business and Professions Code].[34]

The court enforced the provisions of the partnership agreement.

The California Supreme Court had occasion to consider the issue and to revisit the decision in *Haight* two years later in *Howard v. Babcock*.[35] There, the partnership agreement had language resembling that in *Haight*. In 1982, the partners of Parker, Stansbury, McGee, Babcock & Combs entered into a partnership agreement containing a clause providing as follows:

> Should more than one partner, associate or individual withdraw from the firm prior to age sixty-five (65) and thereafter within a period of one year practice law . . . together or in combination with others, including former partners or associates of this firm, in a practice engaged in the handling of liability insurance defense work as aforesaid within the Los Angeles or

33. *Id.*, 234 Cal. App. 3d at 969, 285 Cal. Rptr. at 848.
34. *Id.*, 234 Cal. App. 3d at 971, 285 Cal. Rptr. at 849.
35. 6 Cal. 4th 409, 863 P.2d 150, 25 Cal. Rptr. 2d 80 (1993).

> Orange County Court system, said partner or partners shall be subject, at the sole discretion of the remaining non-withdrawing partners, to forfeiture of all their rights to withdrawal benefits other than capital as provided for in Article V herein.

Subsequent to the execution of that partnership agreement, several new partners were elected, although they did not sign the partnership agreement. Three other partners then terminated their relationships with the firm and announced they would begin practice in competition with the firm. The other partners of the firm replied that they would withhold a portion of the withdrawing partners' withdrawal benefits due to violation of the noncompetition clause. A battle then ensued over the withdrawing partners' share of the accounts receivable, work in progress, and unfinished business of the firm.

The trial court decided that although the partnership was dissolved by operation of law when the withdrawing partners terminated their relationships with the firm, the partnership agreement, including the noncompetition clause, remained binding in all its terms. On appeal, the court declared the noncompetition clause void on the ground that Rule 1-500 of the Rules of Professional Conduct banned the noncompetition agreement. A further appeal to the California Supreme Court followed.

The supreme court noted that there was a conflict among the courts of appeal in California and that the *Haight* court had found that clause enforceable. As for the Business and Professions Code, the court found "no demonstrated legislative intent to create a silent exception for lawyers" and said that it would apply the statute according to its terms. It concluded that the statute applies to partners in law firms.[36] The court then had to deal with the issue concerning whether the Code of Professional Responsibility, Rule 1-500, prohibited the clause. Said the court:

> We are not persuaded that this rule was intended to or should prohibit the type of agreement that is at issue here. An agreement that assesses a reasonable cost against a partner who chooses to compete with his or her former partners does not restrict the practice of law. Rather, it attaches an economic consequence to a departing partner's unrestricted choice to pursue a particular kind of practice.[37]

---

36. *Id.*, 6 Cal. 4th at 417, 863 P.2d at 154.
37. *Id.*, 6 Cal. 4th at 419, 863 P.2d at 156.

Significantly, the court said "we agree with the Court of Appeal in *Haight* declaring an agreement between law partners that a reasonable cost will be assessed for competition is consistent with Rule 1-500."[38]

The court's opinion, written by Justice Mosk, then launches into an extended exposition of the rationale for allowing law firms to include noncompetition clauses in their partnership agreements. The opinion notes that although it has been the traditional view that noncompetition clauses violate the rules of professional conduct, changes in the way law is practiced allow these clauses to address business interests of law firms that can no longer be ignored. The facts that partners and associates no longer have the strong bonds of loyalty to their firms, and that partners with a lucrative practice leave a law firm along with their clients, can place a tremendous financial strain on the firm. Justice Mosk notes that the departure of partners has the further adverse effect of increasing expenses attributable to the remaining partners as withdrawing partners seek to escape liability for mutually incurred debt.

The court takes note of the fact that decisions in other states strike down noncompetition clauses. It recites their reasoning: concern about assuring the theoretical freedom of each lawyer to choose whom to represent and the type of work to undertake, and the theoretical freedom of any client to select his or her lawyer of choice. Justice Mosk declares that both freedoms are actually circumscribed. He says:

> Putting aside lofty assertions about the uniqueness of the legal profession, the reality is that the attorney, like any other professional, has no right to enter into employment or partnership in any particular firm, and sometimes may be discharged or forced out by his or her partners even if the client wishes otherwise. Nor does the attorney have the duty to take any client who proffers employment, and there are many grounds justifying an attorney's decision to terminate the attorney-client relationship over the client's objection. Further, an attorney may be required to decline a potential client's offer of employment despite the client's desire to employ the attorney. For example, the attorney may have a technical conflict of

38. *Id.* (citation omitted).

> interest because another attorney in the firm previously represented an adverse party. Finally, the client in the civil context, of course, has no "right" to any attorney's services, and only receives those services he or she can afford.[39]

Justice Mosk then argues that noncompetition clauses may actually serve clients as well as the financial well-being of the law firm. He notes that firms may be more willing to support the development of a particular lawyer's relationship with a client, and to provide the equipment, library, and other facilities to serve a client, if the lawyer serving that client is precluded from personally usurping the benefits of that relationship. Otherwise, the lawyer may leave the firm, taking the future income from the client, and leaving the firm with the additional expenses.

The opinion states:

> We are confident that the interest of the public in being served by diligent, loyal and competent counsel can be assured at the same time as the legitimate business interest of law firms is protected by an agreement placing a reasonable price on competition. *We hold that an agreement among partners imposing a reasonable cost on departing partners who compete with the law firm in a limited geographical area is not inconsistent with rule 1-500 and is not void on its face as against public policy.*[40]

Before you rush out and insert a noncompetition clause into your firm's partnership agreement, be sure to check the law in your state. Despite California's liberal approach, in many jurisdictions such clauses are prohibited and will not be enforced.

In a 1989 decision, the New York Court of Appeals struck down such a clause as violating the Code of Professional Responsibility, Disciplinary Rule 2-108(A), the same section that is incorporated into California's rule 1-500.[41] In the *Cohen* case, Mr. Cohen had been a partner in Lord, Day & Lord for some twenty years. In 1985, he withdrew from the firm to join another New York City firm. The partnership agreement provided for payment of a share of the firm profits to a withdrawing partner, including those stemming from services performed but not yet billed at time of departure. A withdrawing partner was paid, based on a formula, over a

39. *Id.*, 6 Cal. 4th at 422, 863 P.2d at 158.

40. *Id.*, 6 Cal. 4th at 424, 863 P.2d at 160.

41. Cohen v. Lord, Day & Lord, 75 N.Y.2d 95, 550 N.E.2d 410, 551 N.Y.S.2d 157 (1989).

three-year period, thus avoiding the necessity of a detailed accounting. In addition, the partnership agreement contained this clause:

> Notwithstanding anything in this Article . . . to the contrary, if a Partner withdraws from the Partnership and without the prior written consent of the Executive Committee *continues to practice law in any state or other jurisdiction in which the Partnership maintains an office or any contiguous jurisdiction,* either as a lawyer in private practice or as a counsel employed by a business firm, he shall have no further interest in and *there shall be paid to him no proportion of the net profits of the Partnership collected thereafter, whether for services rendered before or after his withdrawal.* There shall be paid to him only his withdrawable credit balance on the books of the Partnership at the date of his withdrawal, together with the amount of his capital account, and the Partnership shall have no further obligation to him.[42]

When the firm failed to pay Cohen his departure payments, he sued. Lord, Day & Lord relied on the forfeiture-for-competition clause. The firm also complained that Cohen had taken some of the firm clients with him.

The trial court ruled that the noncompetition clause was unenforceable as violating Disciplinary Rule 2-108(A).[43] The appellate court reversed, holding that the clause was valid as a financial disincentive to competition and did not prevent Cohen from practicing law in New York or any other jurisdiction. Cohen appealed.

The New York Court of Appeals reversed, stating that the retirement exception in the disciplinary rule was just that—an exception limited to retirement payments—and did not extend to payments for any other reason. Regarding the firm's argument that the forfeiture clause was justified because of the economic hardship suffered as a result of the withdrawing partner taking clients with him, the court observed:

> While a law firm has a legitimate interest in its own survival and economic well-being and in maintaining its clients, it can-

---

42. *Id.*, 75 N.Y.2d at 97, 551 N.Y.S.2d at 157.

43. Disciplinary Rule 2-108(A) of the New York Code of Professional Responsibility provided: "A lawyer shall not be a party to or participate in a partnership or employment agreement with another lawyer that restricts the right of a lawyer to practice law after the termination of a relationship created by the agreement, except as a condition to payment of retirement benefits."

> not protect those interests by contracting for the forfeiture of *earned revenues* during the withdrawing partner's active tenure and participation and by, in effect, restricting the choices of the clients to retain and continue the withdrawing member as counsel.[44]

Further, the court noted that unless there is an agreement to the contrary, withdrawal of a partner constitutes dissolution of the law partnership. However, when there is an agreement to avoid automatic dissolution, the withdrawing partner may forego the ordinary and full accounting that would take place in the event of dissolution. The court then said that the agreement forged by the Lord, Day & Lord partnership had to be struck down because such an agreement "must not conflict with public policy" as reflected in Disciplinary Rule 2-108(A).[45]

The *Cohen* case was revisited several years later when the New York Court of Appeals decided *Denburg v. Parker, Chapin, Flattau & Klimpl.*[46] In that case, Howard Denburg withdrew from Parker, Chapin, Flattau & Klimpl in May, 1984, and joined a firm in New Jersey. According to the partnership agreement, the capital account of a withdrawn partner was to be paid to him without interest at the end of the fifth fiscal year after his withdrawal. When Denburg had received none of his capital account funds by the end of the fifth year after his withdrawal, he sued the firm. The firm asserted as its defense a paragraph of the partnership agreement that read, in pertinent part, as follows:

> (a) . . . Any active Partner may withdraw from the firm at any time on not less than sixty (60) calendar days notice to the firm. If an Active Partner withdraws from the firm and shall engage in the private practice of law individually, through another law firm, or otherwise . . . the Withdrawn Partner shall, on demand, pay to the firm a sum equal to the greater of (i) 12-1/2% of the share of the firm's profits allocable to him . . . during the two complete fiscal years of the firm immediately preceding the date on which he . . . withdrew from the firm (except that no amounts shall be payable by the Withdrawn Partner whose share of the firm's profits allocable to him . . . during the fiscal year of the firm immediately preceding the

44. *Cohen*, 75 N.Y.2d at 100, 551 N.Y.S.2d at 160 (citation omitted).
45. *Id.*
46. 82 N.Y.2d 375, 624 N.E.2d 995, 604 N.Y.S.2d 900 (1993).

date on which he . . . withdrew from the firm was less than $85,000 provided that such Withdrawn Partner directly or through another law firm renders no services to clients of the firm during the 24 months following the date on which he . . . withdrew from the firm), or (ii) 12-1/2% of the total billings to former clients of the firm made by such Partner or other law firm in which he . . . is a partner . . . with respect to services rendered during the 24 month period following his . . . withdrawal from the firm. The firm shall apply the whole or a portion of the capital account of the Withdrawn Partner to the payment of the obligation referred to in the preceding sentence. Withdrawn Partners shall not be entitled to any accounting or other payment for work in process, uncollected accounts, goodwill or any other matter or cause.[47]

One of Denburg's former partners testified that the Parker firm had moved into new quarters and had borrowed $4.5 million to finance the move. There was also evidence that the partners had agreed to stay together for five years to share the burden of the increased costs and had agreed that any who left would compensate the firm appropriately.

The trial court denied Denburg's motion for summary judgment and he appealed. The appellate court reversed, granting Denburg summary judgment, citing *Cohen v. Lord, Day & Lord*. The court also commented on the evidence regarding application of the partnership provision to the firm's coverage of the $4.5 million loan. It said that was at best only a partial account of the provision's purpose. Whatever other incidental objectives the provision may have had, its principal function was to prevent withdrawing partners from competing with their former firm. The court ordered an accounting, which revealed a capital account of some $24,900, and final judgment was entered in that amount. The law firm appealed.

The New York Court of Appeals agreed with the conclusion of the appellate court that the clause was a forfeiture-for-competition provision and violated public policy. However, the court held that Denburg's oral settlement agreement with the firm, was separable from the forfeiture-for-competition provision and, depending on the facts determined on remand, might be enforceable.[48]

---

47. As quoted in Denburg v. Parker, Chapin, Flattau & Klimpl, 184 A.D.2d 343, 586 N.Y.S.2d 107 (App. Div. 1992) (lower court's opinion).

48. *Denburg*, 82 N.Y.2d at 385, 624 N.E.2d at 1002, 604 N.Y.S.2d at 900.

Thus it is that New York holds to the traditional ban against noncompetition clauses. It is a signal to you to be aware of the policy in your state, should you decide to include such a clause in your partnership agreement.

The effect of a forfeiture-for-competition clause has also been judicially reviewed in New Jersey,[49] which has followed the holdings in New York. Norris, McLaughlin & Marcus is a professional corporation with a law practice in New Jersey. It was sued by two partners who, together with an associate, terminated their membership in the firm and then filed suit to recover sums they claimed were due them under a "Service Termination Agreement." After leaving the Norris firm, they commenced practice under the firm name of Collier, Jacob & Sweet.

The terms of their departure were governed by two agreements the parties entered in 1986. The first was a "Buy-Sell Agreement," which required the firm to buy back the shares of any shareholder whose employment with the firm was terminated for any reason. This agreement was carried out and was not in dispute. The second agreement was the Service Termination Agreement providing for compensation above the member's equity interest in the firm, calculated pursuant to a formula set out in the agreement.

The Service Termination Agreement provided for different benefits depending upon whether the departure was "competitive" or "noncompetitive." A departure was "competitive" if the lawyer, within one year of the date of termination, either (1) engaged in the practice of law involving service to clients of the former firm who were clients of the former firm at the date of termination, or (2) solicited other professional and/or paraprofessional employees of the former firm to engage in the practice of law with the departed lawyer.[50]

The departing partners, Jacob and Collier, together requested $81,125 as compensation under the Severance Termination Agreement. The firm declined the payment, asserting that the lawyers had retained clients in violation of the non-solicitation provision and had solicited employees in violation of the antiraiding provision.

---

49. Jacob v. Norris, McLaughlin & Marcus, 128 N.J. 10, 607 A.2d 142 (1992). *Jacob* arose in the context of an agreement involving a professional corporation, rather than a partnership, but this factor was not discussed by any court that heard the case.

50. *Id.*, 128 N.J. at 15.

The departing lawyers filed suit, arguing that the competitive departure provisions were void as against public policy because they contravened Rule 5.6 of the Rules of Professional Conduct. This rule, similar to Disciplinary Rule 2-108(A) considered in *Cohen*, provided:

> A lawyer shall not participate in offering or making:
> (a) a partnership or employment agreement that restricts the rights of a lawyer to practice after termination of the relationship, except an agreement concerning benefits upon retirement.[51]

The Norris firm defended on the ground that the plaintiffs had engaged in a "competitive voluntary departure" and, under the terms of the Service Termination Agreement, they were entitled to no termination compensation and received only the right to purchase from the law firm certain life insurance. Had the departure been a "noncompetitive departure," the firm would have been obligated to pay the departing member, among other benefits, an amount equal to 25 times 110 percent of the member's annual draw applicable immediately before departure.

The chancery division (the trial court) found that the arrangement under the Service Termination Agreement was a restriction on the plaintiffs' right to practice law under Rule 5.6.

The appellate court reversed the trial court. It found the noncompetition provision struck a reasonable balance between the lawyer's right to practice and the firm's need to protect itself from the consequences of the lawyer's departure. It held that, in any event, based on equitable considerations, the lawyers would not be entitled to compensation under the Service Termination Agreement. The two departing partners then appealed to the New Jersey Supreme Court.

In its opinion, the supreme court traced the history of Rule 5.6 of the Rules of Professional Conduct, and noted it was the progeny of Disciplinary Rule 2-108(A), discussed in the New York cases of *Cohen* and *Denburg*. The court reviewed the case law interpreting Rule 5.6 and its antecedent, and noted particularly those cases that held the view

> that each person must have the untrammelled right to the counsel of his choice. A contrary decision would allow clients

---

51. *Id.* at 17.

> to be unknowingly treated like objects of commerce, to be bargained for and traded by merchant-attorneys like beans and potatoes.[52]

Regarding the financial disincentives built into the Norris firm's agreement, the court held:

> By forcing lawyers to choose between compensation and continued service to their clients, financial-disincentive provisions may encourage lawyers to give up their clients, thereby interfering with the lawyer-client relationship and, more importantly, with clients' free choice of counsel. Those provisions thus cause indirectly the same objectionable restraints on the free practice of law as more direct restrictive covenants. We believe that indirect restrictions on the practice of law, such as the financial disincentives at issue in this case, likewise violate both the language and the spirit of [Rule 5.6]. Any provision penalizing an attorney for undertaking certain representation "restricts the right of a lawyer to practice law" within the meaning of [Rule 5.6].[53]

The law firm argued that the court should distinguish between agreements that require departing lawyers to forfeit their equity interest in a firm and those that merely deprive them of additional compensation unrelated to their vested interest. The court said it did not have to resolve the question of whether the compensation was "earned" or "additional." The court held that if the agreement creates a disincentive to accept representation of a client, it violates the Rules of Professional Conduct. The court declined to accept the distinction in *Cohen* regarding the departing lawyer's right to receive "earned income" as distinguished from "future profits," because either disincentive would discourage client choice.

The court discussed the argument that the old firm had a need to protect its commercial concerns. The court declared:

> Moreover, although law firms are understandably concerned about their financial well-being in view of the increasing fluidity of law-firm membership, that fluidity also justifies a heightened vigilance against any form of restrictive covenant.[54]

---

52. *Id.* at 21 (citation omitted).
53. *Id.* at 22.
54. *Id.* at 27.

Nonetheless, the New Jersey court tossed out a modicum of comfort to the Norris firm, indicating that the value of a departing partner's capital account could be adjusted to reflect the lesser value of the firm resulting from its change in circumstances:

> In computing a withdrawing partner's equity interest in the former firm, accounting for the effect of the partner's departure on the firm's value is not unreasonable. Although the departing attorneys always have a right to receive the value of their capital accounts, in computing the value of any additional interest they have in the firm, the value they contributed can be offset by the decrease in the firm's value their departure causes.[55]

The court referred to its decision in an earlier case, *Dugan v. Dugan*,[56] which had established that goodwill is nothing more "than the probability that old customers will resort to the old place" and the further probability that future patronage can be translated into prospective earnings. The court stated:

> Accordingly, we recognize that if a partner's departure will result in a decrease in the probability of a client's return and a consequent decrease in prospective earnings, that departure may decrease the value of the firm's goodwill. It would not be inappropriate therefore for law partners to take that specific effect into account in determining the shares due a departing partner.[57]

The court then held that the loss of a firm's client revenue following the departure of a member was another of the many factors to be taken into consideration when determining the value of the departing member's share in the corporation.

Next, the New Jersey Supreme Court addressed the issue concerning whether it was a violation of Rule 5.6 of the Rules of Professional Conduct for the departing members to have contacted members of the professional and paraprofessional staff of the Norris firm. The court found that such conduct did not violate the rules. It said the

> "practice of law" consists not only of lawyers' interactions with their clients, but also includes their interactions with col-

---

55. *Id.* at 28.
56. Dugan v. Dugan, 92 N.J. 423, 457 A.2d 1 (1983).
57. *Jacob*, 128 N.J. at 30.

> leagues. Agreements discouraging departing lawyers from contacting those lawyers with whom they would like to associate violate [Rule] 5.6.
>
> The provision unduly constricts the right to practice of those attorneys who would have liked to have accompanied a departing partner, but who were not informed of that partner's interest due to an agreement creating a disincentive against their being contracted. The effect is all the more objectionable when the ignored attorney is an associate who was not a party to the agreement establishing the restriction.
>
> Restrictive agreements have a similarly unfair effect on paraprofessionals.[58]

The court then considered the effect that should follow from striking down the offending clause in the Service Termination Agreement. It noted that the departing lawyers would receive a windfall by receiving compensation despite their violation of the rule in signing the agreement. If they were barred from receiving the additional compensation, the firm would receive a windfall from a covenant that violated public policy. The court indicated that the solution lay in determining whether the public interest would best be served by giving one party or the other the benefit of the decision. It decided that Jacob and Collier should receive the additional compensation:

> We note that equitable principles might bar a plaintiff's recovery if the plaintiff had been a senior partner instrumental in drafting a restrictive agreement, imposing it on his or her fellow partners or employees, and then sought to have the provision declared unenforceable when he or she decided to leave. Nothing in the record indicates that Jacob or Collier played such a role in developing the Agreement. Therefore, Jacob and Collier are entitled to the compensation provided by the Service Termination Agreement.[59]

There are numerous lessons to be drawn from *Cohen, Denburg,* and *Jacob.* First, it is extremely difficult to conceive of a forfeiture-for-competition clause that will stand in the courts. Second, should

58. *Id.*
59. *Id.*, 128 N.J. at 36.

you be the departing partner seeking to escape judicial censure for becoming a party to an agreement containing such a clause, make sure that you had no hand in its drafting. Third, as a partner in a firm seeking to protect itself against the losses following the departure of a rainmaker, note that *Jacob* teaches that a downward adjustment in goodwill can be made when determining the value of the departing lawyer's interest. But beware—as it appears from a number of other decisions, whether goodwill can be valued at all is a question. (Note the later discussion in Chapter IV, under the caption "Goodwill" in connection with matters relating to dissolution.

The *Denburg* decision also illustrates that the rule in New York is more restrictive, and paying the withdrawing competing partner his or her capital account is insufficient. A forfeiture-for-competition clause will not survive judicial scrutiny in New York. The court's language is expansive on the point. Speaking about the language in the partnership agreement, the court said:

> Whatever other incidental objectives the provision may have had, it is evident that its principal function was to prevent withdrawing partners from competing with their former firm. The provision, after all, exacts a penalty only from those withdrawn partners who continue to practice law privately, and, therefore, potentially in competition with the firm, and exempts from the penalty only those who, inter alia, do not in their new situations continue to serve their former firm's clients. Indeed, the exemption is inexplicable if a principal purpose of the provision was not to prevent competition. Moreover, even if the firm's motive in assessing the penalty was benign, it is clear that the effect of the penalty provision would be to discourage departing counsel from continuing to represent clients of the firm and concomitantly to interfere with the clients' choice of counsel. Accordingly, we are of the view that [the provision] is void on its face as a forfeiture-for-competition provision.[60]

If you wish to have a forfeiture-for-competition clause in your firm's partnership agreement, it is wise to check carefully the decisions in your state to determine just how far the courts will allow

---

60. *Denburg,* 184 A.D.2d at 345, 586 N.Y.S.2d at 109.

you to go in building a protective wall against the competing withdrawn partner.[61] It is likely to be only an inch, rather than a mile.

Management of the Law Partnership

As stated at the outset, the partnership agreement is in the nature of a constitution. In many respects, we might follow the example of the Constitution of the United States in establishing a framework for a law firm partnership agreement. Just as the people of the United States have a bundle of rights, a portion of which they parcel out to the government in its basic document, so also should a law firm in its constitution. The partners should reserve the right of decision in all matters not expressly delegated to the management, executive, or other committee that is the depositary for day-to-day operating questions.

There are some items that need addressing but do not belong in the partnership agreement. The partners should agree that each of them is prohibited from doing certain things, even though these things may arise in the day-to-day operation of the firm. These things belong in a separate policy statement, adopted by the partnership and applicable to all partners. Even though each equity partner has the legal authority to act on behalf of the firm, chaos would ensue if every partner in a firm of any size exercised that power. So it is that the firm needs to impose prohibitions on such things as opening bank accounts; borrowing money; selling, transferring, or pledging firm assets; making guarantees or indemnification on behalf of the firm; and making contracts on behalf of the firm. Any such activity would require a prior vote of the partnership to approve it.

Classification of Partners

Assuming that there are to be several classes of partners, it is essential that the partnership agreement spell out quite clearly

---

61. Note that California goes further than most states in upholding forfeiture-for-competition clauses. *See* Note, *Why Anti-Competition Clauses Should Be Unenforceable in Law Partnership Agreements: An Argument for Rejecting California's Approval in* Howard v. Babcock, 8 GEO. J. LEGAL ETHICS 669 (1995). The New York position, which severely restricts such clauses, is supported by a report of the Committee on Professional Responsibility, Association of the Bar of the City of New York. *See* 20 FORDHAM URB. L. J. 897 (1993).

whether partners other than equity partners are to have any vote. If such partners are to have a vote on only some matters, then the document must be clear about which items are within the purview of the nonequity partners.

Notice

The document should be clear about the notice requirements for a partnership vote, the method of giving notice, and the requirements for proof of delivery of notice. All this may not be of great moment in a firm with a small number of partners, but it can assume grave proportions in a large firm with partners spread over a wide geographic area.

Quorum

The partnership agreement should include a clear exposition of quorum requirements. Whether abstentions from voting should be read into the quorum requirement is important. Partners unwilling or hesitant to take a position on a controversial item may refrain from being present and voting on the issue; unless the quorum provision of the agreement is written with this possibility in mind, the result can be at variance with the wishes of most of the partners. For example, assume your firm has fifty partners. The quorum for a vote on opening a branch office in another geographic location is 80 percent of the partners, or forty persons, and a two-thirds majority of those voting is required to approve the office. If the requisite number of partners—say forty-five—vote and thirty vote in favor, the office will open. However, if only thirty-nine partners vote, then even if all voted in favor, the item would fail for lack of a quorum. The solution may be to impose a financial penalty upon any equity partner who declines to vote or to grant a proxy. In the era of electronic mail and facsimile machines, there are few valid excuses a partner may offer for failing to vote.

Proxy Voting

Partners should also have the right to vote by proxy. In areas of known controversy, it is probably desirable for the proxy holder to secure written authorization from the partner granting the proxy, lest the authority be challenged. If you are a partner granting a proxy, you should assure yourself that your partner will exercise the proxy, and will vote it in accordance with your instructions. If you grant a proxy that is not voted, you have failed to vote just as certainly as if you ignored the meeting. Remember, in most cases it is your money!

Telephone Conference

The partnership agreement should also contain a provision regarding attendance at firm meetings via telephone conference. Holding meetings in this manner is so common today that it cannot be ignored as an acceptable method of procedure.

Voting Requirements and Restrictions

The partnership agreement should set forth with some detail the voting required in various instances, such as admitting new partners, borrowing money, leasing office space, and accepting controversial clients.

There is no absolute rule when it comes to voting. Requirements will differ, depending on the size of the firm and its degree of democratization. For example, a two-thirds vote on some matters in a three-person partnership may not offer sufficient protection to all three partners in difficult situations. Suppose that two of the partners propose to enter into a long-term lease, and the third partner considers that his or her resources are inadequate to support such a commitment and does not wish to put these limited assets at risk. It is far more desirable for the three individuals to decide (1) to abandon the idea or (2) to dissolve the partnership, rather than to commit the firm by a two-thirds vote. In this instance, the partnership agreement should specify that unanimous consent is required to proceed in very important matters.

On the other hand, in a large firm, a two-thirds vote may be the only practical way to conduct business. On more significant matters, a somewhat higher percentage vote can be required, but seldom is it desirable or practicable to provide for a unanimous decision by the partners.

In the discussion that follows, the considerations mentioned should be kept in mind.

Admission of New Partners

If the law firm is to function as a truly democratic organization, each equity partner must have a voice in deciding who should become a partner. In fact, even when it may be impractical to provide for votes on this matter by nonequity partners, it is nonetheless desirable to allow them a full opportunity to express their views. When decisions on partner admission are assumed by one individual or group within the firm, and the remaining partners have little or no voice in the decision, there is bound to be a decline in morale. The risk grows that an invisible line will be drawn between the newcomer or newcomers and those who had no part in the invitation to join the firm. The high degree of cooperation among partners that is the hallmark of a competent and successful firm will no longer be present.

Because the relationship among partners should be close, most firms require a very high percentage of those voting to approve admission of a new partner. Put another way, it does not take very many partners to foreclose a lawyer's ability to become a partner. Many firms use a figure of 10 percent; thus, if your firm has fifty partners, at least forty-five of them must vote in favor of admission for an invitation to be extended. As a practical matter, when a firm's partners have a close relationship and it appears that a candidate might have as much as 9–10 percent of the partners in opposition, some others who normally would be supportive will elect to cast a negative vote. This will assure that the candidate will not receive an invitation and the result will help to preserve firm harmony.

Expulsion and Other Discipline

Just as partnership admission is perhaps highest on the list of critical items for partners to consider, perhaps next in line are votes for expulsion or disciplinary action against a partner. To expel or discipline a partner is drastic action and has severe consequences for the firm. Except in the clearest of cases, there is bound to be litigation and the firm will be obliged to defend its position. Moreover, the effect on the individual lawyer is harsh and demands an exceptionally high vote of the partnership to assure fairness. Similarly, any disciplinary action against a firm's lawyer by the partnership—such as a reduction in compensation—should receive the same careful attention. The same vote as required for admission to partnership should be required for expulsion or discipline.

Borrowing

Law firms often find it necessary to borrow money, either for current operations when cash flow is temporarily impaired or for capital improvements, such as modernizing or acquiring new office equipment. Although it is the credit of the law firm that supports the loan, it is really the combined credit of the several partners that is the true collateral. If the resources of the firm are insufficient to satisfy the obligation, the creditor can pursue each partner—all being jointly and severally liable on the debt. For this reason, there should be a partnership vote to approve a firm borrowing. The vote required may be a simple majority or some greater percentage, depending on the structure of the firm. When disparity exists between the financial resources of the partners, so that those of lesser means may be more reluctant to go into debt, perhaps a larger percentage vote to approve a borrowing is justified.

Leases

Every law firm requires a suitable office. With rare exception, that office is leased. In the exceptional situation, the building may be owned by the law firm. Even when the building is owned by one of the partners, he or she is generally the lessor; in such cases, it is even more important that all partners have a voice in deciding whether to enter into the lease. The same considerations regarding borrowing, as discussed above, apply to obligations under the lease. Consequently, the same care should be taken in drafting the provisions of the partnership agreement related to voting on a lease.

Client Acceptance; Litigation with Clients

Many partnerships fail to come to grips with a very sensitive matter—whether a person or firm proposed as a client should be accepted by the firm. This decision in many partnerships is left to an executive or operating committee, and a small committee is often vulnerable to the entreaties of a partner eager to obtain a new client, potentially profitable to the firm, even though there are circumstances that make representation questionable. Often, a partner seeking to keep a new client, attracted over time with some difficulty, will overlook doubts about the character or financial stability of the client. Should there be ethical questions related to potential conflicts-of-interest, the partner will resolve them in his or her own mind in favor of accepting the client. These results might not follow if the question about whether to take on the new client is put to a vote of the partnership. The good news is: the firm is spared possible embarrassment and challenge to its ethics. The bad news is: the firm may lose the revenue the client would produce for the firm.

Similarly, if a partner is giving thought to instituting suit against a client of the firm, the partner should be required to refer the proposal to the partnership. By a vote on the matter, the partners are spared the possibility that the litigation would reflect the vexation of one or two partners of the firm; the case will be brought only if authorized by the firm itself.

The Substance of Meeting Notifications

When partners are busy attending to law practice and not involved in controversy within the firm, arrangements for meetings are carried out with ease and courtesy of the partners toward each other. Let a controversy arise, in which there are conflicting views concerning the proper handling of the matter, and the pleasant tenor of things will disappear. Some partners will resort to any "bag of tricks" to secure a favorable vote on a matter in which they have a strong interest. One trick, of course, is to hold a meeting on very short notice or inadequate notice. Unless the partnership agreement is specific, not only about the time requirements for notice in a particular type of situation, but also about the substance to be disclosed, the rights of many partners will be in jeopardy.

As for time, the solution is to provide adequate opportunity for partners to arrange their schedules so they are able to attend a partnership meeting. Some partners whose practice keeps them "chained to the desk" are not aware that other partners may have travel schedules that take them away from the office for extended periods. The latter's problems must be kept in mind when setting the time period for notice in a partnership agreement.

As for substance, nothing can rankle a partner or group of partners against those who conduct the day-to-day affairs of the firm like the belief that some partners are being "kept in the dark." When a firm is having difficulty in one area of practice, or in its finances, or with one or more partners, it is important that notice of meetings not be perfunctory. The formal notice of the meeting should be accompanied by sufficient explanatory material to allow the recipient to understand the issues to be considered at the meeting. Failing to provide this information may lead a partner to miss the meeting, believing it unimportant. When he or she perhaps later discovers that a vital matter was acted upon, outside his or her presence, it is bound to cause an otherwise avoidable level of animosity. For this reason, the partnership agreement should specify that the notice of the meeting should include, or be accompanied by, such description of the items to be considered at the meeting as will enable each partner to understand the significance of the issues to be voted upon.

As a practical matter, not every meeting will be called by such a proper and complete notice. Many meetings will be arranged quickly and informally by telephone call. Partners will attend and, by their presence, waive any right to challenge the satisfaction of the notice requirements for the meeting. The well-organized firm will, however, follow the example of most major corporations concerning meetings of their directors. Notices will be complete and accompanied by written explanations of items on the agenda and the issues related to them.

Almost every firm of some size has a lawyer experienced in putting together papers for corporate meetings. His or her skill in assembling the proper documents for a well-organized partnership meeting should be utilized. There is no excuse for misunderstanding—or, sometimes, chaos—in the conduct of a partnership meeting. If documentation is understandable and presented in an attractive and usable form, proponents of an action will have less difficulty in obtaining the votes required for implementation. You, as a partner, have a right to receive that kind of paperwork to be able to discharge your duties responsibly.

Accounting Principles

Details of partnership accounting do not belong in a partnership agreement. However, to avoid disagreement, certain fundamental points need to have consensus at the outset. The first is whether the firm will account on a cash or accrual basis. The second is whether major purchases of the firm will be capitalized or expensed.

Accounting principles, and the differences between accounting for tax purposes and accounting for purposes of reporting to the partnership, and between cash basis and accrual basis accounting, are beyond the scope of this volume. However, suffice it to say that firms, large or small, should have the advice of a competent accounting firm before making decisions in this area.

The matter of deciding whether to capitalize or to expense major purchases is a different issue. Again, to avoid disagreement among partners, it is desirable to provide in the partnership agreement that the decision to capitalize or expense an item or group of items, the cost of which will exceed, say, 2 percent of gross annual revenues, must be made by the partnership. Bear in mind that the entire cost of an item that is expensed (and that could be capitalized) comes out of your pocket in the year of purchase. By electing to capitalize, you spread out the misery over time, but, at the same time, decrease the financial results of operations in future years.

Capital Contributions

When a new law firm is organized, the partners may find that a substantial investment is needed to provide a location, office furniture, equipment, and research materials. The new partners may elect to contribute cash for this purpose and some may have furniture and office machinery ("property") that they are able to contribute to the partnership.

The partnership agreement should recite not only that cash is to be credited to the individual partner's capital account with the firm, but the uses to which the cash may be put and the extent, if any, to which it will affect the partner's interest in the firm's earnings. As for property, the partnership agreement should require that the contributing partner provide adequate support for the value ascribed to each item. This can be represented by the appraised value or original purchase cost depreciated in accordance with an acceptable depreciation scale.

As the partnership lives on, additional capital may be required. The partnership agreement should contain detailed sections relating to items such as the vote required to assess partners, the time permitted to complete an additional contribution, and the penalty for failure to do so. Because the burden of an additional capital contribution tends to fall unevenly on partners simply because of their differing circumstances, the vote needed for assessment should be substantial. In the smaller firm, a unanimous vote of the partners would make sense, while in the larger firm perhaps an 80 percent vote would not be unreasonable. In any case, one or more partners may be unable to provide additional capital in response to an assessment, and the partnership agreement should set out the consequences. Other partners should be able to make up the deficiency. The defaulting partner can suffer a reduction in his or her partnership percentage, or the partnership can be considered to have loaned the defaulting partner a sum equal to the deficiency, on which the defaulting partner will be obliged to make principal repayments and interest.

If a partnership is fortunate enough to have one or more partners with greater financial resources than others, the fortunate ones may be able to lend monies to the partnership on more attractive terms than the partnership can obtain from banks or other financial institutions. The partnership agreement should provide that such loans may not be made without a partnership vote, just as in the case of a loan obtained from a public institution. The partnership agreement should also indicate that all the terms and conditions of the loan are to be described to the partnership before the vote.

Partnership Shares

Conditions in any law firm change from time to time. It is impracticable in a large or medium-sized law firm to specify the size of the partnership share of each partner. In a very small firm, the partners may be able to agree on a partnership share that will prevail for a significant period of time. In this case, the shares can be written into the partnership agreement.

Establishment

In the usual case, the partnership agreement will specify that each year, the partnership share of each partner will be determined by a committee of partners, usually elected by the partnership. This is the ideal situation. There are firms where an individual partner—who may have the characteristics of a martinet—makes the decision and the other partners have no voice in the matter.

When the partnership agreement provides for a committee to establish partnership shares, that committee should have specific terms of reference. Nothing aggravates a partner and contributes to deterioration in morale faster than inability to discern what prompted a shares committee to reach the decision it did. The terms of reference should recite the factors to be taken into consideration in awarding a discrete share to a partner and the relative weight to be accorded each factor.

In some firms, a lawyer who is a rainmaker but does no substantial amount of legal work rates better treatment from the committee than a lawyer who produces less business but contributes substantially to the firm's billable hours. In other firms, there are lawyers who are the "worker bees" but their production of business is nil; nonetheless, they receive equal treatment with their brother and sister partners. Whether all groups are to be treated equally or whether one or more factors are to weigh more heavily should be disclosed in the terms of reference of the share committee. Even though the committee may not appear to follow the rules, it gives the partners some comfort to know that the rules are there. When a partner complains about an award, the committee has its terms of reference to which it can point to justify the outcome. Further, the partnership agreement should specify the channels through which there is appeal from a decision of the compensation committee; should the appeal process move to another committee or group, it should be made clear that the same guidelines apply to the deliberations of that committee or group.

But a "warning flare": inclusion of specific terms of reference in establishing a compensation committee will not assure relief from litigation by a dissatisfied partner. Moreover, it is doubtful that one can draft guidelines for the compensation committee that will be sufficiently specific to create enforceable contract rights.

In *Roan v. Keck, Mahin & Cate,*[62] Mr. Roan, a leading rainmaker for Keck, Mahin & Cate in Chicago, was a partner from 1983 through 1988. He retired and moved to Florida to practice law. He filed a complaint against Keck, Mahin & Cate, complaining that the firm breached its fiduciary duty to him by awarding him grossly inadequate compensation from 1985 through 1988, in violation of the firm's partnership agreement. The firm moved to dismiss.

In its unpublished order, the Seventh Circuit adopted the report of the magistrate judge to whom the district court referred the motion for report. (The district judge affirmed the report, recommending dismissal of the complaint. It was from this action that Roan took the appeal.) The Seventh Circuit affirmed the district court.

The Keck, Mahin & Cate partnership agreement provided that recommendations on compensation are made to the elected management committee by the compensation committee. The partnership agreement specified that the compensation committee was to take into account, among other factors, the quality of each lawyer's work, the initiative, industry, and responsibility displayed in han-

62. 1992 U.S. App. LEXIS 12030 (7th Cir. May 18, 1992). This is an "unpublished order" not to be cited according to Seventh Circuit Rule 53. Rule 53 provides: "Unpublished orders: . . . (iv) Except to support a claim of res judicata, collateral estoppel or law of the case, shall not be cited or used as precedent (A) in any federal court within the circuit in any written document or in oral argument; or (B) by any such court for any purpose." 7th Cir. R. 53.

dling firm clients, judgment and experience in the practice of law, new business (if any attracted), the profitability of the lawyer's work to the firm, client development and preservation, and other significant contributions, if any, to the operation and success of the firm. The partnership agreement authorized the management committee to make such changes in the recommendations of the compensation committee as it deemed proper. These recommendations became final unless amended by a consensus at an annual partners meeting. If substantial disagreement existed among the partners, year-end distributions were to be determined by the management committee.

From 1985 through 1988, Roan's average annual compensation was $227,000 and his average annual billings were $2,589,000. Regarding his claim that such "grossly inadequate compensation" was a breach of fiduciary duty, the court said "the determination of partners' compensation is covered in the partnership agreement which specifies procedures to be followed in determining compensation and who is authorized to make final decisions."[63]

Regarding the claim for breach of contract, the magistrate judge noted that the guidelines Roan relied upon applied only to the compensation committee. "There is no reference to the guidelines in . . . the partnership agreement which authorizes the management committee to make such changes in the recommendations of the compensation committee as it deems proper or in the provision that recommendations of the management committee are final absent a different consensus of the . . . partners."[64] The magistrate judge further held that "the guidelines are too indefinite to create any enforceable contract rights. While some of the factors listed in the guidelines such as new business, profitability and industry (billable hours) lend themselves to quantification, a judgment weighing all the factors together is obviously imponderable."[65]

This conclusion is incontrovertible. Any set of guidelines that a firm writes into the partnership agreement will certainly involve subjective analysis and conclusions by the committee members recommending the compensation. Nonetheless, reasonable and workable guidelines, even though legally unenforceable, are, I believe, eminently desirable.

---

63. *Roan*, 1992 U.S. App. LEXIS 12030 at *7.

64. *Id.* at *12.

65. *Id.* (citations omitted).

Partnership "Draws"

In the usual case, a partner will be permitted to make periodic "draws" (monthly or otherwise) against his or her anticipated share in the partnership profits for the year. If we assume that a partner has a 10 percent share in the firm, and the budget indicates that the net earnings for the year will be $1.2 million, then the partner would be able to draw $120,000 at the rate of $10,000 per month. Whether the firm is small and will earn only half that, or large, so that we could add zeros to the number, makes no difference. The accuracy of the budgetary forecast directly affects the partners' draws. When a firm has a type of practice that makes prediction of revenue difficult, the size of the draw available to a partner should be on the conservative side. Should the firm have an unusually good year, the method of disposition of any excess earnings can be determined by the partners at year-end.

The difficulty is in writing principles governing this philosophy into the partnership agreement. However, it should be done. Too often partners expect to receive amounts well in excess of what prudence dictates; if standards of living are geared to expectations rather than reality, bad feelings among the partners can result. This result will be dispelled if the "bad news" is embodied in the partnership agreement.

It is also important that the partnership agreement recognize the distinction between capital contributed by the partners—which is part of the permanent financial structure of the firm—and earnings generated by the legal business. The former is not distributable under any circumstances unless the partner withdraws from the firm; only earnings are available for distribution.

The decision whether to retain a certain portion of earnings as a reserve for various purposes is one that should be made by the partnership, and the agreement should so provide. A significant vote is probably not necessary in this area. In most partnerships, the vote of a majority—or, at most, two-thirds—of the partners should be sufficient.

Every law firm is not necessarily a "cash cow." Some firms have problems in collecting fees from recalcitrant clients. Others conduct their practices from castles when it would be more appropriate to establish their offices in storefronts. In any event, say that the financial results of operations are negative: in some years there is a loss! The partnership agreement should set forth in unmistakable language the consequences to the partners, in terms of their draws, in that situation.

For example, if there is a loss and the partnership must borrow to cover the draws, that borrowing should require a partnership vote. Moreover, to repay the borrowing, the agreement might provide that for purposes of calculating partnership draws in later years, one-fifth of the amount of a loss in any subsequent year in which the firm has net earnings will be subtracted from net earnings of the partnership in determining the amount available for distribution. The amount subtracted would be applied to debt repayment.

As discussed at the outset, the partnership agreement is a constitution for the firm. It is not an operating manual. Many of the details of the firm's financial management need to be arranged in instruments other than the partnership agreement; otherwise, the constitutional nature of the partnership agreement is lost.

Among these details are requirements for reserves, maintenance of adequate working capital, malpractice and property insurance, benefit programs (life and health insurance), vacations, and policies regarding illness and incapacity of partners. Unquestionably, a well-run firm will establish policies in these areas. When a new partner comes aboard, he or she, in addition to signing the partnership agreement, should receive written exposition of the firm's policies in these areas. The new partner should then acknowledge receipt of a copy of this document or documents. It is self-evident that as these policies are developed by the firm, they should be put to a partnership vote.

Activities of Partners

The partnership agreement should declare that each partner is expected to devote all of his or her professional efforts to law practice with the firm, unless, by a vote of the partnership, it is expressly otherwise agreed. Consequently, when a partner is admitted as a member of a firm, the presumption is that he or she will so devote their professional efforts. If a partner is given the privilege of spending a certain amount of time in activities unrelated to the practice of law, particularly if the activities are business-related, such an arrangement should have the prior approval of the partnership and be reduced to a written agreement between the firm and the partner. This sort of arrangement deserves careful scrutiny because, as we have seen, third parties often see an attorney-client relationship when a lawyer does not. The risk is that the "extracurricular" activities of the partner may subject the firm and the other partners to unforeseen consequences. The agreement between the firm and the partner should provide for restrictions on the partner and requirements concerning the "holding out" of his or her position with the third party; these will assist the firm in avoiding liability related to the partner's business transactions.

The firm, in its wisdom, might decide to set out in advance its policy on permitting exceptions from the basic policy in the partnership agreement. Certainly, it should be made clear that the firm will not approve engagement in activity that would constitute competition with the firm, nor in any business that would compete with a client of the firm.

Because of the great risk of violation of insider trading rules, particularly in the large firm that may represent clients that are publicly traded companies, the firm should adopt a policy that (1) permits, in a narrow channel (as an exception to the general prohibition on outside business), limited amounts of investments by partners and their families in publicly traded and privately held companies, and (2) defines those businesses or corporations in which any investment would present a problem for the firm. The policy, which is best drafted by a lawyer skilled in securities law, can require prior approval by designated partners for acquisition or disposition of shares in these companies.

Arbitration under the Partnership Agreement

Most law firms would prefer not to "wash their dirty linen" in public. Disputes between the firm and former partners, associates, or staff members—regardless of which party is in the right—are an embarrassment. To avoid the glare of publicity that a court appearance may entail, inclusion of an arbitration clause in the partnership agreement (and in agreements with associates and staff) may be a solution.

In a case in New York's appellate division, in which my friend, Stephen Axinn of Skadden, Arps, Slate, Meagher & Flom, was counsel for the law firm of Kreindler, Relkin & Goldberg, the court upheld the law firm's arbitration clause in its partnership agreement.[66] In that case, Avrom Vann, after serving as an associate for a year and half, signed a written agreement in December, 1972, making him a "partner in the firm" of Kreindler, Relkin, Olick & Goldberg. His compensation was to be fixed by the man-

66. Vann v. Kreindler, Relkin & Goldberg, 78 A.D.2d 255, 434 N.Y.S.2d 365 (App. Div. 1980), *aff'd*, 54 N.Y.2d 936 (1981).

agement committee as a percentage of the firm's net fees, with a minimum draw. He could not make any commitment in the firm's name without prior approval of the management committee, he was required to make a capital contribution of $5,000, and his liability for firm debts was limited to that amount. The "general partners" agreed to indemnify and hold him harmless from all other ordinary liabilities of the firm. He received no interest in the assets of the partnership, nor its name, clients, or fees. Vann's partnership interest could be terminated upon his suspension or disbarment, conviction of a crime, bankruptcy, or commission of acts of moral turpitude. In the event of dissolution, the agreement indicated what Vann was to receive in the way of compensation and return of capital. The agreement contained a broad arbitration clause covering any "controversy arising out of or in any way relating to this agreement, including . . . any controversy relating to dissolution."[67]

The agreement was signed by Vann, Kreindler, Olick, and Goldberg. Relkin, in an apparent oversight, did not sign.

In March, 1974, Olick left the firm, thus dissolving the partnership, and a new firm, Kreindler, Relkin & Goldberg, was formed. There was no change in the written agreement. In 1977 and again in 1979 a new partner was admitted, but no written agreement existed among the partners. In October, 1979, Kreindler and Relkin presented a proposed partnership agreement to Vann. He was to have no interest in the firm's assets, but would receive a portion of the firm's fees. Vann declined to sign the agreement. He was then offered a junior partnership at a fixed salary, which he also refused. He insisted that he have an interest in the firm proportionate to his interest in the fees he claimed he had enjoyed since 1977. When this was refused, he commenced an action in 1980 for an accounting and damages. Simultaneously, the partnership served a notice demanding arbitration pursuant to the arbitration clause of the 1972 agreement. Vann countered with a proceeding to stay arbitration. The court granted his motion and the firm appealed.

As framed by the appellate court, "the issue is whether the arbitration clause in the 1972 agreement survived the changes in the partnership, and the increase in Vann's salary and drawing account and other financial benefits."[68] The court said, regarding the departure of certain partners and the addition of others, that

---

67. *Id.*, 78 A.D.2d at 255, 434 N.Y.S.2d at 366.
68. *Id.*, 78 A.D.2d at 257, 434 N.Y.S.2d at 368.

"[a]lthough the entity changed, the relationship continued as before, an ongoing continuous partnership. In this context, the dissolution had no real significance. [Kreindler, Relkin & Goldberg] was, in effect, the assignee of [Kreindler, Relkin, Olick & Goldberg]."[69]

The court then said that an assignee of a contract may avail itself of an arbitration clause. More significantly, the court said:

> It is undisputed that there was an arbitration agreement. Even assuming that there is an issue as to termination of the agreement by statutory dissolution of the partnership, due to change in makeup of the partnership, this is an issue for the arbitrators and not for the courts.[70]

Should you decide to include an arbitration clause when drafting a partnership agreement, make certain that it has the scope desired to cover the issues you wish to have included. On the other hand, if you do not want to provide for arbitration of your agreement, it is important that you so state; otherwise, if your firm has a long history, you may find lurking in its background an arbitration clause that may still apply unless you expressly negate its effect.

In New York, at least, the standard for judicial review of arbitration awards is quite narrow. In *Weidman v. Fuchsberg*,[71] New York's appellate division reiterated its position that "when a contract is interpreted by an arbitrator, his determination may be disturbed only if it is found to be completely irrational, violative of public policy, or beyond the scope of arbitration."[72] Weidman and Miller had been partners in Fuchsberg & Fuchsberg, having become partners in 1968 and 1972, respectively, until the firm elected, in 1985, to exercise a buyout provision in a supplementary agreement. Weidman and Miller had each signed a partnership agreement, dealing with general matters, and a supplementary agreement governing payments to a terminated or retiring partner. The partnership agreement contained an arbitration clause.

When a dispute arose about the value of the interest of Weidman and Miller in the firm, arbitration ensued. The court states that the arbitrator found that "petitioners were terminated in bad

---

69. *Id.*, 78 A.D.2d at 259, 434 N.Y.S.2d at 368.

70. *Id.*, 78 A.D.2d at 260, 434 N.Y.S.2d at 369.

71. 177 A.D.2d 342, 576 N.Y.S.2d 232 (App. Div. 1991).

72. *Id.*, 177 A.D.2d at 344, 576 N.Y.S.2d at 234 (citing Matter of Correction Officers Benevolent Ass'n v. City of New York, 160 A.D.2d 548, 549, 554 N.Y.S.2d 198 (App. Div. 1990)).

faith to prevent them from obtaining the benefits of purchasing some of respondent's interests, resulting in an 'undue penalty or unjust forfeiture'."[73] The law firm claimed that the amount of money awarded the petitioners by the arbitrator reflected an improper award of punitive damages, and the firm appealed. The lower court found for the law firm on the punitive damages issue and for the petitioners on other issues. Both sides appealed.

The appellate court restated the decisions of the New York Court of Appeals in its holdings that while punitive damages are prohibited in arbitration awards, whenever compensatory damages are somewhat speculative, they are necessarily punitive. In confirming the arbitrator's award, the court said

> The arbitration award herein also did not authorize punitive damages but damages for bad faith termination, and the Supreme Court was simply unjustified in declaring the two to be indistinguishable.[74]

Thus, drafters of a partnership agreement should not be concerned that enforceable punitive damages might stem from an arbitrator's unfavorable decision.

The New York Court of Appeals has adhered to these standards.[75] A withdrawn partner of Milbank, Tweed, Hadley & McCloy sued his former firm for supplemental payments denied him under provisions of the partnership agreement. Eventually, the dispute went to arbitration on the issue of whether the provisions were invalid forfeiture-for-competition clauses, barred by the *Cohen*[76] case. The arbitrator found that the partnership agreement did not violate the *Cohen* principle, and the Milbank firm appealed. Reversing a vacatur by New York's appellate division, the court said:

> The arbitrator's award here both factually and legally answers the public policy challenge raised by petitioner. Whether or not we agree with his findings and conclusions,

---

73. *Id.*, 177 A.D.2d at 343, 576 N.Y.S.2d at 234.

74. *Id.*, 177 A.D.2d at 345, 576 N.Y.S.2d at 235.

75. *See* Hackett v. Milbank, 1995 N.Y. LEXIS 2229 (N.Y. Ct. App. July 5, 1995).

76. Cohen v. Lord, Day & Lord, 75 N.Y.2d 95, 550 N.E.2d 410, 551 N.Y.S.2d 157 (1989).

the award does not on its face clearly violate public policy, and should not have been vacated on that basis.[77]

Rights and Obligations of Withdrawn and Retired Partners

It might seem incongruous to include in a partnership agreement provisions regarding the rights and obligations of partners who withdraw or retire from the firm. However, you who are a partner have a legitimate interest—while you are a partner—in knowing how the firm will treat you, should you withdraw or retire.

If a firm wants to enjoy good relations with its senior partners, before and after retirement, it is in the firm's interest to address the issue of retirement status in the partnership agreement. Typically, a retired partner will remain "of counsel" to his or her firm. There should be a written agreement between the lawyer and the firm spelling out the details of that arrangement. Such minutiae do not deserve attention in the partnership agreement.

However, the partnership agreement should contain general language that indicates (1) whether the partner is to receive full, or reduced, compensation until normal retirement date, (2) whether there will be compensation thereafter, (3) whether the firm will pay any or all of life and health insurance premiums after retirement, (4) whether office space and office services will be provided, and (5) whether the firm will pay the retired partner's membership dues and expenses in connection with professional organizations. On the retired partner's side, the agreement should indicate his or her obligations to the firm in terms of right to practice, malpractice insurance coverage, and client development activities.

As for a partner choosing to withdraw, the partnership agreement should specify what the partner is entitled to receive from the firm in terms of return of capital, a share of earnings to which he or she has contributed before leaving the firm, and any interest in "work in progress" for which there may have been no previous billing.

These issues will be revisited in Chapters IV and V.

---

77. *Hackett*, 1995 N.Y. LEXIS 2229 at *20.

CHAPTER IV

Dissolution of a Law Partnership

Elements for Consideration

A properly formed and adjusted law partnership is akin to a marriage. When it is dissolved, for whatever reason, it is a traumatic experience for the partners, both from psychological and financial aspects. In examining the causes and consequences of a partnership dissolution, one must look at matters from the viewpoint of the partner or partners separated from the organization and from the viewpoint of those who will continue as partners.

In this connection, it is interesting to observe the changes in partnership law that will be wrought by adoption of the Revised Uniform Partnership Act (RUPA). RUPA was promulgated by the National Conference of Commissioners on Uniform State Laws in 1994, and has been adopted by the legislatures in Connecticut and Florida.

RUPA makes a distinction between certain events (such as withdrawal of a partner, expulsion of a partner, or death or disability of a partner), which result in "dissociation," and other events (such as dissociation in a partnership-at-will, failure of remaining partners to agree to continue after a dissociation by death or bankruptcy, a consent to dissolve, or completion of the term for the undertaking), which result in "dissolution."

Under RUPA, partners have certain fiduciary duties, including the duty of loyalty, the duty of care, and the obligation to act in good faith and deal fairly. The duty of loyalty carries with it the obligation to refrain from competing with the partnership before its dissolution.[1] If there is dissociation, then certain rights and duties of a partner cease.[2] The partner's right to participate in management ceases, as does his or her duty to refrain from competition, while other duties of loyalty and care continue regarding matters that arose before the dissociation. If the dissociation does not result in dissolution of the partnership, the dissociated partner's duties of loyalty and care continue should he or she continue to participate in the winding up of the business.[3] Moreover, the partnership is required to buy out the interest of the dissociated partner pursuant to a formula set out in the statute.[4] The formula specifies that the amount to be paid the dissociated partner is the

> amount that would have been distributable to the dissociating partner [under winding up conditions] if, on the date of dissociation, the assets of the partnership were sold at a price equal to the greater of the liquidation value or the value based on a sale of the entire business as a going concern without the dissociated partner and the partnership were wound up as of that date.[5]

The formula appears to be a practical one for partnerships, but not necessarily for law partnerships. As we will observe in the discussion of goodwill later in this chapter, there are some jurisdictions that do not consider the value of goodwill in calculating the going concern value of a law practice. If the only assets that may be taken into consideration are the "hard assets" (which are not truly significant when looking at the value of a law firm), the dissociated partner will receive a disappointing sum.

Causes of Dissolution

The dissolution of a law firm is a relatively rare phenomenon. When it happens—particularly to a large or well-known firm—it is big news in the business community. During March and April, 1995, for example, *The American Lawyer* carried stories concerning the demise of such leading partnerships as Pettit & Martin of San

---

1. Rev. Unif. P'ship Act, § 404(b)(3) (1994).
2. *Id.*, § 603.
3. *Id.*
4. *Id.*, § 701.
5. *Id.*, § 701(b).

Francisco, Johnson & Wortley of Dallas, and Shea & Gould and Lord, Day & Lord Barrett Smith of New York. The publicly advanced reasons for the decisions to disband in these situations were varied. Each of us can surmise why dissolution might have been necessary: too much emphasis on a small client base or a particular area of practice, so that the loss of a single client or the disappearance of a practice segment placed heavy financial stresses upon the firm; the exodus of one or more rainmakers from the firm; or, as sometimes happens, the inability of the partners to agree upon a proper and equitable division of earnings.

In smaller firms, the decision to dissolve may be based upon reasons less material and more philosophical. The partners may disagree on the future course of the firm. Some may wish to see the firm expand in one fashion or another, while others may believe that the better course is to remain of a particular size. Absent a consensus, dissolution is inevitable so that each group may pursue its own agenda.

Under partnership law, the loss of a partner in a partnership, whether by withdrawal, expulsion, or death, will cause the dissolution of the partnership—*unless* the partnership agreement provides for the continuation of the partnership. When a partnership agreement gives the partners the power to expel a partner and continue the partnership business thereafter, the parties' conduct is subject to the Uniform Partnership Act provision that the expulsion of a partner causes the dissolution of the firm.[6] However, if a partnership agreement specifically provides that the firm will not dissolve upon the withdrawal of a partner, the courts recognize that the partnership continues to exist after a partnership withdrawal.[7] Some of these issues will be discussed in more detail below.

Dissolution can occur by operation of law in other circumstances. For example, "the election of a lawyer to a judgeship, thereby incapacitating him from the practice of law," may dissolve a partnership of which he is a member.[8]

Given these situations, you, as a partner, have an obligation to yourself and to your firm to make sure your partnership agreement correctly reflects the intention of the partners: Under what

---

6. Alan R. Gilbert, Annotation, *Construction and Application of Expulsion Provision in Partnership Agreement between Attorneys*, 72 A.L.R.3d 1226 (1994).

7. Beckman v. Farmer, 579 A.2d 618 (D.C. App. 1990).

8. Michael A. Rosenhouse, Annotation, *Validity and Application of State Statutes Prohibiting Judge from Practicing Law*, 17 A.L.R.4th 829 (1994), Sec. 10(b).

circumstances do you wish the partnership to be dissolved and when do you want it to continue?

Factors in Determining Whether to Dissolve the Partnership

As we have observed, the usual causes for considering the dissolution of a partnership are the financial instability of a firm or the dissatisfaction of one or more partners with their financial arrangements with the firm. Less often, it may be the failure of partners to interact well on a personal level.

Whatever the reason for contemplating dissolution, many factors must be weighed. Will the firm or the individual partner or partners improve their economic situations if the firm is dissolved? One must give much credence to the old saying that "the grass is greener on the other side." Other firms may be having the same economic pressures as your firm. Whether a vote for dissolution will produce a better result may be quite conjectural.

Withdrawal of a Partner

Compensating the Withdrawing Partner

If you are a law firm partner, you have an unfettered right to withdraw from the partnership, subject to whatever restrictions are written into the partnership agreement regarding notice and effective date. When you withdraw, you are entitled to whatever the partnership agreement entitles you to receive. If the partnership agreement is silent on withdrawal or contains no specific provisions governing payments to you from the firm, then the law of partnership as it applies in your jurisdiction will govern your rights.

In general, the Uniform Partnership Act (UPA) makes a distinction between the amount owed a partner upon dissolution of a partnership and the amount due the partner upon his or her death or retirement. The UPA provides that upon dissolution (assuming the partner has not wrongfully caused the dissolution), the partner is entitled to have the partnership property applied to discharge its liabilities; any surplus is then applied to pay, in cash, the net amount owed the respective partners. When partners retire or die, the UPA provides that such partners, or their legal representatives, are entitled to receive as ordinary creditors an amount equal to the value of their interest in the dissolved partnership with interest or, at their option or the option of their legal representatives, in lieu of interest, the profits attributable to the use of their rights in the property of the dissolved partnership. In the absence of any agreement to the contrary, each partner is entitled to an accounting of his or her interest as against the winding up partners or the surviving partners or the partnership continuing the business, as of the date of dissolution.

Because of these provisions in the UPA, which may produce results inconsistent with the desires of the partners, it is important that the partnership agreement spell out the consequences in the various situations that may arise. In short, the agreement should specify when withdrawal of a partner is permissible and what shall happen (in terms of payments and benefits to the withdrawing partner) if withdrawal takes place (1) in accordance with the terms of the agreement or (2) in violation of those terms. It should state, particularly, whether the partnership is to continue or be dissolved. In the discussions of cases that follow in this chapter, other significant points to be covered will become apparent.

Liability for Malpractice of the Withdrawing Partner

Chapter I discusses the liability of the partnership for malpractice of the withdrawing partner, and the withdrawing partner's liability for acts committed before and after the dissolution of the law firm.

Withdrawal Provision in Partnership Agreement; Right to Cause Dissolution

The problems associated with living in a partnership plagued with inability of the partners to agree upon the share of earnings of each are illustrated in the *Cowan* case.[9] The plaintiff, Mr. Cowan, had been an associate in a law firm. In 1974, four of the lawyers in the firm entered into a formal partnership agreement, constituting the firm of Gracey, Maddin, Cowan & Bird. In subsequent years, several partners were added. The partnership agreement provided for annual calculations of three-year historical fee production for each partner to determine his partnership percentage for the ensuing year.

In 1986, Cowan was insisting that he receive a percentage greater than the formula would provide, and was told by one of

---

9. Cowan v. Maddin, 786 S.W.2d 647 (Tenn. Ct. App. 1990).

his partners that this course of action would drive off the younger partners. A few weeks later, another partner attempted, unsuccessfully, to establish a new partnership agreement. Meanwhile, Cowan's percentage was adjusted upward from the formula, although in an amount less than Cowan desired. Accordingly, Cowan stated his intent to submit a plan for his withdrawal from the firm. Several other partners then indicated they would withdraw from the firm. Cowan proposed that he retire and become "of counsel" to the firm, which the partners found unacceptable. Cowan withdrew his retirement proposal and announced he would remain as a partner. Thereafter, Cowan was not notified of partnership meetings and was excluded from partnership decisions. The other partners wanted Cowan "out."

By this time, months had passed. It was May, 1987. Another partner, Mr. Bird, announced that he had a proposal for terminating his relationship with the firm and another for Cowan. He said that if his proposals were not accepted, he would dissolve the firm.

The remaining partners then transferred funds to bank accounts over which Cowan and Bird had no control. However, they set up an interest-bearing account into which they placed funds estimated to equal the maximum amounts to which Cowan and Bird would be entitled. When the transfers were discovered, Cowan and Bird, in late May, 1987, signed and delivered a document to the partners purporting to dissolve the firm. "Suffice it to say that the record reeks of animosity between plaintiff and defendants."[10]

Cowan brought suit seeking a decree that the partnership was dissolved and an order for a judicial winding up of the partnership affairs.

Several issues were involved in the appeal, but in essence the central question was whether, when a partnership agreement is silent on the issues of dissolution at will or for cause, a partner can cause a dissolution by announcing his or her withdrawal.

It is significant that the partnership agreement in the *Cowan* case provided in part that

> [t]his Agreement, and as the same may be amended from time to time, shall continue for an indefinite period and shall not be terminated except in accordance with the provisions stated herein. The death, resignation, withdrawal, retirement or expulsion of a partner shall not terminate the Agreement,

10. *Id.* at 650.

> but the same shall continue in full force and effect for the benefit and government of the remaining partners in a continuing law practice.[11]

Although Cowan argued that the parties did not anticipate the serious disagreements that arose, his argument was unavailing. The court said:

> We are of the opinion, and so hold, that where a partnership agreement is entered into and specifically contemplates that the agreement shall continue until terminated and specifies the rights and liabilities of the partners on withdrawal, the agreement is binding and that this Court should not speculate that the parties did not anticipate that there would be serious disagreements between partners. If a partner wishes to leave the partnership, there is a plain and simple method provided, i.e., "withdrawal." Granted, in the instant case the plaintiff would probably be better off financially if the partnership were dissolved. However, he agreed in 1974 when he entered into the partnership and signed the Agreement that if he wished to leave he would leave pursuant to the Agreement.[12]

The *Cowan* court then went on to discuss the consequences of the withdrawal. Its opinion provides insight into the distinctions among termination of a law firm's operations, formal dissolution, and the effect of withdrawal of one or more partners. The court stated:

> Therefore, gentlemen, it appears to the Court and the Court finds that although there is a technical dissolution or a dissolution of the partnership as to the withdrawing partners, to wit, Mr. Cowan and Mr. Bird, inasmuch as the partnership agreement provides that the partnership will not terminate nor be—and the effect of that is that the partnership will not be liquidated, the partnership will continue for the remaining partners with Mr. Bird and Mr. Cowan paid the net amount due them from the firm and protected [sic] from firm liability [sic].[13]

This factor might have influenced the attitude of the court toward Bird: before leaving his old firm, Bird was sending out

---

11. *Id.* at 651.
12. *Id.* at 652.
13. *Id.* at 655.

mailings to his former clients on behalf of his new firms, Maddin, Cowan & Bird, or Gracey, Maddin, Cowan & Bird.[14]

The lesson of the *Cowan* case is that it is highly desirable to have a specific provision in the partnership agreement dealing with the intention of the partners about the consequences of a withdrawal of one or more partners—particularly whether the partners intend that the partnership will continue its operations with the remaining partners.

The partnership in the *Cowan* case had a provision in the agreement dealing not only with withdrawal, but also with the financial arrangements to which the withdrawing partner or partners would be entitled. As it turned out, this was a fortuitous provision because an argument ensued over the right of a withdrawing partner to receive a distributive share of the firm's recoupment, after his withdrawal, of expenses advanced while he was a partner.

Cowan's firm had advanced certain items of expense for clients and had written off these expenses in calculating taxable income. When the expenses were recouped from clients, the funds recouped were taken as taxable income. Cowan claimed to have an interest in the expenses advanced to the date of withdrawal. In the court below, the chancellor had found that it would be equitable to award a share to Cowan. The court of appeal reversed. It noted that

> [t]he Agreement specifically states that "as of the effective date of withdrawal, the withdrawing partner shall have no further interest or right in the accounts receivable or matters in progress belonging to the firm."[15]

The court decided that the chancellor had erred in holding that Cowan was entitled to an interest in expenses advanced.

A case in the New York Court of Appeals underscores the desirability of addressing, in the partnership agreement, the consequences of withdrawal of a partner and the financial arrangements that are to follow. The case also illustrates that ambiguity in the document can make for misunderstanding and result in litigation to resolve the matter.

The case resulted from the decision of Robert Jackson to withdraw from the firm of Hunt, Hill & Betts in Manhattan. Three part-

---

14. *Id.*
15. *Id.* at 657.

ners, including Jackson, withdrew at the same time. The remaining partners made arrangements with the two other partners, but had made none with Jackson. He claimed he was entitled to participate in fees that were earned but unpaid at the time of his withdrawal, and in the physical assets of the partnership. Jackson won in the trial court, but had his complaint dismissed on appeal to the appellate division. The case then came to the New York Court of Appeals.[16]

As stated by the high court, the decision hinged upon "whether the term 'net profits,' as used in [the partnership agreement], includes fees that are earned but uncollected, or only such as shall have been collected at the time when a partner withdraws."[17] Although Jackson would not have been entitled to an accounting had the firm made an estimate of its "net profits" as of the date of his withdrawal, the court directed an accounting. It also held that Jackson was entitled to share in the fees of the firm that were earned but uncollected at the time of his withdrawal.

Again, the case demonstrates a need for clarity in the partnership document. In the desire for brevity, many firms may neglect to add language that will specify—when a withdrawing partner is entitled to a share of net profits—exactly how net profits are to be calculated. This is a mistake your firm should avoid.

Prohibiting Competition by the Withdrawing Partner

The two cases in New York, reviewed in Chapter III, demonstrate the difficulty a firm may encounter in attempting to prevent a partner from withdrawing and practicing in competition with the firm. These are, of course, the *Cohen* and *Denburg* cases.[18]

Dealing with Law Firm Dissolution

Factors Causing Dissolution

The issue of the circumstances that can cause the dissolution of a partnership has been with us for a long time. For example, the New York Court of Appeals in 1913 dealt with a question concern-

---

16. Jackson v. Hunt, Hill & Betts, 7 N.Y.2d 180, 164 N.E.2d 681, 196 N.Y.S.2d 647 (1959).

17. *Id.*, 7 N.Y.2d at 185, 164 N.E.2d at 683, 196 N.Y.S.2d at 650.

18. Cohen v. Lord, Day & Lord, 75 N.Y.2d 95, 550 N.E.2d 410, 551 N.Y.S.2d 157 (1989); Denburg v. Parker, Chapin, Flattau & Klimpl, 82 N.Y.2d 375, 624 N.E.2d 995, 604 N.Y.S.2d 900 (1993).

ing when incapacity of a partner can cause a partnership to be dissolved.[19]

Reginald Barclay and Alexander Barrie had been partners in a manufacturing business for years—from 1873 until 1908. In February, 1908, they entered into a new partnership agreement for a term expiring in 1913. Just a few months later, in May, 1908, Barrie suffered a stroke, causing paralysis and preventing him from performing his duties in the partnership. Specifically, the court said:

> In my opinion the fair construction of these findings as a whole is that defendant became and continued wholly incapacitated for the discharge of his duties as copartner from May 10, 1908, until March, 1912, and that the most which could be expected in the future was that he would make a "practical recovery within the time limited for the existence of the copartnership," namely, at some time before January 1, 1913.[20]

The opinion states what the court held out as the general principle of law governing the circumstances:

> And in elucidation of the general principle thus stated, the cases and text writers as well as common sense make it apparent that "permanent" incapacity as a ground for dissolution does not and should not mean incurable and perpetual disability during the life of the partner. It means incapacity which is lasting rather than merely temporary, and the prospect of recovery from which is remote; which has continued or is reasonably certain to continue during so substantial a portion of the partnership period as to defeat or materially affect and obstruct the purpose of the partnership.[21]

Because Barrie was unable to perform his duties for three years and eleven months out of the total partnership time of four years and eleven months—with no assurance that he would recover before the expiration of the partnership term—the incapacity was "permanent." The court reversed the judgment below, which had dismissed the complaint. The plaintiff, Barclay, was entitled to dissolution of the partnership.

---

19. Barclay v. Barrie, 209 N.Y. 40, 102 N.E. 602 (1913).
20. *Id.*, 209 N.Y. at 47, 102 N.E. at 604.
21. *Id.*, 209 N.Y. at 49, 102 N.E. at 604.

Similarly, death of a partner is cause for dissolution of a partnership.[22] It has also been certain for many years that the value of unfinished business is an asset of the partnership, a share of which is an entitlement of the deceased partner's estate. In 1894, the California Supreme Court stated:

> While it is certainly true when a professional partnership between attorneys at law is dissolved by the death of one, the survivor is entitled to his own future earnings, and is not required to make an allowance in the settlement of the partnership accounts for what may be termed the goodwill of the partnership, or for the profits of such future business as may have been given to him by former clients of the firm, still, in regard to unfinished business intrusted to the firm, and which the client permits the surviving partner to complete, such contract of employment, although not capable of assignment, is still to be viewed by a court of equity as an asset of the partnership.[23]

Now one would think that, if incapacity and death at common law could cause the dissolution of a partnership, lunacy should, too. But not according to the Illinois Supreme Court in a decision rendered over a hundred years ago.[24] Briefly, the facts were that Samuel Raymond and George Vaugn formed a partnership in 1874 to do a sugar brokerage business. Several years later, Vaugn was committed to an asylum as temporarily insane. Raymond was his conservator and carried on the business until Vaugn was discharged from the hospital. The issue of the effect of the insanity arose when Vaugn sued Raymond because Vaugn was not satisfied with the financial settlement he had arrived at with Raymond. If the partnership were dissolved, the finality of the conservator's report would govern; if it were not, Vaugn would have his day in court. The court held that the partnership could be dissolved only by decree of court.

The UPA changed these concepts slightly. Under the UPA, death of a partner causes the dissolution of a partnership. On the other hand, the UPA requires application to the court and a decree of dissolution when a partner has been declared a lunatic in any judicial proceeding, is shown to be of unsound mind, or becomes

---

22. Little v. Caldwell, 101 Cal. 553, 36 P. 107 (1894).
23. *Id.*, 101 Cal. at 561, 36 P. at 109.
24. Raymond v. Vaugn, 128 Ill. 256, 21 N.E. 566 (1889).

in any other way incapable of performing his or her part of the partnership contract.[25]

Dissolution does not always require such formalistic ritual as an application to, and decree from, a court. Consider what happened in a recent Maryland case.[26] Marr and Langhoff were law partners in a firm known as Marr, Langhoff & Bennett, P.A. After a few years, there were differences about the firm finances. Langhoff decided to leave. The court, in its decision, recites what happened on December 31, 1981:

> On . . . Langhoff's last day with [the old firm], Bennett and Langhoff discussed [the old firm's] work in progress for clients and physical assets. Apparently without difficulty, they reached a very simple agreement. Bennett testified, "I broached the topic, whatever is yours is yours, and whatever is ours is ours, except for the matter of Dr. Kidwell."[27]

The court gave great significance to these words. It said:

> We construe the Langhoff-Bennett contract to have effected an immediate winding-up of [the firm]. It is not suggested that there was any agreement for [the firm] to exist for a fixed term. Nor does any party to this case advance an argument premised on dissolution of the firm breaching the partnership agreement. Whether we view Marr and Bennett as having expressly willed a dissolution, or as having expelled Langhoff, [the firm] was dissolved December 31, 1981. "On dissolution, the partnership is not terminated, but continues until the winding up of partnership affairs is completed."[28]

Thus, *Marr* tells us that no elaborate document is needed to terminate a law partnership. A few simple words, and it is accomplished.

Consequences of Dissolution

There is no question that a partnership agreement may spell out the financial effects of a dissolution and provide in specific terms

---

25. *See* UNIF. P'SHIP ACT §§ 31, 32 (1914).

26. Marr v. Langhoff, 322 Md. 657, 589 A.2d 470 (1991).

27. *Id.*, 322 Md. at 661, 589 A.2d at 472.

28. *Id.*, 322 Md. at 668, 589 A.2d at 475 (citations omitted). Note that the court treated the firm as a partnership, ignoring the fact that it was organized as a professional association.

for the amounts to be received upon dissolution by each of the partners. The problem is to determine what happens when the partners have failed to provide for the situation in their agreement.

California courts have addressed the issue. One spelled out the consequences bluntly:

> In this case we hold that in the absence of a partnership agreement, the Uniform Partnership Act requires that attorneys fees received on cases in progress upon dissolution of a law partnership are to be shared by the former partners according to their right to fees in the former partnership, regardless of which former partner provides legal services in the case after the dissolution. The fact that the client substitutes one of the former partners as attorney of record in place of the former partnership does not affect this result.[29]

The partners in Jewel, Boxer & Elkind had neither an agreement regarding dissolution nor a written partnership agreement. After their decision to dissolve, the four partners each sent to their clients an announcement of the dissolution and a consent to the retention of the individual lawyer in substitution for the old firm. A dispute then arose about how fees from these clients were to be allocated.

Two of the partners, Jewel and Leary, contended the fees were assets of the old partnership. All postdissolution fees should have gone to the old partnership and be distributed according to the partners' interests in the old firm. The other two partners argued that the substitution of lawyers transformed the business into "new business," outside the purview of the UPA; the old firm would be entitled to share only in the fees on a quantum meruit basis related to work performed before the dissolution.

In response to the argument by Boxer and Elkind that clients have an unfettered right to choice of counsel, the court followed California precedent that distinguished between the right of clients to choose counsel and the right and duties of former partners to income from unfinished partnership business. "Once the client's fee is paid to an attorney, it is of no concern to the client how that fee is allocated among the attorney and his or her former partners."[30] The court noted that there were sound reasons for the rule. It would eliminate the extra compensation that would accrue to the

---

29. Jewel v. Boxer, 156 Cal. App. 3d 171, 203 Cal. Rptr. 13 (Ct. App. 1984).
30. *Id.*, 156 Cal. App. 3d at 178, 203 Cal. Rptr. at 17.

lawyer who might dissolve the firm and take the most profitable cases with him or her. It thus prevents partners from competing for the most remunerative cases and then scrambling to solicit the firm's clients upon dissolution. The court held:

> In short, the trial court's allocation of postdissolution income to the old and new firms on a quantum meruit basis constituted error. The appropriate remedy is to remand the cause for posttrial proceedings to allocate such income to the former partners of the old firm in accordance with their respective percentage interest in the former partnership. This will also allow the trial court to allocate fees received since the trial.
>
> Under the provisions of the Uniform Partnership Act, the former partners will be entitled to reimbursement for reasonable overhead expenses (excluding partners' salaries) attributable to the production of postdissolution partnership income; in other words, it is net postdissolution income, not gross income, that is to be allocated to the former partners.[31]

A slightly more complicated fact situation than *Jewel* was presented in a California case decided some ten years later. Alan Grossman brought a personal injury action on behalf of his client (Case Janes I). Shortly thereafter, Grossman formed a law partnership with Laurence Davis. The partnership made a fee agreement with Grossman's client, basing the fees on the client's "net recovery." The partnership was dissolved some months later and, subsequently, Case Janes I was settled. However, at the time of settlement, the client was represented by Davis. Because of judgment-proof defendants in Case Janes I, Davis decided further litigation was necessary and, armed with assignments from the settling defendants in Case Janes I, a second lawsuit (Case Janes II) was instituted. It produced legal fees in six figures after a successful conclusion. The question was: did the former partnership have an interest in the fees produced by "unfinished business"?

Davis contended that Case Janes II was a separate matter. It had been commenced well after the dissolution of the partnership and was not in existence when Case Janes I was settled. Of course, Grossman argued that the fees from Case Janes II were generated through the winding up of the partnership business and must be

---

31. *Id.*, 156 Cal. App. 3d at 180, 203 Cal. Rptr. at 19 (footnote omitted).

allocated to the partnership. The trial court found for Grossman and Davis appealed.

In its opinion, the appellate court said:

> The idea that winding up a legal partnership's unfinished business may require the filing of new litigation is not a novelty. Just as other types of former partnerships may sue to collect debts, so too can dissolved legal partnerships initiate an auxiliary round of litigation to bolster or facilitate predissolution lawsuits to collect debts owed to clients.
>
> The Janes II action was a continuation by other means of the dissolved partnership's unfinished business in Janes I. The trial court was therefore correct in awarding Grossman fees from Janes II proportionate to his partnership interest.[32]

This result may not have been what Davis intended or expected. Again, the importance of a written partnership agreement is demonstrated. It was unfortunate that Davis had rescinded the written partnership agreement with Grossman shortly after its execution.

Dissolution of a partnership does not end the necessity of vigilance regarding the conduct of former partners. Consider what happened when the New York firm of Schmidt, Aghayan & Saide dissolved. Clients of the firm previously sued the firm and its partners in federal court for breach of fiduciary duty and other misfeasance, and had won a judgment of $1.8 million. The firm was dissolved. Thereafter, Schmidt, a former partner, converted some $1.8 million of funds from a client's estate, allegedly to settle the claim against the firm and its former partners. The estate sued. Partner Aghayan moved to dismiss. In a convoluted set of facts, the court determined that "defendant Schmidt's conversion of the Estate's funds after dissolution of the partnership, was an act 'appropriate for winding up partnership affairs or completing transactions unfinished at dissolution' within the meaning of New York Partnership Law Section 66 and therefore binding upon the partners."[33]

To make matters more complicated, the estate's funds had been received in settlement of litigation in a federal court. Because it appeared that the settlement had been procured by Schmidt using the funds converted from the estate, the court declined to

32. Grossman v. Davis, 28 Cal. App. 4th 1833, 1837, 34 Cal. Rptr. 2d 355 (Ct. App. 1994) (citations omitted).

33. Majer v. Schmidt, 169 A.D.2d 501, 564 N.Y.S.2d 722 (App. Div. 1991).

grant Aghayan's motion to dismiss as to him, even though he had a general release from the settling defendants. Further, the court reversed the court below, which had declined to impose a constructive trust upon the $1.8 million. Said the court:

> Surely the instant case, involving allegations of outrageous fraud perpetrated upon his clients by an attorney, who was able to prolong his career of fraud only by settling with one client with funds stolen from another, is one which calls for the intervention of equity.[34]

Majer illustrates the necessity for every partner to be aware of what his or her partners are doing. Should there be a "bad apple" in the barrel, the consequences may spill over onto other, innocent nonparticipants in the partnership—and these consequences last beyond the date of dissolution of the partnership. As in the *Majer* case, partners who wind up the firm may be liable for a former partner's misdeeds that took place after he left the firm. (This points to the necessity of obtaining a malpractice insurance policy that will protect you and your partners adequately for the period of limitation of malpractice claims after termination—not merely dissolution—of the partnership, and that has an exception against exclusion of coverage for partners and associates without knowledge of, or participation in, any act giving the carrier the right to deny coverage. See the discussion of *Home Insurance Co. v. Dunn* in Chapter I.)

The partners of Antonow & Fink, an Illinois law partnership that dissolved, are well aware of the liabilities that can follow a firm dissolution. Before its dissolution, the Antonow & Fink firm had entered into a lease of computer equipment. The firm failed to make payments on the lease. The lessor assigned its rights under the lease. After the firm was dissolved, the assignee sued the individuals who were former partners in the law firm. The assignee moved for judgment on the pleadings against those individuals. In granting the motion, the court said:

> The [Illinois Uniform Partnership Act] provides that all general partners are jointly liable for the partnership's contractual debts. The IUPA further provides that "[t]he dissolu-

34. *Id.*, 169 A.D. at 503, 564 N.Y.S.2d at 725.

> tion of the partnership does not of itself discharge the existing liability of any partner."[35]

Consequently, dissolution is not a prescription for avoidance of liability.

If your firm should be in difficulty—financial or otherwise—and dissolution is contemplated, the law continues to place upon you and your partners the obligation of fiduciary duty to one another. The solicitation of clients by a partner before a decision to dissolve the partnership breaches that obligation. Timing is crucial. Once a decision to dissolve the partnership has been reached, the fiduciary relation between partners ceases to exist. The appellate division in New York stated it thusly:

> Although dissolution occurs when the partners determine to discontinue business, the partnership is not terminated until the winding up of partnership affairs is completed. However, the fiduciary relation between partners terminates upon notice of dissolution, even though the partnership affairs have not been wound up. After dissolution, each former partner is free to practice law individually, and has the right to accept retainers from persons who had been clients of the firm.[36]

The law guards jealously the right of individual lawyers to practice law and the right of clients to choice of counsel. Thus, there are many things you and any of your partners who are dissatisfied with your firm can do to change the situation, and yet not violate any duty of professional responsibility. These matters are discussed in great detail in *Meehan v. Shaughnessy*, an opinion by the highest court in Massachusetts.[37]

THE *MEEHAN* CASE

James Meehan and Leo Boyle were partners in Parker Coulter. Both had been with the firm for many years and were litigators. In July of 1984, dissatisfied with their unsuccessful opposition to a new firm pension plan, they decided to leave and set up their own partnership. First, in anticipation of a July 5 meeting, they made

---

35. Pacificorp Credit, Inc. v. Antonow & Fink, 1990 U.S. Dist. LEXIS 7733 at *6 (N.D. Ill. 1990) (citations omitted).

36. *In re* Silverberg, 81 A.D.2d 640, 641, 438 N.Y.S.2d 143, 144 (App. Div. 1981) (citations omitted).

37. Meehan v. Shaughnessy, 404 Mass. 419, 535 N.E.2d 1255 (1989).

lists of their cases and provided them to a junior partner, Ms. Cohen, whom they intended to invite to join them. Cohen agreed to keep their plans confidential until they were announced. Meehan and Boyle stated that they intended to leave the old firm on December 31. Meanwhile, they proceeded to discuss joinder with the new firm with certain associates at Parker Coulter, and to negotiate with a bank for financing required for the move.

Although during the summer and fall of 1984 Meehan and Boyle continued actively to plan for their departure and the opening of their new firm, they (and the lawyers who proposed to leave with them) did not shirk their duties at Parker Coulter. Their case loads increased, but, as the opinion notes, "[t]hey settled cases appropriately, made reasonable efforts to avoid continuances, tried cases, and worked on discovery. Each generally maintained his or her usual standard of performance."[38]

The cloak of confidentiality the departing lawyers had maintained was finally broken late in November, 1984, and on November 30, they announced their impending departure from Parker Coulter. At this time, the partners who were not leaving began discussing with clients the firm's desire to continue representation. Meanwhile, Meehan began to speak with clients and to mail previously prepared authorization forms that would consent to removal of their cases to the new firm.

On January 1, 1985, the new firm opened its doors. The opinion of the Massachusetts Supreme Judicial Court summarizes what happened:

> [The new firm] removed a number of cases from Parker Coulter. Of the roughly 350 contingent fee cases pending at Parker Coulter in 1984, [the lawyers leaving] removed approximately 142 to [the new firm]. Meehan advised Parker Coulter that the 4,000 asbestos cases he had attracted to the firm would remain, and he did not seek to take certain other major clients. Black removed thirty-five cases; Fitzgerald removed ten; and Cohen removed three. A provision in the partnership agreement in effect at the separation provided that a voluntarily retiring partner, upon the payment of a "fair charge," could remove "any matter in which the partnership had been representing a client who came to the firm through the personal effort or connection of the retiring partner," subject to

38. *Id.*, 404 Mass. at 426, 535 N.E.2d at 1259.

> the right of the client to stay with the firm. Approximately thirty-nine of the 142 contingent fee cases removed to [the new firm] came to Parker Coulter at least in part through the personal efforts or connections of Parker Coulter attorneys other than [the departing lawyers]. In all the cases removed to [the new firm], however, the [new firm] attorneys had direct, existing relationships with the clients. In all the removed cases, [the new attorneys] communicated with the referring attorney or with the client directly by telephone or letter. In each case, the client signed an authorization.[39]

When Parker Coulter did not pay them the amounts they deemed owed, Meehan and Boyle brought suit, not only to recover these amounts, but also to obtain a declaration regarding the amount they owed Parker Coulter for work done on cases before their removal from the old firm. Parker Coulter then counterclaimed, asserting breach of fiduciary duty on the part of the departing partners, breach of the partnership agreement, and tortious interference with advantageous business and contractual relationships.

After a trial, Parker Coulter's claims were rejected and Meehan and Boyle were found entitled to recover amounts owed them under the partnership agreement. However, Parker Coulter was held entitled to recover from Meehan and Boyle for time and expenses incurred on cases removed by Meehan and Boyle to the new firm. Parker Coulter then appealed and the supreme court granted direct review.

In a lengthy opinion, the court enunciated the rights of a partner to dissolve a partnership pursuant to a partnership agreement, his or her obligations under concepts of fiduciary duty, and the consequences of a breach of these commitments.

RIGHTS PURSUANT TO THE PARTNERSHIP AGREEMENT

The court recognized that the rights of a partner under the UPA could be modified by the partnership agreement. It noted:

> Where a partnership agreement provides that the partnership is to continue indefinitely, and the partnership is therefore "at will," a partner has the right to dissolve the partnership, and the dissolution occurs "[w]ithout violation of the agree-

39. *Id.*, 404 Mass. at 427, 535 N.E.2d at 1259.

ment between the partners." In a dissolution which occurs "[w]ithout violation of the agreement," the statute defers to the method of dividing the partnership's assets which the parties bargained for in their partnership agreement. In contrast, where the partnership agreement provides that the partnership is to continue for a definite term, a partner has merely the power to dissolve, and the dissolution occurs "[i]n contravention of the agreement between the partners." If the dissolution occurs in contravention of the agreement, the dissolving partner is subject to certain damages, and the statute does not expressly allow the partnership agreement to control the division of the partnership assets.[40]

In a footnote, the court held that the "wrongful act" alleged by Parker Coulter—dissolving the partnership before its term—was not a "legal wrong." Consequently, Parker Coulter was not entitled to damages.

Moreover, the court found that the partnership agreement prescribed the manner in which the assets of the dissolved firm were to be allocated among the partners, and the court held that these provisions would override those of the UPA. The Parker Coulter agreement provided that the departing partner would receive a share of the firm's current net income and a return of his or her capital contribution. In addition, instead of assigning a value to the firm's expected fees from unfinished business, the partnership agreement provided that the departing partner could remove any case that came to the firm through the "personal effort or connection" of the partner, if that partner compensated the old firm for the services to the client. The Massachusetts court honored that provision of the partnership agreement, not only regarding cases that came through the "personal effort or connection" of the partner, but also those cases removed that had not come to the old firm through the "personal effort or connection" of the departing partner.

BREACH OF FIDUCIARY DUTY

What is particularly interesting about the opinion in *Meehan* is the discussion of whether the departing partners breached their fiduciary duty to Parker Coulter. The court noted that "Meehan and Boyle owed their copartners at Parker Coulter a duty of the utmost

40. *Id.*, 404 Mass. at 428, 535 N.E.2d at 1260 (citations omitted).

good faith and loyalty, and were obliged to consider their copartners' welfare, and not merely their own."[41]

Parker Coulter had charged that the departing lawyers had manipulated case assignment to their own benefit. Accepting the trial judge's findings, the court noted that all the departing lawyers worked full schedules from July to November, 1984, and that cases were reassigned on the basis of merit and workload.

Parker Coulter also claimed that the departing lawyers unfairly acquired consent from clients to remove cases to the new firm. It was here that Meehan and Boyle stumbled. Said the court:

> We agree that Meehan and Boyle, through their preparation for obtaining clients' consent, their secrecy concerning which clients they intended to take, and the substance and method of their communications with clients, obtained an unfair advantage over their former partners in breach of their fiduciary duties.[42]

The court faulted Meehan for denying to his former partners that he had any plans for leaving the partnership, when, at the same time, he and Boyle were preparing removal authorizations for clients. In this time frame, the court found, Meehan also traveled to New York to attempt to interest U.S. Aviation Underwriters, a Parker Coulter client, in becoming a client of the new firm.

The court's opinion also notes that the content of the letter Meehan and Boyle sent to clients was unfairly prejudicial to Parker Coulter. The court said, speaking of the findings in the court below:

> The ethical standard provides that any notice explain to a client that he or she has a right to decide who will continue the representation. Here, the judge found that the notice did not "clearly present to the clients the choice they had between remaining at Parker Coulter or moving to the new firm." By sending a one-sided announcement, on Parker Coulter letterhead, so soon after notice of their departure, Meehan and Boyle excluded their partners from effectively presenting their services as an alternative to those of Meehan and Boyle.[43]

---

41. *Id.*, 404 Mass. at 434, 535 N.E.2d at 1263.
42. *Id.*, 404 Mass. at 436, 535 N.E.2d at 1264.
43. *Id.*, 404 Mass. at 437, 535 N.E.2d at 1265.

Thus, held the court, Meehan and Boyle violated the duty of utmost good faith and loyalty they owed their partners. It is interesting, too, that the Massachusetts court found that two lawyers, one a junior partner and the other an associate of Parker Coulter, both of whom had "participation in the preemptive tactics" of Meehan and Boyle, had also violated the duty they owed the partnership.

CONSEQUENCES OF THE BREACH

Suffice it to say that the Massachusetts Supreme Judicial Court, in directing the fashioning of a remedy on remand, reviewed the acts of the departing partners in detail. In essence, the court decided that, regarding the profits the departing lawyers derived from cases unfairly removed from Parker Coulter, a constructive trust should be imposed for Parker Coulter's benefit.

Meehan teaches that the departure of one or more partners and the consequent dissolution of a law firm can be a very disturbing event. A departing lawyer needs to be very careful about what is done before his or her departure; until departure, the fiduciary obligation among partners—including those planning departure—remains in effect. Any profits improperly obtained from cases unfairly removed from the old firm will accrue to the old firm's benefit. The redeeming feature is that the departing partners, as former partners of the old firm, will receive their proper share of the profits returned to the old firm from the constructive trust.[44]

Valuation of a Partnership upon Dissolution

Of major concern to partnerships, and especially smaller partnerships, is the value that will be ascribed to a partnership interest upon dissolution of the firm—for whatever cause.

CONTINGENT FEE CASES

For example, a firm that specializes in personal injury matters may wonder what happens to the numerous contingent fee cases in the files, should a partner die, causing the dissolution of the firm. This was the question presented in *Bader v. Cox*,[45] a Texas case.

44. *Id.*, 404 Mass. at 449, 535 N.E.2d at 1271.
45. 701 S.W.2d 677 (Tex. Ct. App. 1985).

William Cox Jr. and Bertran Bader Jr. formed a partnership in 1978. Another member of the Bader family joined the partnership somewhat later. Bertran Bader died in 1982, automatically dissolving the partnership. The other partners continued the law practice, most of which was represented by contingency fee cases. Bertran's executrix sued the firm, contending that it failed to pay the estate Bertran Bader's percentage interest in the contingent fee cases.

The court found there had been no partnership agreement in place and the provisions of the UPA would govern. Concerning the firm's contention that the estate could not recover for the value of the contingency fee cases, the court said:

> Thus we cannot agree with [the firm's] contention that because the partnership operated on a cash-basis accounting system and because the value of the contingent-fee files at the time of decedent's death is not readily or easily ascertainable, the files are not assets of the partnership. The fact that fees are not earned until a case is concluded by settlement or judgment does not compel the conclusion that the files lose their characterization as partnership assets for purposes of evaluating the interest of a deceased partner.[46]

The court held that the estate was entitled to the present value of the decedent's interest in the contingency fee cases, plus a share of profits derived from those cases from the date of dissolution of the firm to the date of termination of the cases. However, if the amount of work the surviving partners were obliged to contribute to the cases exceeded the work they would have performed had the decedent been alive, an appropriate adjustment should be made in the estate's percentage interest.

GOODWILL

A major issue is whether the value of goodwill may be included in the valuation of a law partnership upon its dissolution. This question was considered by the California Court of Appeal when a partner, ousted from his law firm, brought a complaint against his former partners. Robert Fraser sued Raymond Bogucki and other partners in the dissolved patent law firm of Fraser and Bogucki. Fraser claimed that he had spent thirty years building up a patent

46. *Id.* at 681.

law practice. Finally, he curtailed his law practice to serving a single client, which required him to travel extensively. While he was traveling, his partners dissolved the partnership. Although Fraser did not refer in his complaint to obtaining the value of goodwill, but instead sought to recover his loss to his career investment and future profits, plus emotional damages, the court nonetheless deemed the complaint aimed at goodwill. Fraser also asserted that his former partners acted in bad faith, exploiting his age that would practically and emotionally disable him from competing with them by starting a new law firm. The trial court dismissed the complaint.

The court of appeal distinguished the California cases that allowed recovery for goodwill in matrimonial disputes because the lawyer-spouse in such cases continued the practice as before. The court said:

> We fail to see why a lawyer such as Fraser should be permitted to share in expected future profits from clients who have elected not to retain his services. Nor do we savor the prospect of innumerable lawyers from defunct law firms suing each other because some of them were more successful than others in attracting new business from old clients following the dissolution of a partnership.
>
> Payment for goodwill following the breakup of a law partnership is, moreover, barred by California's Rules of Professional Conduct.[47]

Regarding Fraser's claim that his former partners breached their fiduciary duty to him, the court said that Fraser had not been denied his share of the proceeds from the unfinished business of the dissolved partnership. Rather, he was attempting to share in earnings from future business from the dissolved partnership's former clients who elected to retain the services of the new firm. The court, in considering the activities of Fraser's former partners, held that a partner may not be denied his share of the proceeds of the unfinished business of a dissolved partnership and may, in fact, take for his own account new business from clients of the dissolved partnership. However, he may not take for himself pro-

---

47. Fraser v. Bogucki, 203 Cal. App. 3d 604, 609, 250 Cal. Rptr. 41, 45 (Ct. App. 1988).

ceeds of future business from clients who elect to go with the new partnership.[48]

It thus appears that if you are a California lawyer, the possibility that you can be paid for your share of the goodwill of a dissolved partnership is remote. But not so if you are a partner in New York, particularly if you are forced out of your firm, which is then reconstituted. That was the state of facts in the *Dawson* case, decided by New York's appellate division.[49] In the court's view,

> [t]he proposition that a law practice has no good will is a consequence of ethical concerns that the sale of a law practice would necessarily involve the disclosure of client confidences. We agree with the Special Referee that such concerns do not come into play in contexts other than a sale, in particular a partnership dissolution, and disagree with the dictum to the contrary in *Siddall v. Keating,* 8 A.D.2d 44, 46–47, 185 N.Y.S.2d 630 (1st Dept. 1959), *aff'd* 7 N.Y.2d 846, 196 N.Y.S.2d 986, 164 N.E.2d 860). Indeed, that defendant's remaining partners, after dissolving defendant in order to exclude plaintiff as a partner, immediately reconstituted themselves as a new firm using the same name, address, facilities and client list as the dissolved firm, evidences that defendant in fact had good will to distribute.[50]

Handling the Dissolution Prospect

When a law firm is formed, or has been in existence for a long period of time, the partners usually contemplate that it will "last forever." They are no more thinking about dissolution of the firm than two young lovers entering marriage are preparing for divorce. But a law partnership—while it has an affinity to marriage—is a different relationship. It behooves the partners to think about the consequences of dissolution and to draft provisions in the partnership agreement reflecting their intentions and specifying what will happen in that eventuality.

---

48. *Fraser*, 203 Cal. App. 3d at 610–611, 250 Cal. Rptr. at 45.

49. Dawson v. White, 1995 N.Y. App. Div. LEXIS 1228 (N.Y. App. Div. 1995).

50. *Id.* at *1 (citations omitted).

When a Partner Must Be Expelled

There are times when a law firm finds it necessary to expel a partner.

Two cases illustrate the proper procedure for removing a partner the remainder of the partners find undesirable to retain. The first arose in the state of Washington. The *Holman* case arose out of the expulsion of a partner from a prominent Seattle, Washington, firm in 1969.[51] Francis Holman and his brother, William Holman, sued J. Paul Coie and the other partners of their former law firm, claiming damages for breach of the partnership agreement, breach of trust and conspiracy with a firm client, The Boeing Company, to oust them.

In 1941, Francis (the older Holman) joined the firm, where his father, William, was a senior partner. Francis became a partner in 1954. He worked almost exclusively on legal matters for Boeing. His brother, William, joined the firm in 1949, became a partner in 1957, and worked for Boeing in his early years with the firm but not in the years immediately preceding the expulsion. The father, William Holman, retired from the firm in 1962, before the actions giving rise to the dispute.

When the suit was commenced, the firm had twenty-two partners and other associates. The partnership agreement, to which the Holmans were signatories, provided that the business affairs of the partnership would be administered by an executive committee of ten named partners. Both Holmans were members of the executive committee. The partnership agreement also stated

> that "any member may be expelled from the Firm by a majority vote of the Executive Committee," but [did] not specify whether expulsion [was to] be with or without cause or list any of the grounds for expulsion.[52]

The court's opinion indicates there was testimony in the trial court that before the Holmans became partners, meetings had been pleasant and friendly. William Holman began to question the "inadequacy of the legal rates which the firm charged the Boeing Company. He had also questioned other fee structures and the amount of 'unchargeable time' accumulated by several of the senior partners for other than legal work."[53] In 1965, Francis Holman

---

51. Holman v. Coie, 11 Wash. App. 195, 522 P.2d 515 (Ct. App.), *cert. denied*, 420 U.S. 984 (1975).

52. *Id.*, 11 Wash. App. at 197, 522 P.2d at 517.

53. *Id.*, 11 Wash. App. at 198, 522 P.2d at 517.

was elected to the state House of Representatives and, in 1968, to the state Senate, without seeking the firm's approval. Some partners apparently had unexpressed disapproval of the amount of time spent on state service and the reduced percentage of time spent on partnership business. There was testimony that

> in March 1969, several of the officers of Boeing discussed, with several members of the executive committee, a newspaper article written by a political columnist, which characterized Senator Holman as a "tax reform maverick," and praised him for his independence from his client, principally Boeing. There is also testimony that in April 1969, the president of Boeing took issue with legal fees charged by Francis Holman for legal work which he had done for the company.[54]

In mid-April 1969, a speech by Senator Holman, which apparently aggravated some executives of Boeing, provided information that, according to Boeing, he knew or should have known was erroneous. About the same time, a Boeing executive advised the firm that the company did not want Francis Holman doing any further work for it.

The law firm scheduled a partnership meeting for the evening of May 12, 1969, the day on which Senator Holman would return from the legislative session. According to the court, the meeting

> was convened by the managing partner, who then read aloud a resolution which, without giving cause or reasons, expelled [the Holmans] from the partnership. When they asked the reasons for the resolution, none were stated. A vote was taken; by a seven-to-two result the partners were expelled.[55]

Suit was commenced by the Holmans and the trial court granted the defendant firm's motion to dismiss. The Holmans appealed. Their grounds for claiming breach of contract were that the firm (1) failed to give them proper notice of the executive committee meetings at which they were expelled, (2) expelled them without cause, (3) gave no reasons and stated no cause for their expulsion, and (4) failed to provide them with an opportunity to be heard.

First, the appellate court found that the executive committee complied with the firm's rules concerning notice; the gathering of

54. *Id.*, 11 Wash. App. at 198, 522 P.2d at 518.
55. *Id.*, 11 Wash. App. at 201, 522 P.2d at 519.

executive committee members on May 12 preceding the expulsion, of which the Holmans received no notice, was not a formal meeting. And "to hold otherwise would abrogate any informal discussions the parties might have amongst themselves about other partners."[56]

Second, the Holmans asserted that the rules of procedure of the executive committee called for a notice of meeting, together with an agenda of items to be covered. However, the court observed that under the partnership agreement, it was provided that notice was not a requisite to the validity of any meeting of the executive committee; the rules of the executive committee, it held, must be subservient to the provisions of the partnership agreement when there is a conflict.

Third, the Holmans argued that the actions of the partners on May 13 in expelling them without notice, without stating reasons, and without an opportunity to be heard, violated the Holmans' right to due process. The court noted that the partnership agreement did not contain any of the requirements the Holmans sought to impose on the expulsion process. After reviewing decisions in other states concerning the issue, the opinion states:

> We find this partnership agreement to be unambiguous, and not to require notice, reasons, or an opportunity to be heard. To inject those issues would be to rewrite the agreement of the parties, a function we neither presume nor assume.[57]

Finally, the Holmans challenged their expulsion on the ground that the firm failed to act in good faith. The court considered the definition of "good faith" advanced by courts in other jurisdictions, and then made short shrift of the Holmans' contentions. It said: "In view of our holding that the executive committee had the right to expel plaintiffs without stating reason or cause pursuant to the partnership agreement, there was no breach of fiduciary duty."[58]

The second case arose in Indiana. Kightlinger & Gray practiced law as a partnership in Indianapolis for many years. Gerald Lawlis originally joined the firm in 1966 as an associate, but left in 1969 to join the legal staff of Eli Lilly and Company. In 1971, he was

---

56. *Id.*, 11 Wash. App. at 203, 522 P.2d at 520.
57. *Id.*, 11 Wash. App. at 208, 522 P.2d at 523.
58. *Id.*, 11 Wash. App. at 210, 522 P.2d at 524.

offered a partnership at Kightlinger & Gray and returned there, executing a partnership agreement in 1972.

In 1982, Lawlis became an alcohol abuser and did not practice law for several months in early 1983 and in mid-1984. He did not disclose his problem to the partnership until he advised the finance committee in July, 1983. The committee sought advice from a physician experienced in alcoholism. Lawlis was then asked to, and did, sign a document setting forth certain conditions for his continuing relationship with the partnership. Among other things, the document stated: "It must be set out and clearly understood that there is no second chance."[59] However, in 1984, Lawlis again resumed alcohol consumption and sought treatment, and the firm gave Lawlis a second chance.

The firm's finance committee required Lawlis to meet specified conditions to continue his relationship with the partnership. He was required to meet with specialists selected by the partnership, take treatment and consultations, and obtain reports from the specialist about a favorable outcome of the treatment. He was advised he would be returned to full partnership status if he complied. Lawlis ceased consumption of alcohol in March, 1984.

During Lawlis's struggle with his problem, his compensation was reduced by annual addenda to the partnership agreement. Because of his progress, Lawlis met with the finance committee and proposed, on October 1, 1986, that his participation in earnings be restored in 1987. On October 23, 1986, one of Lawlis's partners told him that the firm's finance committee intended to recommend severance of Lawlis's relationship as a senior partner no later than June 30, 1987. On October 25, 1986, all of the firm's files were removed from Lawlis's office.

At the end of 1986, at a partner's meeting, the recommendation was accepted (with Lawlis not voting) and he was given compensation sufficient to entitle him to status as a senior partner, assist his transition to other employment, and protect his ability to obtain insurance coverage. When Lawlis refused to sign the 1987 addendum to the partnership agreement containing these provisions, he was expelled by a seven-to-one vote of the senior partners on February 23, 1987; Lawlis cast the lone senior partner's negative vote. The agreement required a minimum two-thirds affirmative vote of the senior partners for expulsion of a partner.

---

59. Lawlis v. Kightlinger & Gray, 562 N.E.2d 435, 438 (Ind. App. Ct. 1990).

Lawlis then filed suit for damages. In the trial court, he was denied summary judgment and he appealed. He first contended that the notification by the finance committee on October 23, 1986, and the removal of the partnership files from his office constituted a de facto dissolution of the partnership. This, he claimed, was wrongful and in contravention of the partnership agreement.

The court found that no expulsion occurred in October, 1986, that the firm continued to regard Lawlis as a senior partner, and that Lawlis considered himself to be a senior partner after October 26, 1986.

Article X of the partnership agreement of Kightlinger & Gray provided:

> A two-third (2/3) majority of the Senior Partners, at any time, may expel any partner from the partnership upon such terms and conditions as set by said Senior Partners.[60]

The court noted that because the Indiana Uniform Partnership Act permitted the expulsion of any partner in accordance with power conferred by the partnership agreement, Lawlis was effectively expelled in accordance with the firm's partnership agreement on February 23, 1987.

Lawlis also contended that the expulsion violated the partners' duty of good faith and fair dealing because Lawlis was expelled for the "predatory purpose" of increasing the "lawyer-to-partner" ratio. The court noted several facets of the firm's conduct toward Lawlis that belied any lack of good faith and fair dealing. The court said that from the time the firm first became aware of Lawlis's addiction to alcohol, it sought to assist and aid him through his medical crisis, despite his efforts to conceal his alcoholism from his partners. The court noted that the firm allowed Lawlis to continue to draw on his partnership account, even though he became increasingly unproductive. Despite Lawlis's execution of the agreement that (1) allowed the firm to monitor his work product, (2) recommended he attend Alcoholics Anonymous meetings, (3) set specific times for him to arrive and remain at the office, and (4) specified that there would be no second chance, the court observed that Lawlis resumed the consumption of alcohol. Clearly, said the court, "these undisputed facts present no 'predatory purpose' on the firm's part."[61]

---

60. *Id.* at 439.
61. *Id.* at 440.

Regarding Lawlis's claim that the partnership lacked "good faith" because he was expelled to improve partnership income by changing the lawyer-to-partner ratio, the court found no evidence that the purpose in severing Lawlis was to gain any business or improper advantage over the remaining partners.

Summing up the court's position was its statement that

> [a]ll the parties involved in this litigation were legally competent and consenting adults well educated in the law who initially dealt at arm's length while negotiating the partnership agreements here involved. At the time the partners negotiated their contract, it is apparent they believed . . . the "guillotine method" of involuntary severance, that is no notice or hearing, only a severance vote to terminate a partner involuntarily need be taken, would be in the best interests of the partnership. Their intent was to provide a simple, practical, and above all, a speedy method of separating a partner from the firm, if that ever became necessary for any reason. We find no fault with that approach to severance.[62]

The lessons of *Holman* and *Lawlis* are that a partnership, with a properly drawn partnership agreement, can expel a partner without notice, without cause, and without providing any reason. Whether this is a desirable result necessarily depends on which side of the table you happen to sit.

If you are convinced that you will always relate with the majority in the firm—with the center of power—and want to have the right to expel any partner at any time, then you will want such empowerment written into the partnership agreement. It is, in many instances, a desirable way to eliminate quickly any partner whose actions or failures to act may be adversely affecting the ambiance in the firm.

On the other hand, should you be concerned that a group of your partners might be able to eject you and others—perhaps to garner your legal business they could then take for themselves—you may want to install safeguards within the partnership agreement. These safeguards would prevent precipitous action taken without providing notice or reasons for the proposed expulsion, and would require the partners to act with the utmost good faith.

---

62. *Id.* at 442.

Sale of a Partnership Interest

Sale of a law practice is unethical in many jurisdictions. The restriction is mainly of concern to sole practitioners, whose principal asset is a stable of clients. Seldom is the inability to sell a law practice a problem for partnerships and professional corporations, although, as we shall see, it occasionally crops up in the case law. The restriction is based on the general theory that lawyers should not traffic in their clients.

The inability to sell a practice does not affect the right of lawyers to sell the fixed assets of a firm; it simply is a prohibition on selling the files.

Model Rule 1.17

On February 7, 1990, the ABA House of Delegates adopted an amendment to Rule 1.17 of the Model Rules of Professional Conduct that permits the sale of a law practice by a lawyer or law firm under certain conditions. However, since that date, only a few states have amended their own codes to conform with the model rule.[63]

Effect of a Void and Unenforceable Agreement

Let us assume that, notwithstanding the code provision prohibiting a sale, a partner contracts to sell his practice. What happens?

Sheldon Raphael and Edward Friedman practiced as the two shareholders in a professional corporation, Friedman & Raphael, P.C., in New York. Raphael decided to retire and he and Friedman contracted with Philip Shapiro to sell Raphael's interest in the practice to Shapiro. The old firm was to be dissolved and a new firm, Friedman & Shapiro, P.C., formed. Shapiro arranged to pay over a five-year period and he executed promissory notes, due commencing May 1, 1990, with acceleration clauses that, in event of default, evidenced the purchase price. Shapiro stopped paying the notes on about April 1, 1991, and Raphael brought suit in a New York court.

---

63. Note, *Permitting the Sale of a Law Practice: Furthering the Interests of Both Attorneys and Their Clients*, 22 HOFSTRA L. REV. 969 (1994); *see also* Joanne Pelton Pitulla, *When a Solo Takes Down the Shingle*, in THE LAWYER'S GUIDE TO RETIREMENT ch. 26 (David A. Bridewell ed., 1994).

Noting there was a debate about whether the sale of a law practice should be permitted, the court said:

> While the issue is being debated, the present policy in this State is one of prohibition. Although there appears to be some equitable basis in the arguments of proponents for legalization, without promulgation of specific terms and conditions to regulate the sale of law practices in the Code of Professional Responsibility there is a potential for abuse as envisioned by the legal community of this jurisdiction and as shown in the present case before the Court.[64]

The court noted that Raphael had violated other provisions of the Code of Professional Responsibility in that he divulged, without consent, confidences and secrets of his clients to a third party. Raphael had moved to Nevada and the new firm continued to handle matters formerly handled by Friedman & Raphael, P.C., with Raphael receiving a percentage of fees and recovered disbursements—an arrangement the court said violated the code. Finally, the court noted that Raphael had agreed not to reopen or reestablish a law office or engage in the practice of law in Manhattan for a period of five years.

The court found the contract void and unenforceable. In its opinion, the court said:

> Defendant Shapiro who also knowingly violated the provisions of the Code of Professional Responsibility should not be permitted to reap the benefits of a void and unenforceable contract. The parties, in these circumstances, should be left as they are.[65]

Thus, the New York court gave no relief to the parties in pari delicto.

But, across the continent, a different result occurred. Roger Walsh had a law practice in the state of Washington. He had been practicing some thirty-two years and in 1978 decided to sell his practice. He made a contract with one of his associates, Robert Brousseau, who agreed to purchase from Walsh the goodwill of the business together with its fixtures, furniture, equipment, library, accounts, files, office supplies, and stationery, bank accounts, and accounts receivable. In payment, Walsh received notes providing

---

64. Raphael v. Shapiro, 154 Misc.2d 920, 922, 587 N.Y.S.2d 68, 70 (Sup. Ct. 1992).

65. *Id.*, 154 Misc.2d at 925, 587 N.Y.S.2d at 72.

for monthly payments. When the purchaser fell behind in the payments for the second time in 1988 (the first delinquency in 1986 resulted in an amended agreement), he told Walsh that the agreement was unenforceable and he did not intend to pay anything further.

In January, 1989, Walsh sued. He sought to recover the amounts due under the notes and a sum equal to medical insurance premiums and bar association dues for life, which Brousseau also had agreed to pay. The trial court granted Walsh's motion for summary judgment.

On appeal, the court observed that although the ABA had adopted the rule allowing the sale of a law practice, the Washington Supreme Court had not adopted a similar rule. The court noted that the agreement between Walsh and Brousseau stated that Walsh would

> "continue to make a positive effort to procure and assist in continuing business of the office" and, during the life of the agreement, would not "directly or indirectly, induce any of his former clients . . . to patronize any other attorney or law firm other than the Purchaser." Additionally, Walsh agreed that "[if] requested by Purchaser [Brousseau], Seller shall introduce Purchaser to all clients, and other parties with whom Seller does business. Seller also agrees to make himself available in the future for reasonable consultation regarding clientele of the practice, both future and past."[66]

The court said this arrangement violated the Code of Professional Responsibility in the state of Washington.

The Court then considered what disposition should be made in the case. First it decided that neither party had intended to enter an illegal contract, but it noted that Brousseau's lawyer drafted the agreement. Moreover, Brousseau had waited

> until he had reaped the full benefit of the bargain and then attempted to avoid its burdens by claiming that the agreement was illegal. By reaping the full benefit of the bargain, then repudiating the contract, Brousseau's behavior is the type of conduct that evokes public outrage.[67]

---

66. Walsh v. Brousseau, 62 Wash. App. 739, 744, 815 P.2d 828, 832 (Ct. App. 1991).

67. *Id.*, 62 Wash. App. at 746, 815 P.2d at 833.

The court found that Brousseau was guilty of the "greater moral fault"[68] and should not be allowed to be unjustly enriched at Walsh's expense. The court affirmed the trial court's award to Walsh.

Thus, it becomes almost a game of "Russian roulette" to determine whether a contract of sale of a law practice will be held void and unenforceable. The court may come down on the side of public policy and leave the parties where they are, or it may find that one party (usually the purchaser) should not be unjustly enriched and enforce the illegal bargain nonetheless.

This is not an area where "ignorance is bliss," as Mrs. O'Hara, a nonlawyer, found out when she attempted to sell her husband's partnership interest in a Chicago law firm. Barratt O'Hara II had been a partner in his firm until his death in 1978. A few months later, his widow contracted with Ahlgren, Blumenfeld & Kempster to sell them the goodwill associated with her husband's name and to merge his law firm with theirs. Before the merger, she was to receive one third of the net income from her husband's past, current, and future clients and, after the merger, one quarter of the gross receipts (as defined) from her husband's business. The Ahlgren firm received the right to place her husband's name on their stationery and office door.

When the Ahlgren firm did not pay, O'Hara sued to recover the amounts due under the agreement. The defendants defended on the ground of unenforceability, and O'Hara raised the issue of estoppel. Regarding that issue, the court said:

> An exception to the estoppel theory arising in cases involving some illegal contracts is where the parties are not in pari delicto. In pari delicto is a legal principle that, in some situations, permits the less culpable of various parties to obtain relief from otherwise illegal or tortious transactions or occurrences like those involved in this case. There is case law that indicates a court could grant relief if the parties are not in pari delicto.[69]

The court said that in this case, the defendants raised the argument that the parties were in pari delicto because the plaintiff knowingly sold the goodwill of her husband:

---

68. *Id.*

69. O'Hara v. Ahlgren, Blumenfeld & Kempster, 127 Ill. 2d 333, 537 N.E.2d 730 (1989) (citations omitted).

> The only suggestion that the plaintiff was not in pari delicto with the defendants is that they were lawyers and drafted the agreement and received the benefits of it. That is not enough. There must be some pleading or evidence that plaintiff had no knowledge of the illegality and that the defendants did. Absent such evidence or pleading disclosing plaintiff's lack of knowledge of illegality and defendants' awareness of same, it would appear that the parties were in pari delicto.[70]

The court then held that because the contract was void as against public policy, the trial court should have left both parties where it found them. O'Hara was out of luck.

Is an Ouster a Forced Sale?

After a series of disagreements and confrontations of varying degrees of acrimony among the partners of Stewart, Wimer & Bump, P.C., Mr. Bump was informed by a handwritten message from his partners on September 8, 1976, that he ought to leave the firm. On October 1, 1976, one of Bump's partners wrote him a letter advising him that his position in the firm was terminated as of September 30, 1976. Although the other partners were willing to compensate Bump for his shares, an agreement on a value was never reached.

Bump claimed that because two of the lawyers in the firm, Hudson and Flynn, had never actually become shareholders, Bump was entitled to one third of the corporation's value. If the two were not shareholders, then on the date of termination Bump would have held one hundred shares out of three hundred; but if the other two were shareholders, Bump would have held one hundred shares out of four hundred. The testimony showed that at a February, 1976, shareholders' meeting, two of the three shareholders voted in favor of a motion to issue fifty shares each to Hudson and Flynn; Bump, the third shareholder, did not vote.

Bump made a number of allegations in support of his one-third interest claim. He said that formalities were overlooked in establishing Hudson and Flynn as shareholders: there were no corporate minutes on the stock issuance, the stock was not paid for until September, 1976, and the corporate name (to reflect the new ownership) was not changed until January, 1977, although the cor-

---

70. *Id.*

poration held itself out as having the new shareholders. However, the Martindale-Hubbell directory service was notified of the corporate change, and new signatories were authorized on bank accounts. Bump raised no objections to these events.

The trial court found that Hudson and Flynn were, in fact, shareholders and that Bump was entitled to a one-quarter interest in the firm. The court also refused to allow Bump any compensation for goodwill. He appealed.

The Iowa Supreme Court first decided that equity would regard substance over form. Ignoring the technicalities, Hudson and Flynn were, in fact, shareholders as of Bump's termination date and Bump was entitled to only a one-quarter interest in the firm.[71]

Concerning goodwill, the court noted that the Iowa Code provided that the purchase price of shares should be book value adjusted for work in process and accounts receivable; it said that goodwill was not mentioned. Although recognizing that goodwill is often included in valuation of a law practice in divorce settlements, the court said it was not proper to include goodwill in other contexts. It explained:

> The legal profession stands in a peculiar relation to the public and the relationship existing between the members of the profession and those who seek its services cannot be likened to the relationship of a merchant to his customer. Other courts have recognized that the attempted purchase of a law firm's goodwill includes the expectation of future patronage from former and current clients, but the attorney-client relationship is personal and confidential. Clients cannot be forced to accept the services of a particular attorney.[72]

The court also considered whether the other members of the corporation had tortiously interfered with Bump's employment agreement with the corporation. In deciding that Bump had no claim, the court noted there were no written or oral agreements in the nature of employment contracts between the lawyers and the firm and, "absent a contract, a valid claim of tortious interference with a contract cannot exist."[73] Because Bump's income from the firm had doubled following his separation, he would have had no

---

71. Bump v. Stewart, Wimer & Bump, P.C., 336 N.W.2d 731 (Iowa 1983).
72. *Id.* at 736 (citations omitted).
73. *Id.* at 737.

damage to claim, had there been a contract. "No claim for damage lies for relief predicated on the tort of contractual interference if damage is not generated."[74] And because the members of the firm would have been justified in terminating an employment contract, there was no tortious interference.[75]

Thus it is that Bump's ouster from Stewart, Wimer & Bump, a professional corporation, became a buyout of Bump's stock interest. The Iowa Supreme Court held that Bump was entitled to the value of his stock, computed in accordance with the Iowa statute (that is, with no goodwill) plus interest from the valuation date until paid.[76]

An Illinois lawyer, who withdrew from a professional corporation after differences with his fellow shareholder, did not fare as well. Walter Trittipo and Donald O'Brien formed a law partnership. Then, in 1972, they incorporated the firm, with O'Brien holding 62.5 percent of the stock and Trittipo the remaining 37.5 percent. Later, two other lawyers joined the firm, and each of the four members had a 25 percent interest. On May 1, 1976, Trittipo withdrew from the firm and tendered his shares, which were cancelled. He remained as a tenant in the office.

Over the next two years, the parties negotiated but were unable to agree on a value for Trittipo's shares. Therefore, in 1979, Trittipo filed a complaint seeking an accounting and an order for specific performance of the firm's obligation to pay him the fair value of his 25 percent interest.

The Illinois statute regulating professional corporations provided that

> [i]f the articles of incorporation, by-laws or separate agreement fail to state a price or method of determining a fixed price at which the corporation or its shareholders may purchase the shares of a deceased shareholder, or a shareholder no longer qualified to own shares in the corporation, then the price for such shares shall be the book value as of the end of the month immediately preceding the death or disqualification of the shareholder. Book value shall be determined from the books and records of the corporation in

74. *Id.* (citation omitted).
75. *Id.*
76. *Id.* at 731.

accordance with the accounting methods used by the corporation.[77]

The trial court entered judgment for Trittipo and the firm appealed. Trittipo's former fellow shareholders contended that the statute did not mandate a purchase from a shareholder who withdrew from the firm, as "disqualification" referred to loss of a license to practice. Trittipo argued that "disqualification" encompassed the voluntary termination of employment with the corporation because, he contended, one had to be a shareholder to practice law on behalf of the corporation.

The appellate court, in a long discussion of various aspects of the "disqualification" issue, rejected Trittipo's interpretation of the statute. Succinctly stated, the court said that a person needed to be only a lawyer—and not also a shareholder—to practice law with the corporation. Consequently, Trittipo did not become "disqualified" by virtue of his ceasing to be a shareholder. The court held that

> [i]n the instant case, there is nothing in the articles of incorporation, the bylaws or in a separate agreement among the parties for the redemption or purchase of the shares of a shareholder who is neither deceased nor disqualified by reason of the loss of his or her license. There being no such provision or agreement, the trial court was not empowered to impose an obligation, on the basis of "equitable principles," to compel the corporation or its remaining individual shareholders to purchase plaintiff's shares in the corporation upon the voluntary termination of his employment with the corporation.[78]

As for the oral agreement of the members to purchase Trittipo's shares, the court said that, without an understanding as to price, the agreement was illusory. Trittipo was left without relief.

Trittipo v. O'Brien carries the lesson of the importance, in a shareholders' agreement governing a professional corporation, to include a provision describing the circumstances under which the firm has an obligation to purchase the shares of a member who leaves the corporation, for whatever reason. That provision should spell out in detail the formula for computing the value of the member's shares for which he or she is to be paid.

---

77. Trittipo v. O'Brien, 204 Ill. App. 3d 662, 666, 561 N.E.2d 1201, 1204 (App. Ct. 1990).

78. *Id.* at 671, 561 N.E. 2d at 1206.

CHAPTER V

Retirement of Partners

When Are You Retired?

"Retirement" in the Modern Age

When most senior lawyers entered law practice, it was, genuinely, a profession. Law firms were not run by a committee or committees but by the partners, albeit sometimes by one or two partners who were martinets. But, more often than not, there was a sense of family in the firm. Once aboard, a lawyer stayed unless guilty of some material breach of ethics or discipline or clearly displayed incompetency. A few firms were training grounds for lawyers; in these offices, only a small percentage were expected to survive. The remainder received excellent tutelage for a few years and then went on to practice elsewhere.

It was rare for a law firm to raid another office and lure a rainmaker or a group of specialists. Each firm built its own cadre of experts. It was not cricket to invade another's "territory." Nor was it proper to sever one's partner from the partnership just because the fellow might have aged a bit and lost some of the spring in his step or, perhaps, seen some of his clients gone astray.

Many factors have contributed to the loss of professionalism in law practice. A whole generation of Americans has grown up with a significantly reduced respect for authority; consequently, senior partners and partners in general gain less respect than was true of their forebears. Greater economic pressures on families have driven younger lawyers to seek higher compensation, even when it has meant putting self-needs ahead of firm needs.

Clients also have themselves to blame for this loss of professionalism. Law firms are treated somewhat the same as "discount houses." Clients shop for lawyers in much the same fashion as they look for a new television set—price is the main thing, with service coming in second. The law firm's reputation, character, and personnel selection have diminished importance in the eyes of clients, who want only to get a desired result at the cheapest price.

As a result of all this, there have been dramatic changes in the legal profession. In essence, two groups of firms have tended to survive: the largest firms, which serve corporate clients able to afford significant legal bills, and the smallest firms, which provide a boutique service in a carefully carved-out niche of the law. Medium-sized law firms discovered they were unable to deliver an acceptable level of service to large clients, and were too expensive for smaller clients. Many found it necessary to merge with other medium-sized firms to achieve the size and breadth of coverage desired by large corporate clients. At the same time, many of the largest firms, subjected to the constant necessity of cutting costs to win bidding wars for business, were downsizing. This is a euphemism for firing lawyers, along with support staff.

Partners have not been immune in the restructuring process to date. There is no reason for partners to expect immunity in the future. In this chapter we will examine what happens to partners who are "downsized" or forced to "retire" from their firms. We will also consider steps that law firms and their partners can take to assure fair and equitable treatment of partners who are retiring or otherwise departing from their firms.

Apart from downsizing (and, after all, that by no means happens except in relatively few firms), there is no pattern of law firm behavior regarding retirement. Some partners simply never retire as partners; we all hear tales of lawyers who continue active in the management and operation of their firms well into their eighties. Other firms require partners to retire according to a rigid set of rules. There are still others that have no policy, and each partner decides for himself or herself when it is time to depart as a partner.

In a tax case involving Vinson & Elkins, one of the country's major law firms,[1] interesting expert testimony was presented con-

1. Vinson & Elkins v. Commissioner, 99 T.C. 9 (1992), *aff'd*, 7 F.3d 1235 (5th Cir. 1993).

cerning retirement trends among U.S. law firms. The expert was James Rabenhorst, managing partner of the national law firm consulting group at Price Waterhouse. Rabenhorst had been a partner there since 1976. He was also a member of the ABA Economics of Law Practice (now Law Practice Management) Section at the time he testified.[2] Concerning the trend among large law firms,

> Rabenhorst further explained that the trend toward earlier retirement in the general population was evident also among partners in large law firms and at [Vinson & Elkins] in particular. He based this conclusion on the changing retirement policies of large law firms. Based on his extensive experience dealing with large law firms, Rabenhorst determined that the firms were decreasing their normal retirement age and establishing early retirement policies to encourage their partners to retire by age 62 or younger. Rabenhorst attributed this trend to several factors which have led to the changing nature of the practice of law. One significant factor was the ever-increasing number of lawyers. For example, he noted, "From the mid-1970s to the early 1980s, the population of lawyers in the United States increased by more than 25,000 lawyers per year." This growth has increased the competitiveness of practicing law and placed greater pressure on lawyers to be more productive and more profitable. Rabenhorst determined that because of the increase in competition in the legal profession, firms were forced to become more formalized and to operate more like traditional businesses, pushing issues such as retirement to the forefront. In addition, he explained that the increased use of sophisticated economic analysis enabled firms to measure the productivity of partners. According to Rabenhorst, "This new emphasis on management often exposed unproductive older partners and put pressure on firms to devise ways of dealing with them."
>
> Moreover, Rabenhorst cited an increasing disenchantment among older partners. He noted that most of these older partners had anticipated a decrease in their workload later in their lives; however, instead, they were pressured to continue to produce at high levels because firms felt they could no longer pay high salaries to older partners who were not producing at the same level as younger lawyers. Rabenhorst

---

2. *Id.* at 21.

> determined that older partners were increasingly faced with pressures to make room for the younger partners. He concluded that all of these pressures led to the desire on the part of both the firms and the older partners for provision for earlier retirement. Finally, he determined that, due to the increased earnings levels of large law firms, partners were financially able to establish retirement plans that would provide sufficient income for earlier retirement. Based on his analysis of the trend toward earlier retirement, Rabenhorst concluded that the retirement age assumption of 62 for the [Vinson & Elkins individual defined benefit plans] was reasonable.[3]

We must recognize that small and medium-sized law firms may not have the luxury of financial ability to fund adequate retirement packages for their older partners; nonetheless the same pressures on older lawyers exist in these firms as in the large law firms. The problem of how and when to retire older partners exists in these firms as well.

Should a Lawyer Be Forced to Retire?

There are many arguments in favor of forced retirement of lawyers.

There is no gainsaying that most humans deteriorate physically and mentally with age. Although many people retain their mental acumen into advanced years, others lose their sharpness or their ability for any cognitive work; mental disability is common in older society. The loss of mental ability in a lawyer is disastrous for a client. It is vital for the profession that clients receive advice from only competent advisors. If lawyers are not required to retire at a particular point in life, then other persons, in or out of the legal profession, must make a judgment in each case about whether a particular lawyer is no longer qualified to practice. In a firm where collegiality is important, few are willing to tell a colleague that he or she is no longer competent. If there is a rule that everyone must retire at a particular age, the unpleasant decision need never be reached.

In some situations, older lawyers continue to be successful rainmakers. Retirement for them would be a decided financial disadvantage, both to them personally and to their firms. On the other hand, circumstances may result in the loss of an older lawyer's

---

3. *Id.* at 43.

client base. For example, the lawyer who has been counselor to corporations, and who relied on corporate general counsel for business, may discover that as general counsel mature, they either retire or move into management positions. They are replaced by younger lawyers who prefer to award legal business to their own contemporaries. In this situation, the corporate client has abandoned the older lawyer, and the law firm can no longer afford to carry the senior lawyer; either he must retire voluntarily or be forced out of the firm. Again, if there is a mandatory retirement age, this difficult decision can be avoided.

Adoption of a mandatory retirement age also has its negatives.

First, there is the loss of wisdom. Once an experienced lawyer is no longer practicing with a firm, the firm can no longer point to that individual as having expertise in his or her area of practice. If several lawyers in a particular practice area happen to reach a mandatory retirement age simultaneously, it can turn out to be a crippling blow to the firm. I am aware of one firm, in line to secure a substantial amount of mass tort defense business, when the firm discovered that the only two partners in its trial department who had a background in that area of work had both retired. To avoid catastrophe, if a mandatory retirement policy has been adopted, it may be desirable to assure that the retirees are, at minimum, available on some reasonable basis for consultation with active lawyers in the firm. Should it be necessary to have the retirees consult with clients or potential clients, the firm should assure that the retiree involved is covered by the firm's malpractice insurance; often such coverage is dropped for retirees upon retirement.

Another negative in a mandatory retirement policy is loss of continuity with long-term and valued clients, particularly if such clients tend to keep their executive group intact despite their advancing years. Just as in the situation when older and retiring general counsel are replaced by younger people with their own cadre of legal advisors, so in the case of the company whose older chief executive controls the legal business, it is the proper contact with the company, kept or lost, that is important. In the latter case, it is the senior lawyer's relationship with the older chief executive that assures the legal business. Adopt a mandatory retirement policy and the senior lawyer is gone—and so is the legal business that he or she maintained for the firm.

The firm that contemplates a mandatory retirement policy must review its client base against the lawyers responsible for keeping it and, well ahead of the retirement dates of those lawyers, start to introduce other partners into the client relationship. Bear in mind, it is the client who chooses the partner to handle the client's affairs—it is not the firm's prerogative to decide who shall advise the client. Therefore, the client must be induced to choose to remain with the partner or partners who the law firm wants to work on the client's matters.

Arrangements upon Retirement

Just as opinions vary about the desirability of forced retirement, so are there many possible arrangements that can be, and have been, made between the retiring lawyer and the law firm.

Probably the most common arrangement is for a gradual reduction in compensation of the lawyer approaching retirement. In the usual situation, the reduction commences at age sixty-five, with a reduction of 20 percent each year through age sixty-nine. Using this formula, in the fifth year the partner would earn 32.77 percent of his or her partnership share at age sixty-five. At age seventy, the lawyer must retire from the partnership. There appears to be no common method for fixing the lawyer's compensation thereafter. In some firms it is a matter of negotiation with the retiree; in others, the partnership agreement establishes a formula for calculating the retiree's compensation. The formula may call for payment of a percentage of average partner income, or of the income of some particular class or group of partners. When the retired partner contributes services to the firm or its clients, compensation after retirement may be tied to the amount of work performed. The firm must be careful to relate the payments to work accomplished and not to the rainmaking aspect of the retiree's contribution; otherwise, the firm and the retiree may both be guilty of fee-splitting, which is barred in many states.

In addition to compensation, most firms provide retired partners with office space (albeit reduced in size from the amount allotted to active partners) and secretarial and other office services.

There is one fillip in the "compensation-after-retirement" picture that must be kept in mind. Many firms do not want retired partners to continue practicing law or soliciting clients. However, as we have observed from the discussion of forfeiture-for-competition clauses in Chapter III, Rule 2-108 of the Model Rules of Professional Responsibility does not permit a firm to place restrictions on the law practice of any lawyer leaving a firm, except when the firm pays the lawyer a retirement benefit. We will discuss this subject at some greater length later in this chapter. It is not clear whether the mere provision of secretarial assistance, office space, and services is sufficient to allow the restrictions or whether the rule requires some specific periodic cash payment in lieu of, or in addition to, the other benefits.

Many firms, usually those with long tenure and of substantial size, provide retiring partners with pension benefits. Most often, these payments are a matter of contract between the partner and the firm, rather than pursuant to a formal pension plan. Lawyers who are firm founders and have long tenure generally are the beneficiaries under these plans. Younger partners usually are not entitled to such payments.

The firm's pension benefit payments supplement Keogh plans, which most firms have adopted. These became available when Congress adopted the Keogh legislation in the mid-1970s. In recent years, the formula under the Keogh regulatory scheme permitted a lawyer with sufficient income to set aside approximately $30,000 before income tax, contributing the amount to an account in which income would be exempt from income taxes until withdrawn. The principal of a Keogh account must be withdrawn in an amount calculated by formula, and taxes paid on the withdrawal, commencing the year after the taxpayer reaches age seventy and a half.

Most firms distribute the amount in the partner's "capital account" to the partner upon his or her leaving the firm. The amount of the payment depends, of course, on the size of the account and whether the firm distributes the amount as a lump sum or in installments. In the latter instance, the installments are generally paid over no more than five years, commencing in the first year after retirement.

Retired partners thus have various sources of "unearned" income: social security, the family's personal investment portfolio, the Keogh Plan, and, in some instances, supplemental payments from the law firm.

Disaster—Reasons for the Casualties

In the late 1970s and early 1980s, the booming economy generated substantial work for the larger law firms. As business increased, corporations required additional funds, and lawyers who counseled lenders and borrowers (those who represented the seekers of equity money from the public), and lawyers for vendors of the myriad of products required for expansion, all benefited. Law firms measured their success by their size. Associates were hired from mushrooming numbers of law school graduates and, in some cases, "raiders" proselytized partners in the competition. Then, the bubble broke.

With an economy heading downward and with the decline in acceptance of the "junk bond," the trend toward business combination slowed to a trickle. Many firms with large merger-and-acquisition departments found they had over-hired and were over-partnered. At the same time, general counsel of corporations were receiving approval for expansion of law departments and, as a means of cutting costs, there was a resultant shift away from "outside counsel." Other departments of law firms also saw a loss of business. All of this caused the downsizing of the law firm to be perceived as a method of survival. Many partners and associates alike were terminated. It was euphemistically called "restructuring the firm."

It is possible to restructure a law firm gracefully. Longtime partners can be treated with deference and given the opportunity to leave the firm with dignity and an opportunity to remain active, should that be their choice. This may require a sacrifice on the part of the partners who will remain in the restructured firm, but, in the long run, the sacrifice is worth it; there will be a perception in the marketplace that the firm's remaining partners are honorable people. Most firms believe it is good business to be thought of as a "class act."

Unfortunately, many law firms have restructured inartistically. Partners have been unceremoniously evicted from their offices, with no severance or supplemental retirement benefits provided, and there has been inadequate compensation for work performed before their ousters. The restructuring has been peremptorily accomplished with associates and support staff. The result is that the firms that have conducted themselves in this manner are held in low esteem by their colleagues and have lost reputation in the marketplace.

The Finley, Kumble Disaster

When professionalism is lost and a sense of fraternity leaves a law firm, disaster can strike, and has struck, even the megafirm. Read with dismay the account by Steven Kumble and Kevin Lahart of "the rise and ruin of Finley, Kumble" in their book, *Conduct Unbecoming.*[4]

---

4. STEVEN J. KUMBLE & KEVIN J. LAHART, CONDUCT UNBECOMING: THE RISE AND RUIN OF FINLEY, KUMBLE (1990). At its zenith, the full name of the firm was Finley, Kumble, Heine, Underberg, Manley, Myerson & Casey. Among its partners were former Senators Joseph Tydings, Russell Long, and Paul Laxalt, former New York Governor Hugh Carey, and former Mayor of New York, William O'Dwyer.

The firm had been founded in 1968 through a merger in New York of two relatively small firms, Amen, Weisman & Butler and Finley & Gore. In less than twenty years, it had grown to a colossus of 240 partners, 450 associates, and 2,000 employees in sixteen cities. According to Kumble and Lahart, as more and more power was acquired by fewer and fewer partners, greater credit was given through compensation to rainmakers than to the working lawyers, gaps between partner distributions grew wider (allegedly, some partners received seventeen times the draw of other partners), and individuals stopped thinking of what was best for the firm and began thinking only of what was in their own interests. The firm management brought in well-known names as partners, assuring them of high earnings. When the revenues (and earnings) to provide the distributions did not materialize, the partners at the top chose to validate their promises to the new partners by paying their distributions in part from capital contributions from other partners. Funds for the capital contributions were, of course, borrowed by those other partners, and their loans were guaranteed by the firm. Once the borrowings got out of hand, and the banks began to wonder how they would be repaid, things for Finley, Kumble began to fall apart rapidly. The banks froze the firm's credit line and would not relieve it of the guarantee of partners' borrowings. With fee collections insufficient to meet the firm's obligations to creditors and for partner distributions, the firm filed for reorganization under Chapter 7 of the Bankruptcy Act in February, 1988.

These events were the result—not the cause—of the firm's undoing. *Conduct Unbecoming* tells many sad tales of lawyers' mistrust of one another, of fighting for an unfair advantage, of keeping for themselves advantages that properly belonged to the firm. Even though their understandings had been reduced to writing and partnership agreements were in place, these writings could not make up for the loss of respect and lack of admiration and confidence of one partner for another.

As one reads the sad account written by Kumble and Lahart, it becomes clear that the most unfortunate partners were not those among the group that had managed to obtain extremely high compensation by their machinations, but rather the pedestrian group of middle-rank and junior partners whose borrowings had allowed these payments. When the firm broke apart, these mid-rank and junior partners were cast adrift and had to reshape their careers, in addition to satisfying their obligations in the firm's bankruptcy reorganization. From the account in *Conduct Unbecoming,* it would appear that some 220–30 of the firm's 270 partners were responsible for a contribution to creditors of over $20 million, or an average of about $100,000 per partner—no mean sum.[5]

In the story of the rise and fall of Finley, Kumble, the authors' portrayal of one of the firm's partners, Harvey Myerson, as being a major contributor to its demise stands out. In *Conduct Unbecoming,* there are at least three pages of material describing Myerson in what are, at best, uncomplimentary terms. One wonders how a law firm could function with such "bad blood" among its partners. And one speculates about whether any partner could be as difficult as Myerson is portrayed to be.

After Finley, Kumble broke apart, Myerson and Bowie Kuhn, former Commissioner of Baseball, formed Myerson & Kuhn. For reasons alleged by Kumble and Lahart in *Conduct Unbecoming,* Myerson & Kuhn lasted just under two years. Myerson & Kuhn filed for protection from creditors under Chapter 11 of the Bankruptcy Act in December, 1989. Myerson was subsequently charged criminally in a multicount indictment, including three counts of defrauding clients by overbilling them. His conviction in federal court was affirmed by the Second Circuit Court of Appeals.[6]

The experience of the lawyers in these two firms strongly suggests that to have assurance that a firm will endure the vicissitudes of law practice, one must choose one's partners with great care and for the right reasons, particularly if, as a partner, you want to avoid being sued, protect yourself against liability, and provide a foundation for a peaceful retirement. Strength of character, mutual respect for that character and legal ability in a partner, and the loyalty to other partners that results, are the best reasons—perhaps the only reasons—for choosing a law partner.

Planning Ahead

Even though your law firm is moving along smoothly, with little prospect for the loss of any significant client or clients, there is always the possibility that fortunes will change. There may be a loss of business through no fault of the firm; a valuable client may fall victim to a hostile takeover or a rainmaker partner in good health may suddenly die. The financial impact upon the firm in any such scenario is severe. Yet, the confusion and fear the event may generate can be avoided.

---

5. *Id.* at 281–82.

6. United States v. Harvey Myerson, 18 F.3d 153 (2d Cir.), *cert. denied,* 115 S. Ct. 159 (1994).

The best place to provide for such an eventuality is in the partnership agreement. It should deal, separately, with the issue of the living partner who withdraws at the request of the firm and of the deceased partner to whose estate the firm must also make some payment.

Involuntary Withdrawal

We discussed some aspects of expulsion of a partner in Chapter IV, in connection with problems of firm dissolution. There are times when a partnership will decide that one of its members—unwilling though he or she may be—must be forced to retire. It must be recognized too that the decision may be less than unanimous. Some partners may oppose turning one of their own out. The firm needs to have a mechanism to deal honorably with the situation.

Consequently, one of the major problems that must be addressed in the partnership agreement is the procedure to be followed by the partnership if the question of the ouster of a particular partner is raised. There will be enormous difficulties and a great possibility that bad feelings will be generated should the firm wait until it is confronted with an ouster situation before taking steps to deal with it. Rather than already having a procedure with broad applicability, the firm will wind up with one tailored to the specific problem confronting it; the solution may not be desirable when applied to other problems that may arise subsequently.

One thing seems to me to be quite clear. The criteria for ouster of a partner should be no less strict than those established for election of a partner in that class. For example, most firms require more than a majority vote—at times a two-thirds, three-quarters, or even 90 percent vote—to elect a person to partnership. The partnership agreement should provide that if a partner is to be removed, the same vote of the partnership is required as that for his or her election. To do otherwise may possibly allow a cadre of dissident partners to lead the firm toward a decision it will later regret. In a matter as serious as removal of a partner, there should be a consensus of the entire partnership, with allowance for only a small minority.

Valuation Schemes

Whether a partner is leaving the firm by way of ouster or through normal retirement, the firm must value the departing partner's interest in the firm and pay that amount to him or her.

The first, and basic, sum that must be paid is the balance standing to his or her credit in the capital account. Again, because of the very substantial differences in the way various law firms treat capital infusion, the amount of capital to be returned in particular cases will differ. Occasionally, a firm will find that a partner has a negative capital account. In a Connecticut case,[7] a partner withdrew from the firm (although he did not retire) with a negative capital account of almost $47,000. Despite demands from his former firm, he refused to pay the balance. The firm sued. The court found for the firm on grounds of unjust enrichment.[8]

Apart from the capital account, a retiring partner may have an additional interest in the firm. Depending on the manner of accounting adopted by the firm, the partner may have a percentage interest in its fixed assets and intangible assets (such as a valuable leasehold) not entirely represented by his or her capital account. There are many schemes for valuing that interest, one of which may include defining it as goodwill. Every so often, a firm considers that a partnership interest has goodwill and attempts a valuation on that basis.

As we have seen from the discussion of goodwill in Chapters I and IV, except in the context of a divorce, courts rarely will place a value on the goodwill of a law firm. This is a sensible rule (although the exception for the divorce situation makes little sense). Goodwill is really the value attributable to the likelihood that the firm's clients will return with additional business. Clients, even corporate clients, usually relate to one or several partners in a law firm. When a partner leaves the firm, the client must do some soul-searching to determine whether to move the legal business elsewhere. Neither the law firm as an institution, nor an individual partner, controls the client. In this state of affairs, the partner in the selling firm really has no goodwill to sell.

Another possible formula for determining the value of a departing partner's interest is to calculate the amount of annual savings to the firm by elimination of the partner; after all, the remaining partners will no longer have to compensate the withdrawing partner, there will be one less name on the list of lawyers for which a malpractice premium must be paid, there will no longer be a need

---

7. Moran, Shuster, Carignan & Knierim v. August, 43 Conn. Supp. 431, 657 A.2d 736 (Super. Ct. 1994).

8. The firm had also sought additional damages on the ground that the former partner had violated the Connecticut Unfair Trade Practices Act. The court found that the internal dispute of the partners did not amount to a controversy in "trade or commerce" as the act required for applicability.

to provide for services from support staff, and the departure of the lawyer will cause some reduction in other overhead costs. All of these savings can be aggregated. They then need to be offset by the revenues produced by the lawyer to determine the net savings to the firm. This calculation must be performed with care. Revenues that are controlled by other partners and remain with the firm do not offset savings, while revenues that are controlled by, and will leave with, the departing partner are such an offset. This may seem like a non sequitur because such a payment calculation results in a larger payment to the lawyer without his or her own client base and a smaller payment to the lawyer who has clients who will no longer retain the firm when the lawyer departs. However, it parallels the economic effect of the change in the partnership.

Then there are also some severance payments that bear no relation to revenues retained or cost savings. The departing partner, particularly one with long service with the firm, may receive a payment that reflects that longevity. The payment is in the nature of a reward for past performance and a generous thank you from the partners who remain. The payment may be in an amount equal to the departing partner's draw for anywhere from six months to several years. Needless to say, for such a payment to be made, the parting must be amicable; any hostility between the firm and the departing partner will negate any suggestion of a generous severance.

Determining the Amount of the Payment

When a partner leaves due to forced retirement or voluntary withdrawal, some person or group must determine the amount of the payment to the partner. The partnership agreement, properly drawn, will make two provisions. First, it will establish the criteria for a severance payment, and second, it will describe the procedure the partnership will follow in determining the amount.

As noted in the preceding discussion, there are several basic methods of providing for a payment: one relates it to goodwill, which seems unjustified for a law firm, another calculates it on the basis of costs saved and revenues enhanced, and yet another views it in the manner of a gift.

Return of Capital

When a partner leaves a firm, voluntarily or involuntarily, he or she is entitled to return of capital. In some firms, partners contribute very little capital. If it is an "old line" firm, the original start-up capital will have dropped in value in today's dollars due to the sheer impact of inflation. This means that the burden on the firm to return capital to retiring partners is not great. However, other firms require a very substantial capital contribution from partners. This is particularly true of those offices that expanded rapidly during the 1980s and did not have the business on the books to support the required expenditures; the funds had to come from the lawyers who were partners at the time, or from borrowings. These partners, when they retire, will have the right to the return of significant amounts of money. Under these circumstances, the firm may be unable to repay the capital in a single payment. The return will have to be made in installments, over time; a five-year payout seems to have been accepted by some firms as reasonable.

Have You Retired?

There is no simple rule one can apply to determine whether a lawyer has retired. Some lawyers who thought they were "retired," and filed tax returns accordingly, were shocked when the Internal Revenue Service (IRS) took a different view.

There is Nicholas Sloan, a computer analyst with the federal government in Washington, who earned a law degree and wanted to establish a law practice once he retired from government service. Sloan was a veteran of the Korean conflict who held a doctorate in electrical engineering. He taught at George Washington University, entered its law school, and received a law degree in 1977. He then went to work with the U.S. Department of Justice, not as a lawyer, but as a computer systems analyst. He planned to take early retirement from the government in 1981 and set up his own law practice.

In the late 1970s, while working in the Justice Department, Sloan accepted a variety of cases to gain some experience. He assisted clients in matrimonial matters, prepared wills, and handled medicaid and workers' compensation claims. He charged his clients very little or nothing at all. The few records he kept indicated that he spent a high number of hours on a matter for which he charged the client the barest of fees.

In a more committed effort to establish himself, he purchased a house in Chestertown on the eastern shore of Maryland. Because he was working with the government during the week, his wife looked after his mail and answered the telephone. Sloan, who maintained his primary residence in a Washington, D.C., suburb, visited Chestertown on the weekends.

The IRS determined a deficiency of over $11,000, plus a penalty, in Mr. and Mrs. Sloan's tax return for 1981. They filed a petition for relief and the matter reached the U.S. Tax Court. The court reached its decision in 1988.[9]

The court observed that Sloan based his fees on estimates of the time he worked on a case. He carried no malpractice insurance in 1981. He spent $480 in 1981 on bar dues and publications, but did not subscribe to publications that related particularly to the kinds of cases he was handling, and he attended no bar association functions related to those cases. The Sloans purchased a houseboat in 1980 and, in 1981, Mr. Sloan used that boat for his office; he met half a dozen people on the houseboat in connection with his practice. He also used the boat for recreational purposes.

In their tax return for 1981, the Sloans deducted expenses in connection with the houseboat, the cost of publication subscriptions, and legal education courses for Sloan. The Sloans reported gross receipts of $640 from Sloan's practice. However, they reported losses for 1979 through 1983.

When the commissioner determined the deficiency for 1981, it was on the ground that the losses claimed by the Sloans were not incurred in furtherance of any trade or business. The tax court agreed. First, it said that Sloan

> did not conduct his law practice in a businesslike manner. Despite working long hours on cases, he rarely charged his clients for his services. Mr. Sloan failed to keep detailed records of the time that he spent performing legal services. On those few occasions that he did bill clients, he based his fees upon estimate [sic] of the time he worked on each case. Moreover, he charged extremely low fees for his efforts. He testified that on two instances, he charged clients a fixed amount, which worked out to a fee of less than $2 per hour.[10]

The first lesson in protecting your tax position is: Keep accurate records and do not give away your services. Says the IRS: "Sock it to those clients!"

Sloan conceded that his job at the U.S. Department of Justice provided his primary source of income. He indicated that from his

9. Sloan v. Commissioner, 1988 Tax Ct. Memo LEXIS 324, 55 T.C.M. (CCH) No. 1988-294, ¶ 880294, at 1238 (1988).

10. *Id.*, 1988 Tax Ct. Memo LEXIS 324, at *11.

activities in 1981, he wanted to gain legal experience that would be useful when he practiced in earnest after retirement. Said the court:

> Such an intention shows that he was not so much interested in current gain from his practice as he was in attempting to build a foundation for a practice which he hoped to establish in the future. In our judgment, it also indicates that Mr. Sloan did not engage in the practice of law with the primary purpose of earning a profit.[11]

Lesson number two is that you do not get a deduction for amounts spent in anticipation of a "second career." Unless you are already in it, your deductions are at risk.

Regarding Sloan's attempt to establish a law practice in Chestertown, Maryland, the court noted that he was in Chestertown only on weekends when the courts were not in session and that he and his wife did not socialize with members of the community,

> the very individuals who might have hired Mr. Sloan to represent them. In our view, such actions show that he failed to make a serious effort to establish a practice in Chestertown during 1981. In addition, such conduct also indicates that Mr. Sloan was not involved in his law practice with "continuity and regularity."[12]

Another lesson from the IRS. If you want to demonstrate a good faith effort to earn a profit (and earn those deductions), work at it "full time" and show some endeavor in the marketing area. Do not ignore your most obvious potential clients.

Summing up, the Tax Court opined:

> Because we hold that Mr. Sloan did not conduct his legal activities with the primary purpose of earning a profit and was not involved in such activities with continuity and regularity, we conclude that Mr. Sloan's activities in connection with his law practice did not rise to the level of a trade or business. For such reason, the petitioners are not entitled to the deductions claimed by them with respect to such practice.[13]

---

11. *Id.* at *12 (citations omitted).
12. *Id.* at *14 (citation omitted).
13. *Id.*

But there is some solace from the decision. The Tax Court held that because the Sloans had no net earnings from Mr. Sloan's law practice, he did not owe any self-employment tax.

The IRS does not single out for attention taxpayers looking for a second career in the law. Instead, it seems to keep an eye out for lawyers looking for a second career elsewhere. Consider the case of Lew Warden and his spouse, Nadja Warden. Lew Warden, a lawyer, had been a sole practitioner in California for over twenty years when, in 1974, he and his wife acquired from a client, Julius Kahn, a one-sixth interest in an abandoned tennis and swim club. In efforts to partition the property, extensive litigation ensued, with the final result being a sale of the property. The lawsuits were concluded in 1989. The Wardens received payments aggregating over $350,000. They treated half of the property as a business use, and half as residential use, on their 1989 tax return. They then rolled over $85,000 of the business portion of the sale proceeds into a yacht, which they had previously purchased in 1986.

The yacht, christened "Rocking Chair," turned out to be a disaster for the Wardens. When they bought it, Mr. Warden was sixty-six years old, and looking forward to retiring to a warmer climate. He was dissatisfied with his law practice and had decided he and his wife could earn a living from chartering the boat. Mr. Warden was an experienced sailor, had worked as a seaman in his youth, and had been an Air Force navigator and pilot. While practicing law, he and his wife had enjoyed cruising and yacht racing as a diversion in the San Francisco Bay Area and offshore.

Nonetheless, Rocking Chair had numerous major problems after its delivery from its Taiwan builder. The Wardens sued the builder and its agent and won judgments against various parties for substantial amounts, the largest being over $200,000.

Rocking Chair was chartered on only a few occasions despite advertisements in several publications. The Wardens then attempted to sell the yacht between 1989 and 1992, but did not succeed. In the years 1987 through 1992, the Wardens claimed losses in a range of $45,000 to over $81,000 from their chartering activities. In most of these same years, Mr. Warden reported net earnings from law practice, although in 1992 the Wardens showed a zero net income. The IRS disallowed the loss from the yacht claimed by the Wardens for 1989. The case reached the Tax Court. In its opinion,[14] the court said:

---

14. Warden v. Commissioner, 1995 Tax Ct. Memo LEXIS 170, 69 T.C.M. (CCH) No. 1995-176, at 2432 (1995).

> We must first decide whether petitioners' ownership and operation of Rocking Chair were activities that were "not engaged in for profit" within the meaning of section 183(c). Section 183(a) provides generally that if an activity is not engaged in for profit, no deduction attributable to such activity shall be allowed.[15]

The court then reviewed each of the various factors that contribute to that determination. First is the manner in which a taxpayer carries on the activity. The court noted that the Wardens opened a separate bank account for Rocking Chair, although expenses were not always paid from that account. They obtained a business tax declaration, obtained a seller's permit, filed sales and use tax returns, obtained an employer identification number, obtained additional insurance, maintained a telephone on the yacht, advertised the yacht's availability, and attempted to sell the yacht. However, they had no written business plan, nor did they attempt to verify the chartering income forecasts or the income's sufficiency to cover expenses that were made by the yacht builder's agent. The Wardens made no showing that they used data from their records to try to improve the profitability of the operation.

Second is the expertise of the taxpayer or his or her advisers. No evidence showed the specific nature of the information Warden obtained from talking with others in the boating fraternity or from studying yachting magazines.

Third is the time and effort spent by the taxpayer in carrying on the activity. The court said that the time spent by the Wardens in cleaning and maintaining Rocking Chair was consistent with use of the yacht for recreation.

Fourth is the taxpayer's expectation that the assets used in the activity would appreciate. In this case, the Wardens offered no evidence about what they anticipated.

Fifth is the taxpayer's success with other similar activities. The Wardens had no "track record" in this respect.

Sixth is the historical record of income and losses and any occasional profits. The court observed:

> A record of substantial losses over many years and the unlikelihood of achieving a profitable operation are important factors bearing on the taxpayer's intention. The presence of such

15. *Id.*, 1995 Tax Ct. Memo LEXIS 170 at *15.

> losses in the formative years of a business is not inconsistent with an intent to achieve a later profitable level of operation; however, the goal must be to realize a profit on the entire operation, which presupposes sufficient future net earnings from the activity to recoup the losses. In the present case, petitioners reported losses over six years of operation totaling $370,377.[16]

Next is the financial status of the taxpayer. In 1986, when the Wardens purchased Rocking Chair, they had a net worth of $1,027,000. Mr. Warden's law practice and some securities supplied income while the Wardens wrestled with the Rocking Chair problems. The court noted that the Wardens "did obtain a tax benefit from the losses generated by the chartering activities."[17]

Finally, the Tax Court considered the presence of elements of personal pleasure or recreation:

> Mr. Warden was no longer happy in his practice of law, and he was at an age where he was ready to retire. Petitioners wanted to live in a more pleasant, recreational setting. They clearly enjoyed sailing and had engaged in sailing activities for recreation for at least 20 years prior to purchasing Rocking Chair. The yacht was custom built and was equipped with all the amenities. Beginning in 1988, Mr. Warden lived on the yacht and used it as his residence. Petitioners admittedly used Rocking Chair for activities unrelated to chartering, but did not document these trips in their operating log. Petitioners' documented trips on Rocking Chair were to locations such as Sacramento, Santa Cruz, Monterey, Santa Barbara, Newport, Ventura, San Diego and Ensenada, Mexico. Petitioners often stayed for extended periods of time at these locations.[18]

The Tax Court said that to prevail, the Wardens must show their activities with Rocking Chair were primarily to make a profit. The court said it was not enough that the Wardens had profit as one objective of their activity. Moreover, the court said when the Wardens purchased the yacht Mr. Warden was still generating income from his law practice, and the purchase of the boat had a recreational element. Moreover, the Wardens were ready to retire

---

16. *Id.* at *22 (citations omitted).
17. *Id.* at *23.
18. *Id.* at *23–24.

and wanted to live in a pleasant recreational setting. Said the court, "these factors strongly indicate a personal objective."[19]

The court said when the taxpayer has both a personal and profit objective in an activity, a court must decide which activity is "primary." Based on the entire record, the court was not "convinced that the petitioners' primary objective was to make a profit."[20] Consequently, the deduction of the loss associated with the yacht would have to be limited (in accordance with section 183 of the Internal Revenue Code) to an amount equal to the gross income of the activity.[21]

Perhaps you are a lawyer anticipating retirement and you are eager to conduct, after retirement, some professional or business activity that has long been your dream. If your objective is to engage in a profitable enterprise, but you foresee a period of buildup before the business turns the corner, stop and review your income tax picture. Should you be counting on losses from your new activity to cushion the income tax burden on your other earnings, you might first consult the tax experts in your law firm. Hopefully, they will be able to supply the answer to the question about what you should do, in light of cases like *Sloan* and *Warden,* to protect your position.

Have you "retired" when your postretirement activities are such that one does not need to be a licensed lawyer to perform them? Maybe so, but maybe not—if they are activities lawyers sometimes undertake. This was the situation confronting Robert Mahoney, an Iowa lawyer.[22]

Mahoney was a partner in a seven-person law firm. He had practiced some thirty-three years and was fifty-eight years old. When he failed to turn over some estate assets to a successor, he was disciplined by the state bar and his license was suspended. Before his license was to be reinstated, he withdrew from his law firm. In his probation report, he formally advised the disciplinary committee that he had retired from the general practice of law, and that the firm name had been changed. Mr. Mahoney's partners

---

19. *Id.* at *25.

20. *Id.* at *26.

21. The Tax Court made certain other rulings regarding the "carry-forward" of the loss related to the sale of the real property. These rulings are only tangentially related to the discussion in this chapter.

22. Comm. on Prof. Ethics & Conduct of the Iowa State Bar Ass'n v. Mahoney, 402 N.W.2d 434 (Iowa 1987).

agreed to give him a pension, under the terms of which he was not to compete with the firm in the practice of law, but could perform tax work and labor negotiation work.

Mahoney formed a corporation, called ConsulCorp. From its office, he drafted tax returns and acted as a labor negotiator. He also obtained a real estate license. In addition, he rendered business and investment advice, and prepared real estate documents, some contracts, and one will. He appeared in court on a pro bono basis. He obtained the necessary continuing legal education and maintained the client security fund necessary to keep his law license current.

The state bar's Committee on Professional Ethics & Conduct brought a proceeding against Mahoney, particularly on the ground that his formal announcement of retirement from the practice of law was misleading. In upholding the committee's recommendation for further disciplinary action against Mahoney, the court rejected Mahoney's contention that he was no longer in the general practice of law:

> [Mahoney] did not terminate his status as a practicing lawyer when he changed offices. Doing tax preparation and labor negotiation is not necessarily the practice of law and properly may be done by nonlawyers. When these tasks are done by a licensed lawyer, however, they constitute the practice of law. In *Committee on Professional Ethics & Conduct v. Toomey,* 236 N.W.2d 39 (Iowa 1975), we delineated activities that are considered to be the practice of law and in which a suspended lawyer may not engage as including but not limited to the examination of abstracts, consummation of real estate transactions, preparation of deeds, buy and sell agreements, contracts, wills and tax returns as well as any court appearance or counseling clients with regard to the same.[23]

The court held that Mahoney's statement to the committee was misleading and it suspended him for six months.

As noted in the discussion of forfeiture-for-competition clauses, it often happens that retired partners receiving pensions from their law firms are restricted from law practice. Many such practitioners elect to do things merely related to the general practice of law. The case involving Mahoney is a warning. Make sure that what you do is not a violation of the restriction in your state.

---

23. *Id.* at 436.

Many retired lawyers become involved in serving as arbitrators and mediators. Because an arbitrator is not required to be a lawyer—virtually anyone can serve as an arbitrator—that activity is usually thought not to constitute law practice. Yet, the language used by the Iowa Supreme Court in *Mahoney* ("When these tasks are done by a licensed lawyer, however, they constitute the practice of law") must give pause. When this conclusion applies, there is also the question of the need for malpractice insurance. If the activity constitutes the practice of law, the lawyer engaging in it is at risk and needs protection.

It is important to know whether you are "retired." As observed in the *Bane* case, discussed in Chapter I, your partners have no fiduciary duty to you once you retire. If they fail to pay you a pension as agreed, it may be a breach of contract but it is not a breach of fiduciary duty. Furthermore, as Bane found out, the partners have no obligation to forego a dissolution of the firm to pay a pension.

For the partner who wants to retire and receive a benefit from his former law firm, it is important to know that he or she has actually retired. For the law firm planning to impose a legitimate restriction on the retired partner's ability to continue law practice, it is vital to assure that the partner is, in fact, retired. If a payment is structured in a way that it is characterized as a payment for his or her law practice, in all but a few states it will be illegal. As seen in the discussion of forfeiture-for-competition clauses in Chapter III, they are legal in most states only when coupled with payment of a retirement benefit.

The Retired Partner's Name

As a continuing partner in a law firm, you have a special interest in the use of your former partner's name after he or she retires. If it has a value in the marketing of your firm's professional services, the firm must be careful about the structure of agreement concerning its use after the partner retires. Even though the retired partner may not continue to practice law, the firm nevertheless may continue to use his or her name as part of the firm name—provided the firm obtained the retiring partner's consent. When payment to the retired partner for such consent is proposed, the firm should assure itself that there is no prohibition against payments for the goodwill of a professional practitioner in that jurisdiction. The problem can be avoided if the partnership agreement contains an express provision granting consent to continued use of the partner's name after retirement.

Voluntary Versus Involuntary Retirement

Law firms wrestle with the problem of whether to force the retirement of partners or to make the decision elective. When there is a mandatory retirement policy, it is easily spelled out in the partnership agreement. The policy should also include the option for partners to retire earlier than the mandatory age whenever they deem it appropriate. Hence, the firm policy does not relieve each partner of making an election.

What are the factors governing the decision? Of paramount importance to the older lawyer is the question of health, both physical and mental. Certain ailments can be overcome by practitioners in certain disciplines, but not by others. For example, the trial lawyer, dealing daily with the stress of courtroom trials, may be forced to retire—or at least forego trial work—if afflicted with serious hypertension.

Some older lawyers never suffer any diminution in their mental powers, while others gradually "go downhill." When partners see any physical or mental disability in one of their own, there is an ethical obligation to do something about it before any client is harmed. The afflicted partner may respond to reason and remove himself or herself from any opportunity for malpractice; if not, the partnership will have to act.

Younger lawyers will also influence the retirement decisions of older members of the firm. As long as the more venerable lawyers in the office are still around, younger lawyers see them as obstacles to their own advancement. Retirement of the older people represents opportunity for the young. Many older lawyers recognize that, do not resent it, and are willing to turn over the practice to younger members of the firm.

Retirement Provisions in Partnership Agreements

Scale-down of Compensation

One of the more accepted provisions in modern-day partnership agreements is a scale-down clause. To ease the transition of partners from active to retired status, the partnership agreement or the firm's stated retirement policy provides for a gradual reduction of partner compensation beginning in the year after the partner reaches age sixty-five and continuing through age seventy, when the partner is required to retire.

An example of a scale-down in a major firm is set out in the previously discussed *Vinson & Elkins* case.[24] It was described as follows:

> Further, the partnership agreement provided that after reaching fixed-basis status and continuing into retired status for the remainder of the partner's life, former percentage partners would be paid as a guaranteed payment a percentage of their base compensation. This guaranteed payment was to be 75 percent of their base compensation in the first year and 50 percent the second year, and ultimately would reach 25 percent in the fifth year and thereafter.[25]

Not all firms are able to be, nor are they, as generous as Vinson & Elkins. And there are variations of the Vinson & Elkins formula. Perhaps the scale-down will be 20 percent in each of the years after the partner reaches age sixty-five through seventy, with some specified minimum, such as a percentage of the lowest partner draw in the firm. More importantly, payments usually cease after age seventy.

Supplemental Retirement Benefits

If a firm has no mandatory retirement age, it is unlikely that it will provide any retirement benefits to retired partners. Each partner will have to rely on a combination of resources (such as Keogh plans, individual retirement accounts, social security, and personal investments) usually without firm assistance. When retirement is mandatory, whether retired partners receive anything after reaching the firm's retirement age is dependent upon the firm's financial resources.

In any event, whether the firm provides the benefit or the partner is left to his or her own resources is really a distinction without a difference. Remember, to a partner "it is your money." Consider the elaborate plan that landed Vinson & Elkins in the Tax Court in the above-mentioned case.

---

24. *See* Vinson & Elkins v. Commissioner, 99 T.C. 9 (1992), *aff'd*, 7 F.3d 1235 (5th Cir. 1993).

25. *Id.* at 45.

Beginning in 1984, Vinson & Elkins established 132 individual defined benefit plans (IDB) for its partners (though certain partners elected out of the arrangement):

> These plans were virtually identical except for the benefit formula and the identity of the participants. Each of the 132 plans created a trust to provide for the investment and administration of the plan assets. Each partner for whom a plan was created was appointed as the investment cotrustee for his or her plan. Each of the partners for whom a plan was created entered into an agreement with [Vinson & Elkins (V&E)], which outlined the acceptable investments for the plan assets and set forth rules regarding the handling of plan funds. Effective September 1, 1986, 49 of the 132 plans were amended to add a new preretirement death benefit, which was to be insured by a life insurance policy purchased by the plan trustee for each plan.
>
> Each partner bore the cost of funding his or her plan by making available to V&E sufficient funds to make the annual contributions or by allowing V&E to deduct the minimum funding amount from his or her distributive share of V&E profits. V&E allocated to each partner the full expense of any V&E contribution to the plan and the related income tax deduction.[26]

Whatever the Vinson & Elkins partners receive from his or her IDB comes from his or her own earnings—not from "the firm" or some other partner. Whether there is any payment to the retired partner thereafter depends upon the financial status of the firm. In most instances, each retiree is on his or her own.

Long-Service Partners Versus Others

In today's world of law firms, there is a difference between the lawyer who joined the firm forty-five years ago upon graduation from law school and the "lateral partner," who became part of the organization within, for example, the last ten or fifteen years. The person who has given his or her entire life to the firm may receive more generous treatment in the form of a supplemental retirement benefit than those retiring partners with less service.

Such supplemental payments do not put a great strain on the budgets of larger firms. Forty-five years ago, the number of part-

---

26. *Id.* at 11.

ners in most firms was quite small, compared with the number of partners in those firms today. Thus, the supplemental payments to a small number of "old-timers" is spread over a large number of active partners. They can afford it!

Forfeiture-for-Competition

The ethics and enforceability of forfeiture-for-competition clauses were discussed in Chapter III in the context of drafting a partnership agreement, and in Chapter IV in the context of withdrawal of a partner from a law firm. May a law firm enforce a forfeiture of retirement benefits against a partner who does not merely withdraw, but actually retires, and then resumes the practice of law?

We leave aside cases of misrepresentation of the intent to retire and other ethical violations, as in *Mahoney*, previously discussed.

A reading of the cases in New York would indicate that a properly drawn clause can be judicially enforced against a retired partner, provided the payments to him or her are, in fact, retirement benefits. When Robert Silagi retired from the firm of Guazzo, Perelson, Rushfield & Guazzo, P.C. in 1981, he received certain benefits. Then, after a six-month leave of absence, he decided to return and a new agreement was executed. Under this agreement, Silagi would act as counsel to the firm, with use of an office and services, and receive half salary; in addition, he would receive 25 percent of the fees in two matters. He agreed he would not solicit any past, present, or future clients of the firm for a four-year period, nor, for one year, accept any clients whose interests were in conflict with interests of the firm's existing clients. The agreement provided for binding arbitration of disputes.[27]

Silagi sought arbitration of his claim for a share of a fee. When the trial court ordered arbitration, the law firm filed an answer seeking damages against Silagi for competing in violation of his agreement. Silagi then moved for a stay of arbitration, contending that the applicability of Disciplinary Rule 2-108 was not subject to arbitration. The firm filed a cross-motion requesting a hearing on whether Disciplinary Rule 2-108 applied. The trial court denied the hearing, and ordered arbitration of Silagi's claim and a trial of the firm's counterclaims.

---

27. *In re* Silagi, 146 A.D.2d 555, 537 N.Y.S.2d 171 (App. Div. 1989).

In reversing the trial court, the appellate court distinguished the *Silverberg* case,[28] saying as follows:

> That case involved an agreement to terminate a partnership and not the retirement of a partner from an ongoing firm, as is alleged by respondent herein. Should this threshold issue be resolved in respondent's favor, there would be no public policy barring arbitration of the claims and counterclaims. Respondent's motion for a hearing should therefore have been granted and the arbitration stayed.[29]

On the other hand, New York courts have followed the *Cohen* case[30] and permitted enforcement of a forfeiture-for-competition clause when the retiree abandoned practice in exchange for benefits, and then was permitted to resume practice by agreeing to relinquish the retirement benefits. In *Graubard, Mollen, Horowitz, Pomeranz & Shapiro v. Moskovitz,* the court said:

> A more important consideration is the purpose behind [Disciplinary Rule] 2-108. Restrictive covenants are limited in the case of attorneys in order to serve the greater social purpose of providing clients with full and free choice of counsel. The retirement benefits exception therefore ought to be narrowly read. A firm may, for instance, require an attorney not to represent its client or not to practice law at all while receiving retirement benefits, but if the attorney decides to forego those benefits, then he may practice and clients may freely avail themselves of his services.[31]

The Kansas Supreme Court has addressed the issue, albeit somewhat indirectly.[32] Malcolm Miller was a partner who did not retire in a literal sense, but was forced out of his firm. A dispute arose after his expulsion when the firm did not pay certain fees to him, which he claimed were due him. Miller sued.

---

28. *In re* Silverberg, 81 A.D.2d 640, 438 N.Y.S.2d 143 (App. Div. 1981).

29. *Silagi,* 146 A.D.2d at 556, 537 N.Y.S.2d at 172.

30. Cohen v. Lord, Day & Lord, 75 N.Y.2d 95, 550 N.E.2d 410, 551 N.Y.S.2d 157 (1989).

31. Graubard, Mollen, Horowitz, Pomeranz & Shapiro v. Moskovitz, 149 Misc. 2d 481, 485, 565 N.Y.S.2d 672, 676 (Sup. Ct. 1990).

32. Miller v. Foulston, Siefkin, Powers & Eberhardt, 246 Kan. 450, 790 P.2d 404 (1990).

The partnership agreement provided that any partner who was expelled and who, under certain provisions of the agreement was entitled to retirement rights, would not be regarded as an expelled partner, but considered for all purposes as being a retired partner. The agreement further provided that to be entitled to retirement rights, a partner had to meet one of three criteria: (1) attainment of age sixty, (2) service with the firm for thirty years, or (3) inability to continue because of physical or mental disability. These retirement rights were subject to forfeiture, and required the retired partner to return any benefits paid to him, if the retired partner "without the express consent of all continuing partners, re-enters the practice of law or becomes otherwise gainfully engaged or employed at an occupation associated with or related to the practice of law."[33] Miller qualified for retirement benefits because he had attained age sixty and had been with the firm for over thirty years.

The Kansas Supreme Court held that Disciplinary Rule 2-108 allows restriction of the practice of law if it is a condition to payment of retirement benefits. The court held that the application of the provision to Miller was within the exception.[34]

In attempting to settle the issues between the firm and Miller, one of the firm's continuing partners wrote to Miller, offering to continue payment of retirement benefits to him if he would restrict himself to certain permitted activities:

> You may rent office space and employ a secretary, with the understanding that you will identify and utilize it as a "private office" and not a law office. You agree that you will not list or advertise yourself by stationery, letterhead, building address, telephone listing, or otherwise as a lawyer or attorney. Within that setting you may consult with persons and counsel them, but you may not represent them in judicial or administrative proceedings. If you refer such persons to other lawyers, you will either make no charge for any service rendered by you either before or after the referral or you agree that it shall not be your practice to make such referrals to any particular lawyer or law firm.[35]

---

33. *Id.*, 246 Kan. at 455, 790 P.2d at 408.
34. *Id.*, 246 Kan. at 459, 790 P.2d at 411.
35. *Id.*, 246 Kan. at 460, 790 P.2d at 411.

If Miller observed these restrictions, the firm would pay him $2,000 a month for ninety-six months.

The Kansas Supreme Court held that the facts were distinguishable from those in the *Cohen* case (discussed in Chapter IV), because Cohen was not "retiring" but "withdrawing" from Lord, Day & Lord. Here, Miller was qualified for retirement benefits and was being treated as if he were retiring from the Foulston firm. Said the court:

> Nor was the offer of retirement benefits here coercive. Plaintiff did not voluntarily withdraw from Foulston-Siefkin. He was forced to leave under threat of being expelled. Because of his longevity with the firm, he qualified to receive retirement benefits. To receive these benefits, however, plaintiff had to meet certain conditions. Plaintiff had to choose between retiring, including stopping the practice of law and receiving over $190,000 in retirement benefits, or continuing the practice of law, in which case he lost retirement benefits. The provisions of the 1965 agreement making the payment of retirement benefits conditional upon plaintiff's retirement by not continuing to practice law was not unethical or unenforceable and did not violate [Disciplinary Rule] 2- 108(A).[36]

A partner about to retire and the continuing partners should have a clear understanding about what limitations, if any, are to be placed upon the retiring partner's right to continue to practice law after retirement. All need to be cognizant of the ethical restrictions imposed by Disciplinary Rule 2-108 and be aware that no restrictions are permissible unless, and only as long as, retirement benefits are paid to the retiring partner.

Client Relations

An important factor deserving the attention of all partners as the retirement age for any partner (or partners) approaches, is the proper attention to clients' matters. The retirement of partners inevitably will be viewed differently by the firm and clients. If a partner has served his or her clients well, the partner, from the client's view, is "*my*" lawyer. From the firm's view, the client is "*our*" client.

---

36. *Id.*, 246 Kan. at 462, 790 P.2d at 412.

Thus, the "buzzword" in the profession today is "institutionalize." Law firms want to "institutionalize" the clients—that is, try to make the clients loyal to the firm, rather than to any individual lawyer. Clients resist such attempts; even large corporate clients, speaking through their general counsel, will say that they do not retain law firms, they select lawyers.

Under these circumstances, continuing partners should plan, well in advance of their partner's retirement, to gather his or her clients into the inner circle. Clients should be exposed to other partners and senior associates in the firm, both professionally and socially, to establish good rapport. The retiring partner should be part of this effort. If the firm waits until the retirement date has arrived before commencing the "institutionalization" process, there is a gap in time before good relations can be cemented. This gap in time can prove disastrous for retention of the business.

Even though a partner has retired, the firm should provide incentives to him or her to remain active in the client retention process. An occasional invitation to join a business conference with the client, or a social gathering involving the client, will assist in moving the client toward the view that there has been no real change in the "tender loving care" provided by the firm.

Provision of Services to Retirees

Partners about to retire need to consider, and to discuss with the continuing partners, the services that will be provided after retirement. Most law firms will offer retired partners an office (albeit, often much smaller than when the partner was active), secretarial assistance, and office services. Other items can be offered by the firm, depending upon its philosophy, generosity, and financial resources. The firm might elect to pay membership dues in professional associations or social clubs on the theory that the retired partner's participation in these organizations is a good marketing tool. The firm may permit the retired partner to participate in employee benefit plans, particularly life and health insurance programs, after retirement. The retired partner may also be permitted to attend partnership meetings and to continue having access to firm financial and operating information following retirement.

Whatever these arrangements, they should be agreed upon in advance of retirement and included in a separate agreement to cover the postretirement status of the individual lawyer. If the retiree is to serve as "Of Counsel" to the firm, the agreement should define the duties and responsibilities of the position and, in particular, the understanding about malpractice insurance coverage should the lawyer be providing legal advice other than to other firm lawyers.

* * *

EPILOGUE

The law—despite all the "lawyer-bashing"—remains an honorable profession. Without the law and lawyers, the great constitutional protections that we have in this country would soon vanish. We have only to look at those countries with the lowest ratio of lawyers-to-population and we see the places where there is little individual liberty.

Because law is not an exact science, lawyers need discourse with one another to understand their clients' problems and to frame the arguments favoring their clients. The complexity of problems in modern life and the volume of data affecting their solutions many times requires the attention of more than one lawyer. These reasons often impel lawyers toward partnership, to share these problems, these burdens, and their solutions.

For the young lawyer embarking upon a career, the prize after graduation is often a position with a law firm as an associate. The "brass ring" is his or her invitation to join the partnership.

As I said at the outset, a partner cannot claim the rights and privileges of the position without accepting its duties and responsibilities. Sometimes, the duties and responsibilities appear to outweigh the rights and privileges. With careful attention to the events of every day, and an understanding of the rules that apply to them, that simply will not happen.

As a partner, you are a proprietor in America, one who has succeeded in your calling, and you are a contributor to our society.

Be proud of it.

APPENDIX A

Hiring of Associates

Short Form of Offer Letter

Dear XXXXX:

This confirms that we would be happy to have you join us as an associate in our office next year. We are confident that you will find the opportunities at our firm interesting and challenging. We also believe that you will reinforce our talented group of lawyers.

We will advise you when our starting salary for next year has been established. The enclosed description of our firm should answer most questions about us, but please feel free to call me or any other lawyers here at any time if you have questions you would like to discuss.

This offer will remain open until December 1. Please notify us whether you accept, preferably by telephone and as soon as you can, but in any event before December 1. All of us at our firm very much hope that you will decide to accept our offer.

Very truly yours,

[Firm]

By [Partner]

Long Form of Offer Letter[1]

Dear XXXXX:

On behalf of the firm, I am very pleased to extend to you an offer to become an associate with our law firm following your graduation from law school. All of us agree that you will be a highly valued contributor to our firm's success. We believe that your personal attributes, coupled with the legal skills you have demonstrated, ensure that you will have a very successful legal career. We look forward to a long-term association with you as a lawyer at our firm.

Accordingly, we are pleased to invite you to join our firm as an associate. We are sure you will understand that our offer is subject to resolution of any conflict that may exist as a result of your work or knowledge concerning any matter handled by any other firm or employer in which that firm or employer represented a position adverse to that of a client of our firm. For example, you might have been involved with such a matter in your capacity as a summer associate or paralegal with another firm. To assist us in determining whether any possible conflict exists, please let Mr./Ms. XXXXXXXX, the administrative assistant to the hiring committee, or me know as soon as possible if you have ever worked on, or obtained confidential information regarding, any matter in which our firm has represented an opposing position.

The date when you would actually commence work can be determined by mutual agreement, based upon your individual circumstances. Normally new associates do not begin work until after they take the bar examination. This policy is intended to provide everyone ample time to prepare for the exam. Because we believe that new associates should have some income, we pay a stipend to those who have not already taken the bar examination. This stipend for next year will be $0,000, with $0,000 payable in [month] and the balance approximately the first of June. However, we anticipate and expect that you will begin work and go on payroll immediately after Labor Day, but will consider alternative arrangements. We request that you notify us of your plans as early as possible, so that we can make the necessary office logistical arrangements.

The starting salary we have established is in the amount of $00,000 per year.

No vacation time is allotted for first-year associates for the remainder of the calendar year in which they join us. As of the first of the following calendar year, however, associates are entitled to four weeks' vacation.

---

1. This form represents the essential pattern of a letter actually used by a large midwestern law firm; certain clauses, used by other large law firms covering other subjects, have been added by "editorial fiat."

Because associates may wish to have some free time during the holidays at year-end, we permit the borrowing of up to one week of vacation time at the end of the calendar year in which they join us from vacation allowed in the succeeding year.

Health and accident coverage is provided from the first day of employment. Dependent coverage is available and, if elected, the firm pays half the premium cost, with the other half being paid by the associate on either a pre-tax or after-tax basis. There are two life insurance programs available, which upon becoming effective, provide, as to the first policy, coverage of $50,000 with double indemnity for accidental death, and as to the second policy, $100,000 without double indemnity.

The firm maintains a tax-qualified profit sharing plan, in which all employees are eligible to participate after one full year of employment with the firm. Contributions by the firm are discretionary, but historically have been made on behalf of participants, who are not required to make any contributions. Details of the plan are available upon request.

The firm also offers a 401(k) plan. Employees who have satisfied the eligibility requirements for the profit sharing plan may defer a portion of their compensation on a tax-free basis.

Once you are admitted to the bar, the firm will pay your annual bar association dues for the county bar, the state bar, and the American Bar Association. Costs for attending continuing legal education programs for which your attendance has received prior approval will be paid in full. In addition, if you become involved in one of the substantive committees of the state bar or the American Bar Association, the firm will pay the expenses associated with those activities.

In connection with your move to our city, the firm will pay the reasonable and necessary moving expenses, subject to certain limitations; details of what is covered and what is not are available upon request. The firm will also pay the actual and reasonable personal travel expenses to our city for your spouse and children.

The firm also pays for the cost of parking in the garage in our building.

Elements of the firm's fringe benefit program are constantly being reviewed and modified. The foregoing brief summary describes the components of the programs presently in place, but the firm reserves the right to change any element of the program at any time and without further compensation to the firm's employees.

Under current firm policy, you would be considered for partnership after you have been with the firm for seven years. Your election would depend not only upon your prior performance and the firm's expectations concerning your future contributions, but also the needs of the firm at the time your candidacy is voted upon.

This offer is open to you through October 15. Naturally we would appreciate receiving your response at the earliest date possible. If you anticipate difficulty in reaching your decision by October 15, please let us know, and we will attempt to accommodate your needs.

We believe that our firm offers unique opportunities for your development as a professional in a congenial and cooperative atmosphere. I urge you to give us a favorable reply to our offer.

If you have any questions, please feel free to call me to discuss them. We look forward to hearing from you.

Very truly yours,

[Firm]

By [Partner]

APPENDIX B

Form of Partnership Agreement

Partnership Agreement[1]

SECTIONS OF THE AGREEMENT

1. This form of partnership agreement has been drafted by the author, employing ideas suggested by the case law and by copies of partnership agreements from various law firms that, anonymously, supplied copies of their internal documents.

THIS AGREEMENT (hereinafter "this Agreement") is made as of the __ day of _______, 19__, having been executed on the dates set forth by each of the signatories hereto at the places indicated adjacent to his or her signature. Each signatory, for the purposes hereof, is designated a "Regular Partner," as hereinafter defined.

Sec. 1. PURPOSE OF AGREEMENT. The parties hereto desire to form and constitute a partnership solely for the practice of law (hereinafter "the Firm"). The Firm may acquire interests in other partnerships and corporations engaging in activities other than the practice of law but only if, in the opinion of legal counsel for the Firm, legal liability for such other activities is within the coverage of malpractice insurance covering the Firm and its partners.

Sec. 2. EFFECTIVE DATE. This Agreement shall be effective as of the date hereinabove first set forth, notwithstanding that one or more parties hereto may not execute and deliver this Agreement until a date subsequent thereto, except that any person executing this Agreement on a date after the date hereinabove first set forth shall be liable only for those acts or omissions of the Firm occurring after said date of execution; any such person shall be entitled to defense and indemnity by the Firm against claims arising out of any act or omission that occurred before said date of execution.

Sec. 3. NAME. The Firm shall be called "Jones, Smith & Roe." Each signatory hereto acknowledges that none of the names in the Firm name (except "_______") is intended to represent the surname of such signatory. Each signatory, on his or her own behalf and on behalf of his or her

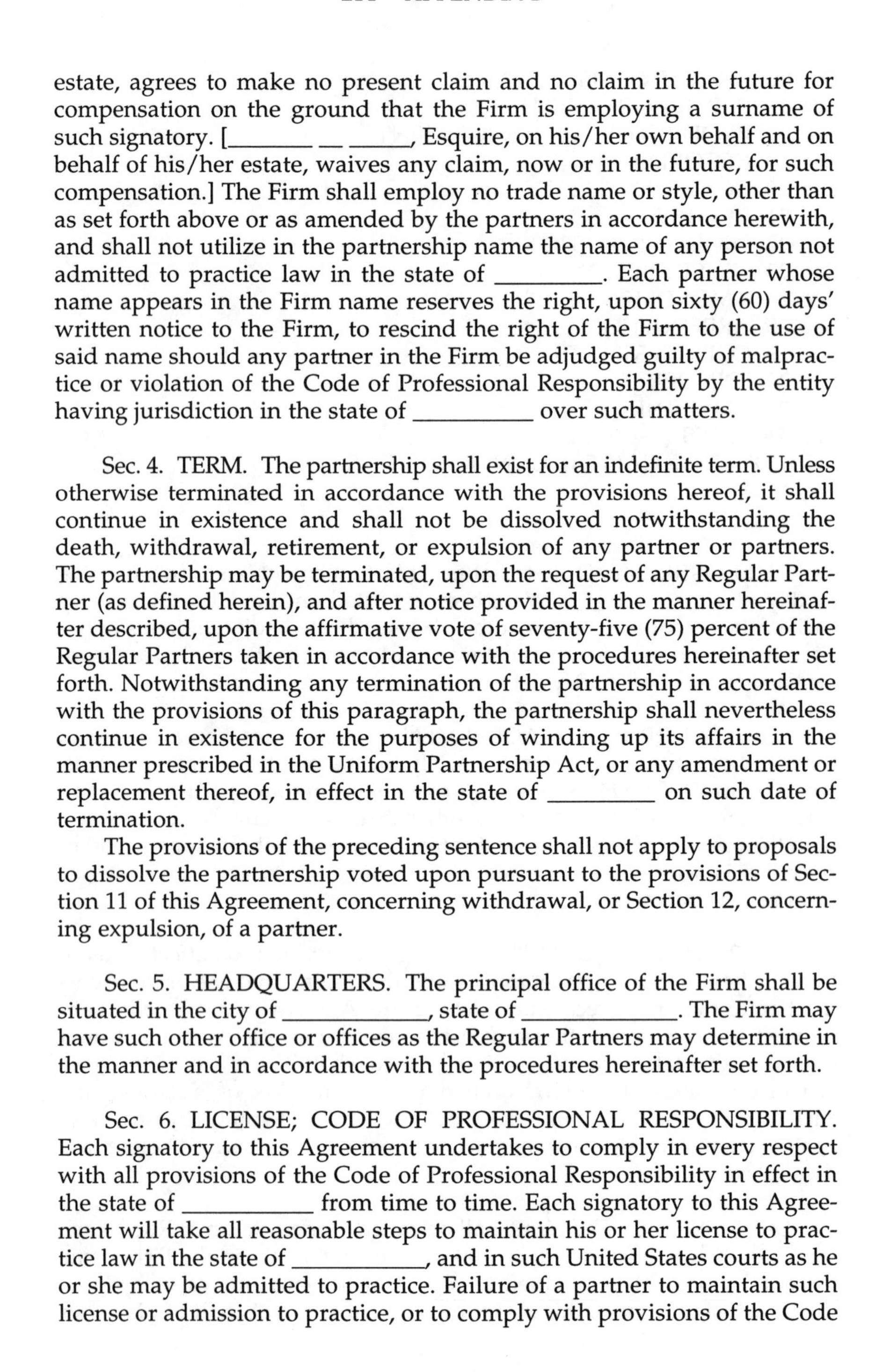

estate, agrees to make no present claim and no claim in the future for compensation on the ground that the Firm is employing a surname of such signatory. [_______ __ _____, Esquire, on his/her own behalf and on behalf of his/her estate, waives any claim, now or in the future, for such compensation.] The Firm shall employ no trade name or style, other than as set forth above or as amended by the partners in accordance herewith, and shall not utilize in the partnership name the name of any person not admitted to practice law in the state of _________. Each partner whose name appears in the Firm name reserves the right, upon sixty (60) days' written notice to the Firm, to rescind the right of the Firm to the use of said name should any partner in the Firm be adjudged guilty of malpractice or violation of the Code of Professional Responsibility by the entity having jurisdiction in the state of __________ over such matters.

Sec. 4. TERM. The partnership shall exist for an indefinite term. Unless otherwise terminated in accordance with the provisions hereof, it shall continue in existence and shall not be dissolved notwithstanding the death, withdrawal, retirement, or expulsion of any partner or partners. The partnership may be terminated, upon the request of any Regular Partner (as defined herein), and after notice provided in the manner hereinafter described, upon the affirmative vote of seventy-five (75) percent of the Regular Partners taken in accordance with the procedures hereinafter set forth. Notwithstanding any termination of the partnership in accordance with the provisions of this paragraph, the partnership shall nevertheless continue in existence for the purposes of winding up its affairs in the manner prescribed in the Uniform Partnership Act, or any amendment or replacement thereof, in effect in the state of _________ on such date of termination.

The provisions of the preceding sentence shall not apply to proposals to dissolve the partnership voted upon pursuant to the provisions of Section 11 of this Agreement, concerning withdrawal, or Section 12, concerning expulsion, of a partner.

Sec. 5. HEADQUARTERS. The principal office of the Firm shall be situated in the city of ____________, state of _____________. The Firm may have such other office or offices as the Regular Partners may determine in the manner and in accordance with the procedures hereinafter set forth.

Sec. 6. LICENSE; CODE OF PROFESSIONAL RESPONSIBILITY. Each signatory to this Agreement undertakes to comply in every respect with all provisions of the Code of Professional Responsibility in effect in the state of ___________ from time to time. Each signatory to this Agreement will take all reasonable steps to maintain his or her license to practice law in the state of ___________, and in such United States courts as he or she may be admitted to practice. Failure of a partner to maintain such license or admission to practice, or to comply with provisions of the Code of Professional Responsibility, shall be grounds for expulsion of such partner from the Firm or other disciplinary action against such partner taken in the manner and in accordance with the procedures hereinafter set forth.

Sec. 7. CLASSES OF PARTNERS. The partnership shall comprise the Regular Partners who are signatories hereto, and such other Regular Partners as may be admitted to the partnership from time to time hereafter. The Firm shall also include Special Partners, Transition Partners, and Retired Partners.

Sec. 7.1 Regular Partners. A "Regular Partner" is a full-time working partner with an ownership interest in the Firm and the right to vote upon all matters pertaining to, and brought to a vote by, the Firm. A Regular Partner may be admitted to the Firm by vote of the Regular Partners in the affirmative number required and taken in the manner provided hereinafter in this Agreement. The admission of a Regular Partner shall not cause a dissolution of the partnership. Each Regular Partner shall devote substantially all of his or her working time and attention to the affairs of the Firm, except as the Executive Committee (hereinafter described) shall otherwise approve. If any Regular Partner requests part-time status or absence in excess of normal vacation or for purposes other than business of the Firm, he or she shall request the prior approval of the Executive Committee, which shall approve or disapprove the request; the Executive Committee shall recommend to the Percentage Draw Committee (hereinafter described) whether any adjustment in the Regular Partner's compensation during such change in status or absence is appropriate.

Sec. 7.2 Special Partners. Any person not voted upon or, if voted upon, not voted upon favorably, for admission to the Firm as a Regular Partner may be admitted as a "Special Partner." Any person so admitted shall be a member of the class of Special Partners, but may have such other designation (such as Contract Partner, Nonequity Partner, or the like) as the Executive Committee shall determine. The vote for admission as a Special Partner shall be in the affirmative number required and taken in the manner hereinafter provided in this Agreement.

Sec. 7.2.1 Voting by Special Partners. Special Partners shall receive notice of, and the right to attend, all meetings of the partnership, except a meeting, or such portion thereof, at which the distributive shares of the Regular Partners are to be discussed or voted upon. Special Partners shall have the right to vote upon all matters presented to the Regular Partners for vote, except that Special Partners shall have no vote upon any of the following:

(i) Admission of partners of any class
(ii) Matters related to the borrowing of money by the Firm

(iii) Matters related to the leasing of office space, furniture, or equipment by the Firm
(iv) Revocation of the authority of a partner of any class to act on behalf of the Firm
(v) Expulsion from the Firm or other discipline of a partner of any class
(vi) Establishment or amendment of the distributive share of any Regular Partner

Sec. 7.2.2 Financial Interests. Special Partners shall have no share in the net profits and losses of the Firm, and no interest in Firm Capital or Firm Inventory. The term "Firm Inventory," as used herein, shall mean the Firm's accounts receivable and unbilled work in process, including work performed pursuant to contingent fee agreements.

Sec. 7.2.3 Power and Authority. Special Partners shall have the power and authority to act in all client matters on behalf of the Firm and to sign opinions of counsel on behalf of the Firm, provided, however, that Special Partners shall have only such express powers to sign on bank accounts and trust accounts of the Firm as shall be granted individually to the Special Partner concerned by the Executive Committee. By the affirmative vote of the same percentage of Regular Partners as were required to vote affirmatively for admission of the Special Partner to the Firm, the Special Partner's association with the Firm may be terminated, without prior notice to the Special Partner and without specification of any reason therefor. By the affirmative vote of not less than two-thirds (66 and 2/3 percent) of the membership of the Executive Committee, any express power granted to the Special Partner may be terminated, without prior notice to the Special Partner and without specification of the reason therefor. In the event of an affirmative vote to terminate the Special Partner or to rescind any express power previously granted, the Executive Committee may take such action on behalf of the Firm as it considers reasonable or advisable to assure the Firm and the partners of the protection of such vote, including such publication thereof as the Executive Committee deems necessary to protect the interests of the Firm.

Sec. 7.2.4 Indemnification of Special Partners. The Firm shall at all times hold each Special Partner and his or her estate harmless from, and indemnify him, her, or it against, all obligations of the Firm incurred before as well as after his or her retirement, death, or disability, except such obligations of the Firm as arise in whole or in part from the actions of the Special Partner and as are excluded or excludable from coverage (other than by reason of such policies' deductible amount) under the terms of the Firm's liability insurance policies otherwise available to indemnify the Firm against such obligations.

Sec. 7.2.5 Other Matters Pertaining to Special Partners. The Executive Committee may, from time to time, establish such policies relating to the compensation, benefits, powers, and responsibilities and limitations thereof, regarding the Special Partners, as the Committee deems appropriate. Any Special Partner aggrieved by such action may bring the policy to the attention of any meeting of the Regular Partners, who shall have the authority to amend, modify, or rescind the policy by such vote of the Regular Partners as hereinafter specified.

Sec. 7.3 Transition Partners. A Regular Partner who elects to retire, may, upon not less than six (6) months prior written notice to the Firm, retire before age sixty-five (65), and if he or she has attained his or her sixty-fifth birthday, shall retire, commencing on the first day of the fiscal year of the Firm next following said election or birthday. Upon such retirement, he or she shall become a "Transition Partner," and shall continue in such capacity until attaining Retired Partner status. A Transition Partner is encouraged, but is not required, to continue to practice law as a partner in the Firm, but is expected to reduce his or her hours of active practice, to introduce to other members of the Firm those clients with whom the Transition Partner is most familiar, and to turn over to other members of the Firm such legal work on behalf of his or her clients as it may be feasible and appropriate to do. As soon as practicable after achieving the status of Transition Partner, such person shall resign all fiduciary positions (for example, trusteeships and conservatorships) held at the behest of clients of the Firm. A Transition Partner shall no longer be eligible for nomination or election to the Partnership Draw Committee or the Executive Committee of the Firm, but shall be entitled to attend all partnership meetings and to vote at such meetings. A Transition Partner shall not be liable for a capital assessment at any time from and after the date he or she attains the status of Transition Partner. The Firm reserves the right, upon the recommendation of the Firm's Executive Committee, to change the status of a Transition Partner to that of a Retired Partner by a vote of the Regular Partners in the percentage and manner hereinafter set forth. A Transition Partner whose status is thus changed shall continue to receive payments from the Firm equivalent to the payments he or she would have received, and during the same period he or she would have served, as a Transition Partner, but shall not be a partner in the Firm for any purpose whatsoever.

Sec. 7.3.1 Compensation of Transition Partner. A Transition Partner shall receive a distribution each year by applying the percentages in the table below to such partner's "Previous Annual Income." The term "Previous Annual Income" shall mean the dollar amount of the partner's average distribution received during the five years, not necessarily consecutive, out of the last ten years, in which such partner's compensation was the highest, and any other monies received by or credited to him or her in the form of taxable income reported to the Internal Revenue Service on Form K-1.

PERCENTAGE

Age at Payment	*Age at Retirement*					
	60	*61*	*62*	*63*	*64*	*65*
61	61.5					
62	41.0	64.2				
63	20.5	42.8	66.9			
64	20.5	21.4	44.6	69.6		
65	20.5	21.4	22.3	46.4	72.3	
66	20.5	21.4	22.3	23.2	48.2	75.0
67	20.5	21.4	22.3	23.2	24.1	50.0
68	20.5	21.4	22.3	23.2	24.1	25.0
69	20.5	21.4	22.3	23.2	24.1	25.0
70	20.5	21.4	22.3	23.2	24.1	25.0

[COMMENT: The above table is illustrative of a scaling down of payments to a retiring partner. Another, less complicated version might reduce the retiring partner's compensation in each year after retirement by an amount equal to 20 percent of his or her compensation in the preceding year.]

Sec. 7.3.2 Other Benefits. A Transition Partner shall continue to enjoy all of the benefits and emoluments pertinent to him or her as a Regular Partner, including the right to attend and vote at (to the extent permitted by the provisions hereof) all meetings of the partnership.

Sec. 7.4 Retired Partners. Any person who has retired from the Firm pursuant to the provisions of this section is a "Retired Partner." A Regular Partner or a Special Partner may retire from the Firm at the end of any fiscal year of the Firm in which he or she attains age sixty (60), or at such later date as he or she selects. Any expression of intent to withdraw before age sixty (60) shall be deemed an election to withdraw from the Firm and shall be subject to the provisions of Section 11 hereof. A partner must retire from the Firm not later than the end of the fiscal year of the Firm in which he or she attains age seventy (70). Unless the retiring partner and the Executive Committee of the Firm shall otherwise agree, such partner's membership in the Firm in the case of a Regular Partner, and the partner's association with the Firm in the case of any other partner, shall terminate at the end of the Firm's fiscal year in which retirement is requested.

Sec. 7.4.1 Benefits to Retired Partners. Each partner who retires from the firm shall be entitled to receive a retirement benefit, calculated in accordance with, and subject to the conditions expressed in, Section 15 hereof. In addition, the Firm will use its best efforts to enable each Retired Partner to participate, at his or her election, in the Firm's medical plan; provided, however, that the entire cost of his or her coverage under such plan shall be paid by the Retired Partner. A Retired Partner will not be covered under the Firm's life insurance plan for classes of partners other than Retired Partners; should the Firm decide to make available any form of group life insurance to Retired Partners, the Firm will use its best efforts to advise each Retired Partner of such availability. The Firm will purchase and pay the premium upon such malpractice insurance as may be necessary to provide defense for, and indemnity to, the Retired Partner against any claim, regardless of when made, regarding matters arising on or before the effective date of his or her retirement.

Sec. 7.4.2 Partnership Obligations. No Retired Partner shall have any liability whatsoever for any liability or indebtedness of the Firm, regardless of whether the liability or indebtedness arose before or after the retirement from the Firm of the Retired Partner. The provisions of Section 22 of this Agreement, regarding indemnity, shall apply to such liability.

Sec. 7.4.3 Of Counsel Status. Unless a retiring partner notifies the Firm of his or her desire not to do so, any partner who retires from the Firm shall continue in "Of Counsel" status with the Firm until the end of the Firm's fiscal year in which such Retired Partner attains age seventy-two (72). The Executive Committee may, in its discretion, terminate the Of Counsel status of any Retired Partner at any time following two (2) years after the effective date of his or her retirement if it shall determine that continuation of such status is not in the mutual best interests of the Firm and such Retired Partner. The Executive Committee may, in its discretion, invite a Retired Partner to extend Of Counsel status beyond age seventy-two (72), on a year-by-year basis, if it determines that such extension would be of significant benefit to the Firm.

Sec. 7.4.4 Of Counsel Agreement. Each Retired Partner shall be entitled to receive from the Firm, in addition to the benefits hereinabove mentioned and such other benefits as mutually may be agreed upon, an office and office services, provided that the Retired Partner and the Firm enter into an Of Counsel agreement that sets forth a description of benefits to be provided the Retired Partner pursuant to Section 7.4.1

and Section 7.4.2, and a specification of status pursuant to Section 7.4.3 and of duties pursuant to Section 7.4.5.

Sec. 7.4.5 Duties. Each Retired Partner continuing in Of Counsel status shall be expected to be available to the Firm upon request for reasonable periods of time for client development and for assistance with special Firm projects as requested by the Executive Committee. The amount of time to be devoted to such matters without compensation, and the rate of compensation to be provided for time expended in excess thereof, shall be set forth in the Of Counsel agreement between the Firm and the Retired Partner. A Retired Partner shall not be expected to perform legal services for clients of the Firm. Such Retired Partner may, however, perform reduced levels of legal services to such clients to the extent authorized by the Executive Committee.

Sec. 7.4.6 Malpractice Insurance; Indemnity. Should the Retired Partner be requested or authorized to perform legal services or to assist with special Firm projects, the Firm will provide, at Firm expense, malpractice insurance to defend and indemnify the Retired Partner through the period of limitation for the commencement of any legal action against the Retired Partner. Such Retired Partner shall be indemnified by the Firm and held harmless from and against any liability, loss, cost, or expense arising in connection with the performance of any such duty.

Sec. 7.5 Restrictions on Authority. No partner of the Firm, of any class, may perform any of the following acts on behalf of the Firm without the prior express written approval of the Executive Committee of the Firm:

(i) Open a bank account
(ii) Sell, transfer, or pledge any asset of the Firm
(iii) Issue a guaranty or agree to indemnify any person or firm
(iv) Lease any real or personal property, except as permitted by subparagraph (v), below
(v) Contract for any goods or services not required in the ordinary course of representation of a client (Examples of permitted contracts required in the ordinary course of representation are those related to the rental of temporary office space during extended court trials, hiring of court reporters, utilization of electronic research data services, provision of temporary office services, service of process, and printing of court records, briefs, and other documents.)

Sec. 8. PROCEDURAL MATTERS.

Sec. 8.1 Notice. Each partner shall be entitled to receive a notice of each meeting of the partnership, except as stated in Section 8.2, below, addressed to him or her at such place as he or she shall specify in writing from time to time to the Secretary of the Executive Committee, or such other employee of the firm as the Executive Committee shall from time to time designate. Such notice may be delivered by mail, facsimile transmission, or computer, unless a partner has indicated that notice may not be given by one or more of such means. Such notice shall state the time, place, and purpose of the meeting and shall be accompanied by an agenda and brief description of the action to be taken by the partners entitled to vote. Failure to give such notice to any partner not entitled to vote at such meeting shall not invalidate any action taken by the partnership at such meeting. Failure to deliver such notice at least five (5) business days before such meeting to a partner entitled to vote at such meeting shall invalidate any action taken at such meeting, unless the partner failing to receive notice shall nonetheless be present at such meeting or shall waive such notice before or after such meeting. Notice by mail shall be deemed delivered on the third (3d) day after the date of postmark; notice delivered by facsimile or computer transmission shall be deemed delivered on the date of dispatch.

Sec. 8.2 Notice Not Required. No notice is required to be given to a partner of any meeting at which the partnership shall consider expulsion of, or shall take a vote to expel, such partner.

Sec. 8.3 Quorum. Unless otherwise specified herein, a quorum at any meeting for the taking of any action by the partnership shall be a majority of the partners entitled to vote at such meeting.

Sec. 8.4 Proxies. Any partner entitled to vote and unable to attend a meeting or any portion thereof at which a vote will be taken may give a proxy to another partner. The proxy may be in writing, at the election of the grantor, and may direct the proxyholder to vote for or against a particular item, or may give the proxyholder discretion to vote as he or she may see fit. In the event of a controversy, the Chair of the meeting shall determine which of two or more partners is the holder of a valid proxy, and shall decide that the holder of a written proxy, signed by the grantor, possesses the valid proxy. If the decision of the Chair is contested, or if the Chair deems no person to hold a valid proxy, the Chair shall not announce the outcome of the vote until he or she has determined, from the grantor, at or after the meeting, which of the persons claiming to be a proxyholder holds the valid proxy.

Sec. 8.5 Electronic Conference Meetings. Meetings of the partnership, noticed in accordance with the provisions of this Agreement, may be held by use of electronic device, as long as such device permits each participant in the meeting to hear each other person when such other person is addressing the meeting.

Sec. 8.6 Voting.

Sec. 8.6.1 Unanimous Votes Required. The unanimous vote, in person or by proxy, of all partners entitled to vote shall be required for approval of the following actions, provided that the vote of the affected partner in the case of votes upon items (ii) and (iii) below, and the votes of the objecting partners in the case of item (viii) below, shall be excluded in determining the partners entitled to vote:

(i) Admission of a Regular Partner
(ii) Expulsion of a partner of any class
(iii) Changing the status of a Transition Partner to that of Retired Partner
(iv) Borrowing of money by the Firm
(v) Leasing of office space, furniture, or equipment for a term of one (1) year or more
(vi) Decision to bring legal action against a client of the Firm
(vii) Decision to resign the representation of a client of the Firm
(viii) Decision to represent a client upon objection of two or more partners of any class
(ix) Assessment of a capital contribution upon the Regular Partners
(x) Decision to (a) change the fiscal year of the Firm, or (b) change the accounting principles from the cash to the accrual method of accounting for the Firm

Sec. 8.6.2 Ninety Percent Vote Required. The vote of ninety (90) percent of all partners entitled to vote shall be required for the following actions:

(i) Approval of the admission of a Special Partner to the Firm
(ii) Adoption of a penalty against any Regular Partner failing to meet an assessment to provide additional capital to the Firm

Sec. 8.6.3 Majority Vote Required. Unless otherwise specifically provided in this Agreement, any other matter voted upon by the partners entitled to vote may be decided by a majority of such partners present and voting, in person or by proxy, at any meeting of the Firm called for the purpose.

Sec. 9. COMMITTEES.

Sec. 9.1 Executive Committee. The Executive Committee of the Firm shall comprise seven persons elected by the Regular Partners from among their number. Each shall serve for a period of three (3) years and until his or her successor has been chosen and qualified. Each such term shall commence on January 1 of the year following election and shall expire on the third December 31st thereafter. Each member of the Executive Committee may serve a second consecutive term in that position if so elected, but may not serve in that position again for at least one (1) year following the completion of the second consecutive term. The Executive Committee shall oversee the financial operations and controls utilized by the Firm; shall recommend to the partnership the structure, form of organization, and personnel to provide the legal and nonlegal staffing of the various departments of the Firm; and shall serve as the supervisory body for the management personnel of such departments. The Executive Committee shall have such other powers and duties as may be assigned to it by the partnership. The Executive Committee shall meet not less than once per calendar month and shall report its activities to the partnership at least once per calendar quarter. The Executive Committee shall select from among its members a Chair and a Vice Chair, and shall choose from the nonlegal staff of the Firm an appropriate person to perform the duties of Secretary to the Committee. The Chair may serve a second consecutive term in that position if so elected but may not serve on the Executive Committee in any capacity for at least one (1) year following the completion of the second consecutive term as Chair or the earlier completion of service in that capacity. The presence of at least five (5) members of the Executive Committee at a meeting thereof shall constitute a quorum. All actions by the Executive Committee, unless otherwise provided in this Agreement, shall be taken by majority vote of the whole committee.

Sec. 9.2 Partnership Shares.

Sec. 9.2.1 Establishment of Shares. The Regular Partners may, by unanimous consent, agree upon the percentage share of each Regular Partner of the Firm, which percentage shall govern for purposes of determining each Regular Partner's interest in Firm assets and in his or her share of distributive Net Income. Such agreed share shall continue until one (or more) Regular Partners advises the Executive Committee that he or she is no longer satisfied with the percentage assigned to him or her. Failing such agreement, the percentage share of each Regular Partner shall be determined by the Partnership Draw Committee.

Sec. 9.2.2 Partnership Draw Committee. The Partnership Draw Committee shall consist of five (5) Regular Partners elected by them from among its number. Each shall serve for a period of three (3) years and until his or her successor is chosen and qualified. Each member of the Partnership Draw Committee may serve second and third consecutive terms in that position if so elected but may not serve in that position again for at least one (1) year following the completion of the second, or, if so elected, a third consecutive term. The Partnership Draw Committee shall select a Chair from among its number. The Chair may serve a second and third consecutive term in that position if so elected but may not serve on the Partnership Draw Committee in any capacity for at least one (1) year following the completion of the second or, if so elected, third consecutive term as Chair or the earlier completion of service in that capacity. The presence of at least three (3) members of the Partnership Draw Committee shall constitute a quorum at any meeting thereof. All actions by the Partnership Draw Committee, unless otherwise provided in this Agreement, shall be taken by majority vote of the whole committee. The committee shall report annually to the partnership the criteria to be utilized by the committee in recommending the percentage of net income of the Firm to be distributed to each Regular Partner during the course of the ensuing fiscal year. The members of the committee shall meet with each Regular Partner during the final quarter of the fiscal year of the Firm and discuss the criteria as applied to such Regular Partner. The committee shall then determine the percentage amounts of net Firm income to be awarded to each individual Regular Partner in the ensuing year, and advise each Regular Partner of the percentage to be recommended for him or her. Any Regular Partner who, within ten (10) days after receipt of such advice, fails to object by letter to the Chair of the Partnership Draw Committee, shall be deemed to have accepted the recommended amount of distribution. The committee shall then report the recommended percentages to the Executive Committee. The Executive Committee shall, within twenty (20) days after receipt of such report, either (a) approve the recommendations as submitted, whereupon they will become the assigned percentages of each Regular Partner for the year, or (b) return the recommendations to the Partnership Draw Committee, indicating the disapproval of the Executive Committee and requesting further review. Within ten (10) days after receipt of any disapproval by the Executive Committee, the Partnership Draw Committee shall complete a review of its recommendations, make such changes therein, if any, as it deems appropriate, and forward any such changes to the Executive Committee. Such reviewed recommendations, as and if amended, shall become the final awards to each Regular Partner for the ensuing year. No individual Regular Partner's percentage shall be changed after determination of a final award as specified in the preceding sentence, except upon the affirmative vote at a meeting of the Regular Partners of eighty (80) percent of the Regular Partners, present in person or voting by proxy, including the vote of the Regular Partner objecting to the recommended percentage.

[COMMENT: As discussed in the text of this book, the manner of fixing partnership draws needs the closest scrutiny to assure that the process will be one having the support of all partners. The initial fixing should be in the hands of a small cadre of well-respected partners. The appeal procedure should be available, simple, and expeditious. The above paragraph suggests just one method of achieving that result.]

Sec. 9.3 Successors. Should seats become vacant on the Executive Committee or the Partnership Draw Committee, for any reason, before the end of the normal term, successors shall be elected by the Firm, in the manner and according to the procedures prescribed for the election of regular members of said committees, for the balance of the unexpired term, except that no such election shall be held if less than six (6) months remain in the term of any member whose seat on either committee has become vacant. Service as a member of the Executive Committee or the Partnership Draw Committee for more than two (2) years in completing an unexpired term shall constitute a term on the respective committee for purposes of the term limitations set forth in the preceding sections concerning the Executive Committee and the Partnership Draw Committee. If the seat of the Chair of the Executive Committee or the Partnership Draw Committee shall become vacant, the remaining members of the respective committee shall forthwith elect a successor to hold the temporary office of Chair until a successor is elected by the Firm and a new Chair is elected and qualified; the full committee shall proceed to elect such Chair promptly upon the filling, by the Firm, of the vacancy on the committee.

Sec. 10. FINANCIAL MATTERS.

Sec. 10.1 Assessments. The Firm may from time to time call upon the Regular Partners to provide additional capital for the Firm. The vote upon such proposal, as provided in Section 8.6, shall be limited to the Regular Partners and must be unanimous. Any such assessment shall allow each Regular Partner a reasonable period of time to deliver the funds required. The proposal shall include a statement of the penalty, if any, to be suffered by any Regular Partner who fails to provide the amount assessed against him or her. Should any Regular Partner fail to provide the additional capital called for by the assessment, any other Regular Partner(s) may agree to supply the deficiency, and that partner (or those partners) shall have his or her capital account adjusted accordingly upon receipt of the additional funds so provided. No penalty shall be imposed upon any Regular Partner whose deficiency is met in full by any other Regular Partner(s).

Sec. 10.2 Compensation of Partners. Partners shall be entitled to draw against their percentage of the estimated Net Income of the Firm for the applicable fiscal year as such percentage is established by the Percentage Draw Committee from time to time. No partner shall be entitled to draw more than such established percentage, and should the actual Net Income of the Firm for the applicable fiscal year be less than the estimated Net Income upon which the percentage draw of the partner was based, the difference between the amount to which the partner would have been entitled based upon actual Net Income and the amount actually drawn by the partner shall be carried upon the books of account of the Firm as a loan to such partner, to be repaid as the Executive Committee and the Percentage Draw Committee, acting as a single committee, shall by a two-thirds vote determine.

[COMMENT: In providing for partnership draws, many firms assume that each year will always produce net income. For some firms, in some economic times, that may not be true. Consequently, if the firm is to borrow money in a particular year, then the funds forwarded to the partners should be considered loans to them and a method of repayment should be adopted to parallel the firm's obligations. Alternatively, the agreement can provide that there will be no partnership draws in any year in which the firm fails to have sufficient net income.]

Sec. 10.3 Firm Capital.

Sec. 10.3.1 Capital Contributions. Each Regular Partner shall contribute to the Firm the amount of capital, in cash, as specified in the Schedule of Capital Contributions annexed hereto. Each person admitted to the Firm as a Regular Partner shall contribute an amount equal to the least amount shown on such annexed schedule. Capital so contributed shall be used only for the purpose of making capital expenditures and in no event may be used for normal operating and maintenance costs of the Firm. Whether a particular expenditure is a capital expenditure shall be determined by the Firm's certified public accounting firm.

Sec. 10.3.2 Working Capital. The Executive Committee shall have the authority to borrow, from time to time and for a period not exceeding one (1) year, sufficient funds to meet the cash requirements of the Firm for its operating expenses, *provided* that any borrowings in excess of $__________ shall first be approved, at a meeting of the Firm, by the unanimous vote of the Regular Partners.

Sec. 10.4 Net Income. The term "Net Income," whenever used in this Agreement, shall mean net income determined by the Firm's independent certified public accountant applying uniform accounting principles on a consistent basis under the cash method of accounting.

Sec. 10.5 Insurance. The Executive Committee shall have the responsibility to solicit bids for coverage of the Firm and its partners against the risk of claims for malpractice and other risks of liability, losses due to injury to property, workers' compensation claims, and the like. No partner shall make any statement or withhold any information on any application of the Firm for insurance that would tend to make such application false; any partner in violation of this provision may be expelled, and shall be liable in damages to the Firm for such conduct. The Executive Committee shall report to the partners the bids for coverage received, and shall recommend approval of such bids as the committee deems appropriate. Any bid so recommended may be approved at any meeting of the Firm, and the insurance purchased upon the affirmative vote of a majority of the partners entitled to vote.

Sec. 10.6 Benefit Programs. The Executive Committee shall solicit, review, and recommend to the partnership such benefit programs, for coverage of partners and employees of the Firm regarding life and health insurance, as the committee may deem advisable. Any employee benefit program recommended by the committee may be approved at any meeting of the Firm, and the program implemented upon the affirmative vote of three-quarters of the partners entitled to vote.

Sec. 10.7 Vacations and Sabbatical Leave. Each partner shall be entitled to the equivalent of one (1) calendar month of vacation during each calendar year, which vacation may be taken at one time or in increments of time during the year. Each partner with ten (10) or more years of service as a partner with the Firm shall be entitled to a sabbatical leave not to exceed six (6) months in duration. During such sabbatical leave, such partner shall receive an amount equivalent to fifty (50) percent of such partner's compensation during the preceding fiscal year. No partner may enter upon sabbatical leave without the prior approval of the head of the department to which he or she is assigned, and the concurrence of the Executive Committee in such approval. Each partner is expected to arrange for proper attention, by another partner or other partners during his or her absence on vacation or sabbatical leave, to matters for which the partner on vacation or leave normally would be responsible. The provisions of this Section 10.7 may be amended by the affirmative vote of two-thirds of the Regular Partners.

Sec. 11. WITHDRAWAL; EFFECT. A partner may withdraw from the Firm at any time upon not less than three (3) months' notice in writing, addressed to the Chair of the Executive Committee. Unless otherwise mutually agreed between the Firm and the withdrawing partner, all interest of the withdrawing partner in the Firm shall cease as of the date given in the notice (hereinafter "Effective Date"), except the right of the partner to receive such payments as may be due him or her pursuant to provisions of this Agreement. Unless otherwise determined by the unanimous vote of the remaining partners, the withdrawal of a partner shall not cause the dissolution of the partnership.

Sec. 11.1 Payments to Withdrawing Partner. A partner who withdraws from the Firm pursuant to Section 11 of this Agreement shall be entitled to receive the payments described in this Section 11. A partner who withdraws and fails to give the notice specified in Section 11, shall be subject to any penalty voted in the manner prescribed and in accordance with Section 8.6.2 of this Agreement.

Sec. 11.2 Capital Account. The Firm shall pay to the withdrawing partner, in one (1) payment or, at the Firm's option, in calendar quarterly installments over a period not to exceed three (3) years (together with interest on the unpaid amount at not more than the prime rate then prevailing), the amount, if any, standing in the capital account of the withdrawing partner as of the Effective Date.

Sec. 11.3 <u>Percentage Draw; Compensation.</u> The Firm shall pay to

(a) the withdrawing Regular Partner or Transition Partner, within sixty (60) days after the Effective Date, that portion of the percentage draw of the withdrawing partner earned by him or her to the Effective Date and not theretofore paid to him or her, or

(b) the withdrawing Special Partner, within thirty (30) days after the Effective Date, that portion of the compensation of the Special Partner earned but unpaid as of the Effective Date,

less any amounts owed to the Firm by the withdrawing partner for repayment of sums theretofore advanced to him or her by the Firm, or for services performed by the Firm for him or her, *plus* any amounts owed by the Firm to the withdrawing partner for reimbursement of expenses incurred by the withdrawing partner on behalf of, and theretofore unpaid by, the Firm. Notwithstanding the foregoing, the payment to any partner who withdraws from the Firm at any date within five (5) years of the date of his or her return from a sabbatical shall be reduced (but not to an amount less than zero) by an amount equal to the total paid to such partner while he or she was on sabbatical leave, multiplied by the following fraction: 1 minus N/60, where N is the number of months (not to exceed sixty (60)) worked after such return.

Sec. 11.4 <u>Interest in Inventory</u>. The Firm shall pay to the withdrawing partner, in quarterly installments over a period not to exceed three (3) years as the Firm in its discretion shall determine, the amount of the interest (hereinafter "Percentage Interest"), if any, of the withdrawing partner in the Firm's accounts receivable and unbilled work in process (together with interest on the unpaid amount at the prime rate then prevailing). It is agreed that such Percentage Interest shall be determined as of the last day of the Firm's fiscal year if it coincides with the Effective Date or, otherwise, the last day of the Firm's fiscal year preceding the Effective Date. It is agreed that to the extent the withdrawing partner would have a Percentage Interest in any contingent fee unearned at the Effective Date, the obligation of the Firm to pay the withdrawing partner's Percentage Interest in respect thereof, including the privilege of installment payment, shall be deferred until the amount of the fee is determined and received by the Firm.

Sec. 11.5 <u>Personal Effects</u>. The withdrawing partner shall remove from the premises of the Firm, on or before the Effective Date, all personal furniture, office equipment, effects, and files, and shall not remove any such items that are the property of the Firm. All files, records, forms, discs, tapes, software, memoranda, correspondence, and all documents and writings of any kind or nature pertaining to the business or clients of the Firm shall, as between the Firm and the withdrawing partner, remain in the sole and exclusive possession of the Firm.

Sec. 12. EXPULSION. A partner may be expelled immediately and without cause by the affirmative vote of that same number of partners required for his or her election to partnership if the vote for election were taken at the same time the vote for expulsion is taken. No notice of such meeting shall be required and, if given, such notice need state only the date, time, and place of the meeting. Upon such expulsion, the partner so expelled thereafter shall have no right or interest in the Firm or any of its assets, clients, files, records, or affairs. Payments to a partner expelled shall be as set forth in Section 11 regarding a withdrawing partner. The expulsion of a partner shall not cause a dissolution of the partnership unless otherwise determined by vote of the remaining partners taken in the same manner as provided in Section 8.6.1 of this Agreement.

Sec. 13. DEATH OR PERMANENT DISABILITY OF A PARTNER.

Sec. 13.1 Death. The death of a partner shall terminate all of his or her interest in the Firm, its property and assets, and, in the case of a Regular Partner, in the partnership. The Firm shall pay to the designee of the deceased partner, within thirty (30) days of the date of death,

(a) in the case of a partner other than a Special Partner, the percentage interest of the partner earned but unpaid plus his or her interest in Inventory, as of the date of death, and

(b) in the case of a Special Partner, the compensation earned by him or her and unpaid as of the date of death,

less any amount representing funds advanced to the partner for expenses unaccounted for by the deceased partner, *plus*, at the request of, and against presentation of appropriate bills from the designee of the deceased partner, any amount representing amounts expended by the deceased partner for client or Firm matters, and for which the deceased partner previously was not reimbursed. In addition, within sixty (60) days after the date of death, the Firm will pay to the designee of the deceased partner, other than a Special Partner, his or her capital account as shown on the books of the Firm. The surviving Regular Partners of the Firm shall indemnify the estate of the deceased partner against any liability for bank or other debt of the Firm existing at the time of death.

Sec. 13.2 Permanent Disability. A partner may be determined to be permanently disabled upon the affirmative vote of eighty (80) percent of the partners entitled to vote, including the partner whose permanent disability is in issue. Upon a determination that a partner is permanently disabled, effective on the date of the vote so determining, the partner shall have no further interest in the Firm and shall receive the payments otherwise payable to the designee of a deceased partner, as in Section 13.1 above provided.

Sec. 14. TAX EFFECT. It is contemplated by the parties to this Agreement that any payments hereunder for the interest in the Firm of a withdrawing, permanently disabled, or deceased partner are, to the extent that they represent payment for partnership properties, capital payments falling under Section 736(b) of the Internal Revenue Code. All other payments for the interests of such persons are intended by the partners as payments of partnership income under Section 736(a) of the Internal Revenue Code. Each partner covenants for himself/herself and his/her heirs and assigns that he or she will make no claims or representations with reference to the income tax nature of any such amounts that are inconsistent with the intent expressed in this Section 14.

Sec. 15. RETIREMENT BENEFIT.

Sec. 15.1 Amount Payable. Each partner who retires from the Firm pursuant to Section 7.4 shall be entitled to a retirement benefit from the Firm. A partner who has served as a partner of the Firm for ten (10) or more years at the time of retirement shall be paid an amount equal to seventy-five (75) percent of such partner's Average Earned Income (as defined). In the case of a partner who has served as a partner of the Firm for less than ten (10) years at the time of retirement, the retirement benefit shall be reduced to an amount determined as follows: the amount calculated by the formula in the preceding sentence shall be multiplied by a fraction, the numerator of which is the number of years the retired partner served as a partner in the Firm and the denominator of which is ten (10).

Sec. 15.2 Condition to Receipt. Any partner who retires from the Firm shall, as a condition of receiving payments under Section 15.1 hereof, agree with the Firm that he or she will not engage in the practice of law in competition with the Firm in the state of ________, or in any other state where the Firm then has an office, for the time period during which retirement payments are being made under Section 15.1. Any partner who does not so agree shall be treated as a withdrawing partner and entitled only to the payments provided in Section 11 hereof. If the Executive Committee determines that any retired partner who is receiving benefits determined under this Section 15 is engaging in activities in competition with the Firm or has solicited or received other than an insignificant amount of business from clients of the Firm, the Firm may, forthwith, terminate the remaining payments to such retired partner.

[COMMENT: The provisions above regarding retirement payments suggest an uncomplicated formula. Other provisions can be drawn to cover other arrangements to offer more generous payments to founding members, or members with longer service, of the firm. Some firms have related adjustments in the amount of the payment to changes in the cost-of-living index, or to variations in partners' average annual income, or to some combination of both. It may also be desirable to provide a cap on the total amount of benefits the firm is obligated to pay. This will obviate a situation where, following the retirement of a large group of very senior partners, the burden on the income of the firm might leave an amount insufficient to meet the compensation needs of the remaining active partners. In short, considerable thought, ingenuity, and innovation needs to go into the design of the retirement pay provision of the partnership agreement.]

Sec. 15.3 Consent. No amendment of the provisions of this Section 15 made after the retirement of a partner may change the method of calculating the amount of the benefit payable to a partner who has retired from the Firm, if the calculation required by such amendment would result in a reduction in the amount of the benefit receivable by the retired partner.

[COMMENT: Just as it may be desirable to protect the firm by including a cap on payments, so also it is appropriate to include this, or a similar, provision to prevent a reduction in benefit payments to a retired partner, other than through the normal operation of the formula in existence when the partner retires.]

Sec. 16. ACCOUNTING. Any partner (or, in the case of a deceased partner, his or her estate) who shall withdraw, be expelled, or die, who is not satisfied with the amounts determined by the Firm to be payable to him or her pursuant to the provisions of this Agreement, shall be entitled to an accounting, to be rendered by the firm of certified public accountants retained by the Firm. Should the partner (or, in the case of a deceased partner, his or her estate) be unwilling to accept such firm of certified public accountants, a representative of that firm and the representative of a firm selected by the unwilling party shall select a third firm of certified public accountants that shall conduct the audit and render the accounting.

Sec. 17. PRIOR AGREEMENTS. Any and all agreements by or among the parties hereto made before the date hereof, excepting only such agreements as pertain to the life insurance, health insurance, and retirement plans of the Firm, are hereby rescinded, replaced, and superseded by this Agreement.

Sec. 18. PROHIBITION ON ASSIGNMENT. No partner shall directly or indirectly sell, assign, or encumber such partner's interest in the Firm, nor shall such partner permit such interest in the Firm to be directly or indirectly sold. No partner whose membership in the Firm shall have terminated, nor any person claiming on such partner's behalf, shall have any interest in the Firm's practice, business, assets, or profits other than for payments specifically provided for herein.

Sec. 19. RECORDS. All records, reports, files, computerized data, case materials, research memoranda, correspondence, and similar documents, compiled in the course of the performance of services with or for the Firm, except to the extent that a client or clients of the Firm may have rights thereto, shall be the exclusive property of the Firm. Any retired, withdrawn, or terminated partner shall have no rights in or with respect to any such records upon and after such partner's withdrawal, retirement, or other termination from the Firm, and, after the death of any partner, no personal representative of such partner or his or her estate shall have such right, except as expressly granted, in writing, by such client(s) or by the Executive Committee of the Firm.

Sec. 20. CONFIDENTIALITY. Any retired, withdrawn, or terminated partner shall maintain in strict confidence all information concerning the Firm's business and the business of its clients, its internal operations, profitability, and related matters, and shall not, without the express written consent of the Executive Committee, disclose any such information to any person not associated with the Firm.

Sec. 21. REVIEW. The provisions of this Agreement shall be reviewed by the partners, with a view to possible amendment or modification, during the second half of the Firm's fiscal year ending in the year 20__. Notwithstanding the foregoing, any partner may request a reconsideration of any provision of this Agreement by written petition to the Executive Committee, which petition shall set forth the requested change in the provision. The Executive Committee shall consider the proposal within sixty (60) days after receipt. If the Executive Committee, by majority vote, recommends consideration of the proposal by the Regular Partners, it shall be placed on the agenda of a regular meeting of the Firm for such consideration not later than one hundred twenty (120) days after receipt of such recommendation from the Executive Committee.

Sec. 22. INDEMNIFICATION. Each retired, withdrawn, or terminated partner, other than a partner expelled pursuant to the provisions of Section 12 hereof, shall be indemnified and held harmless by the Regular Partners from and against any Firm liability incurred after the date of such partner's retirement, withdrawal, or termination.

Sec. 23. SEVERABILITY. In the event any provision of this Agreement shall be held invalid or unenforceable by any court of competent jurisdiction, such holding shall not invalidate or render unenforceable any other provisions hereof.

Sec. 24. AMENDMENT. This Agreement may be amended at any time by the vote of two-thirds of the Regular Partners, unless otherwise specifically provided herein with respect to discrete issues, and provided that no provision hereof requiring a greater vote than two-thirds of the Regular Partners may be amended except by the same greater vote.

Sec. 25. ARBITRATION. Any dispute or controversy arising under this Agreement, if not resolved by mutual agreement of the parties hereto, shall be submitted to arbitration before a panel of three arbitrators in the city of _____________ for settlement under the commercial arbitration rules of the American Arbitration Association as then in effect, and judgment upon the award may be entered in any court of competent jurisdiction, *provided, however,* that the panel of arbitrators shall be chosen as follows: the Firm shall select one arbitrator and the other party to the controversy shall select one arbitrator, each of whom shall be a partner in a law firm in the United States having not less than the number of partners of the Firm; the two arbitrators thus selected shall select a third arbitrator, who shall also be a partner in a law firm in the United States having not less than the number of partners of the Firm. If the two arbitrators selected by the Firm and by the other party to the controversy are unable to agree upon the third arbitrator within thirty (30) days after their selection, the third arbitrator, satisfying the criterion aforesaid, shall be selected by the American Arbitration Association.

Sec. 26. COUNTERPARTS. This Agreement may be executed in several counterparts, each of which shall be deemed an original, and all of which shall constitute one and the same agreement.

Sec. 27. JOINDER. Each partner admitted to the Firm after the effective date hereof shall execute a joinder agreement to this Agreement, as it may be amended from time to time. Each such partner shall be deemed a party to and bound by this Agreement as of the effective date of his or her admission to the Firm.

Sec. 28. GOVERNING LAW. This Agreement shall be governed and interpreted in accordance with the laws of the state of __________.

IN WITNESS WHEREOF, the partners have executed this Partnership Agreement as of _______ ___, ____.

[Names, typewritten, and signatures of all partners]

ATTACHMENT: Schedule of Capital Contributions (Name of partner, amount of contribution, and date of contribution).

APPENDIX 🕮 C

Of Counsel Agreement

[Letterhead of Law Firm][1]

[Month , Year]

John J. Doe, Esq.
1000 Broadway
Major City, ZZ 00000

Dear John:

As you will retire as a partner of our firm at the end of this fiscal year, the firm invites you to remain associated with us as Of Counsel, under the following terms.

1. *Title.* Your title will be "Of Counsel." The firm will be permitted to list your name in that capacity, as it deems fit, on letterheads, brochures, professional listings (such as Martindale-Hubbell), and other promotional materials.

---

1. This is a draft of a simplified, but adequate, agreement for a retired partner who will cease practice, but will have an office and other benefits provided by his or her law firm. For a more detailed discussion of the "Of Counsel" agreement and a wider range of samples of types of agreements, see HAROLD G. WREN & BEVERLY J. GLASCOCK, THE OF COUNSEL AGREEMENT: A GUIDE FOR LAW FIRM AND PRACTITIONER (1991), published by the ABA Senior Lawyers Division.

2. *Status; Health and Life Insurance Coverage.* Your status will be that of an independent contractor, but we shall nevertheless take such steps as may be necessary to assure that you are eligible to remain, and remain, a member of the group covered by the firm's health and life insurance policy. In this connection, you will have the opportunity to purchase from the firm's health and life insurance carrier such coverage as the carrier offers at group rates, and at your own expense. If the firm, rather than you, is billed by the carrier, then the firm, in turn, will bill you for the amount that shall be reimbursable to the firm.

3. *Duties of the Firm.* In addition to offering the insurance coverage aforementioned, the firm will provide you with an office in the firm's __________ [location] facility, equivalent in size to an associate's office, as long as you make minimal use thereof. The firm will also provide secretarial assistance, limited to (a) handling of correspondence related to professional organizations of which you may be a member, (b) forwarding of mail to you, and (c) responding to telephone calls made to you. You will also have access to all the firm's office services (telephone, computer on-line service, facsimile, photocopy, and so forth). The firm will pay or reimburse you for the use of parking facilities in the building where your office is located. The firm will pay or reimburse you for the dues of the American Bar Association, the [state] Bar Association, and the [local] Bar Association. Reimbursement, if any, of your expenses for attendance at meetings of such organizations will require the firm's approval before you incur such expenses. You are invited to attend meetings of the partnership. Upon your request to the secretary of the Executive Committee, you will receive copies of agenda materials for such meetings.

4. *Compensation.* You will receive no compensation from the firm for your service as Of Counsel. In consideration of the provision of services mentioned in paragraph 3, above, you agree to assist the firm, to a reasonable degree, with client development efforts upon request by the firm, but not to exceed the expenditure by you of more than five hours per month. Should you incur any out-of-pocket expenditures for such activity (such as, for example, expenses for client entertainment or meals), you will be reimbursed by the firm therefor.

5. *Retirement Benefit; No Competition.* During your service as Of Counsel, the firm will pay to you the retirement benefit provided for Retired Partners under the firm's partnership agreement. As long as the firm is paying such benefit to you, you will refrain from the active practice of law. "Active practice of law" means the provision of legal service or advice to clients, whether or not for compensation; however, it does not include serving as an arbitrator or mediator in your personal capacity and not as a representative of this firm (and off its premises), nor writing articles or making addresses to professional organizations. Should the firm

request that you perform any legal services, by way of providing advice to other lawyers of the firm or to clients of the firm, the firm will first agree with you upon an appropriate method and amount of compensation, and will undertake to provide and pay for legal malpractice insurance for you. Except as stated in the preceding sentence, and except to the extent otherwise required by provisions of the partnership agreement, the firm will not provide you with any legal malpractice insurance.

6. *Arbitration.* Any dispute between us arising out of this agreement shall be settled by arbitration in the city of ____________, state of _______, according to the commercial arbitration rules of the American Arbitration Association, before a single arbitrator who shall be a partner in a law firm with at least seven (7) partners, and who shall have been a member of the bar of the state of _________ for at least thirty (30) years. Judgment upon any arbitration award may be entered and enforced in any court of competent jurisdiction. Notwithstanding the foregoing, either party to this agreement, by notice to the American Arbitration Association, may insist that the arbitration be conducted by three arbitrators and that the arbitrators be selected as prescribed in the partnership agreement.

7. *Term.* This agreement shall extend for a period of one (1) year from the date hereof, but shall be renewable from year to year for additional periods of one (1) year, upon your application to the Executive Committee of the firm, submitted at least sixty (60) days before the anniversary date hereof. The Executive Committee shall act upon the application within thirty (30) days after its receipt, but failing such action, this agreement shall be renewed on the same terms for the further period of one (1) year from the date hereof.

If the foregoing is satisfactory, please sign and return one counterpart of this letter to me to evidence our agreement. We look forward to your acceptance and to a continuation of our long and pleasant relationship.

Sincerely,

JONES & SMITH

By ___________________

A Partner

TABLE OF AUTHORITIES

A. Cases

B. Statutes

C. Treatises and Periodicals

INDEX

ABOUT THE AUTHOR

GEORGE H. CAIN retired in 1990 as a partner of Day, Berry & Howard, a major New England law firm, where he concentrated in corporate law and business litigation. Now Of Counsel to the firm, he is using his more than forty-five years of experience at the bar to write and speak on subjects of interest to the profession. *Law Partnership: Its Rights and Responsibilities* is his second book; his first, *Turning Points: New Paths and Second Careers for Lawyers*, was published by the Senior Lawyers Division of the American Bar Association in 1994. A graduate of Georgetown University and Harvard Law School, he served as an Air Force officer in both World War II and the Korean War. He continues to be active in a number of professional organizations, including the Senior Lawyers Division of the American Bar Association, where he is a member of the Council, the Division's governing body. In 1995–96, he is serving as Chair of the Senior Lawyers Section of the Connecticut Bar Association. His biography appears in *Who's Who in America*. Mr. Cain lives in Connecticut with his wife, the former Constance Sullivan Collins. He has four sons by a previous marriage, a stepson, and three stepdaughters, all of whom are busily engaged in their own careers.